8.75

GP6-29-72

DATE DUE

APR 26 1986			
NOV 1 5 1990			
GAYLORD			PRINTED IN U.S.A.

STUDIES IN HUMANISM

STUDIES IN HUMANISM

By
JOHN WILLIAM MACKAIL

Essay Index Reprint Series

 BOOKS FOR LIBRARIES PRESS
FREEPORT, NEW YORK

First Published 1938
Reprinted 1969

STANDARD BOOK NUMBER:
8369-1092-3

LIBRARY OF CONGRESS CATALOG CARD NUMBER:
73-84322

PRINTED IN THE UNITED STATES OF AMERICA

TO
MARGARET

PREFATORY NOTE

THIS volume contains a selection of papers written at various times over a good many years, all dealing with humanism as an expression of the human spirit. They follow at conspicuous points, indicated and illustrated by representative figures, the long chain of lights which extends from ancient Greece and Rome down to the present day. For reasons which will be obvious, the original date of each paper is given; but all have been revised, and some of those which had been already separately printed largely re-written.

They are introduced by a discourse given at the inauguration of one of the new institutions of university rank in the United States. It endeavours to set forth and vindicate the function of poetry, as the form of creative art in which the spirit of humanism displays itself most fully and intimately, in its relation to the problems and conditions of the present day and the actual world. Following it are a defence of the value of Greek, and an appreciation of an Ode of Horace; essays dealing with Dante as the central figure of the Middle Ages; with Erasmus and Ariosto as almost exact contemporaries in the full flowering of humanism; then, passing on to our own country, with the *Paradise Lost* as handled by Bentley, and with an English classic of no less eminence and vitality, the *Pilgrim's Progress*; with the foundation, a generation later, of the Chair of Poetry at Oxford, in its relevance towards the movement of the eighteenth century in English letters; with points in that movement marked by the Romantic Revival originated in Scotland by Allan Ramsay, and, when a wholly new orientation was already being given to poetry, by the little-known but significant work of Hurdis, the pupil of Cowper and the contemporary of Wordsworth. Fluctuations of humanism since then are illustrated by a study of Ruskin,

vii

by a review of the re-integration of Shakespeare which is a notable feature of modern scholarship, and by a note on Tradition and Design in their application to art.

I have to acknowledge with thanks permission to reprint matter already published, from the President of the Rice Institute for *The Pursuit of Poetry*; from the Delegates of the Clarendon Press for *The Good of Greek* and *Henry Birkhead*; from the Classical Journals Board for *An Ode of Horace*; from the University of London Press for *The Italy of Virgil and Dante*; from Macmillan and Company for *Dante's Paradiso*; from the Merrymount Press, Boston, Massachusetts for *Erasmus on War*; from the Empire Review for *Ariosto*; from the Council of the British Academy for *Bentley's Milton*; from the English Association for *Allan Ramsay*; and from the Lecture Recorder for *Tradition and Design*.

J. W. M.

6 Pembroke Gardens, London, W. 8.
March 1938.

CONTENTS

THE PURSUIT OF POETRY

[*Written for the inauguration of the Rice Institute, Houston, Texas, September, 1915*]

I

THE FUNCTION OF A UNIVERSITY

THE inauguration of a new institution of university rank is a fitting occasion for reviewing the field which such institutions exist in order to cover; for going back for a moment to first principles, and endeavouring to state, in the simplest terms, why such institutions exist, and what they may effect towards the moulding of a new generation, and the elevation of civic and national life. Different universities, according to the circumstances of their foundation and history, can show different reasons for their existence and for being such as they are. But all of them, whatever the date of their origin, whatever the place of their settlement, have come into being in response to certain demands of the place and the time. All of them have been founded with a purpose single in its nature, though diverse in its manifestations. That purpose is to make stated and secured provision for the higher needs of a civilized community. The needs, like the pursuits, of a community are many. But its civilization is one. It is the object of a university to gather up that civilization, to analyse and study its separate elements in order to recombine them at a higher power, and thus to give conscious direction to the human mind in its knowledge of the past, its understanding of the present, and its power over the future. Its office is to store up, to sort out, and to impart knowledge; and by doing so it accumulates, organizes, and gives forth power. Knowledge is power, according to the old saying; it is latent or stored power. Conversely, power is knowledge transformed into energy; it is knowledge in action. Education, the process which goes on in a concentrated form and at

I   B high pressure in a university, is a mechanism by which the potential energy of the human mind is developed, disciplined, cleared for action. Knowledge is indeed an end in itself, and one which has a value that may properly be called inestimable, since it cannot be expressed in the terms of any other value. Riches, comfort, health, fame, influence, beneficence, are things of which knowledge pursued for its own sake and as an end in itself takes no heed. But while knowledge is or may be an end, education is only a means: a means to knowledge, for such as desire knowledge for its own sake; but for all who pass through it and undergo its influence, a means to the practice and conduct of life.

Hence in any community the idea of a university, the sort of education which a university will be planned to give, will depend on the kind of life which that community desires, aspires towards, sets before itself as worth attaining. In the ancient world the earliest institutions to which the name can in any sense be applied were religious colleges—schools of the prophets, as they are called in the Old Testament, or training-colleges of the priests, as they existed and flourished in Babylonia or in Egypt. The knowledge and power after which they sought, which they accumulated, recorded, and transmitted, were the knowledge of and the power over supernatural forces. For these supernatural forces were then, according to the common belief, what governed the life of mankind and held it at their mercy; to understand them and their ways, and thus to gain the power of foreseeing their action, propitiating their favour, giving this or that direction to their working, was no mere matter of abstract study or idle speculation: it was most severely and immediately practical; it lay at the root of individual and national prosperity. Without education in this all-important and all-embracing knowledge, industry and commerce, arts and manufactures, the conduct of war and peace, were blind and helpless: in a word, life was impossible.

Out of that world rose, after many ages, what we know as the classical civilization. This was the work of Greece, carried on and consolidated by Rome. The universities of the Graeco-Roman world belong to the same period which saw, for the first time, the rise of a trained governing class of organizers and administrators. Hence in these universities the subjects pre-eminently studied were those necessary for such a class: oratory, law, politics, and finance. At the same time the creation of a trained governing class set free those who did not belong to it, whether excluded by birth and fortune or holding aloof by choice from active pursuit of the duties attaching to the work of government. These, and especially the latter class, those who deliberately abstained from active public life, might now pursue knowledge for its own sake; and other universities arose which, in response to this new demand, devoted themselves to the sciences: on the one hand, to the pure or abstract sciences, those of the human mind, like grammar and logic and metaphysics, and those of the physical world, like botany or chemistry or astronomy; and, on the other hand, to the applied sciences, such as engineering or mechanics or medicine, or to those sciences which are also arts, like rhetoric or music.

When, in the Middle Ages, men began to gather together the wreckage of the ancient civilization and to reorganize life on a fresh basis, their notion of a university was fundamentally different. For the medieval notion of the world was that it was something limited, precise, and ascertainable. It was something of which complete knowledge was possible; and to give this complete rounded knowledge was the function of education. The forms of life were prescribed by dogma; and the substance of life, on all its sides and in all its manifestations, was what could be comprehended in these forms. Just as theology was fixed and bounded by the authoritative doctrines of a universal or Catholic Church; just as political and social life was fixed and bounded by the equally authoritative constitutions of that universal Roman Empire, which held sway over men's minds long after it had itself ceased to exist except as a memory of the past or a dream of the future: in like manner and to a like degree were the form and the content of all knowledge determined and limited. Treatises were written *de omni scibili*, "concerning everything which is capable of being known." This was an ideal, in so far as few, if any, had the vigour of mind, the industry, acuteness, and patience, that were required for its attainment. But it was, given these qualities in the student, an attainable ideal. A university professed to offer, its students came prepared to receive, universal knowledge. The medieval curriculum of the Seven Liberal Arts, which included the Sciences—the *trivium* and *quadrivium* of educational legislators—was the same everywhere; was one, complete, and unalterable. Study might be pursued further in certain branches of it than in others; but that was only in so far as the student failed to complete the full course, which would leave nothing more to learn or to know. The *Summa Theologiae*, the sum and substance, over all its range and into all its details, of divine knowledge, was actually put together and written down; the *Summa Scientiae*, the sum and substance of secular knowledge, was the under side, as it were, of that other fabric, and could not extend beyond its limits. That is to say, all learning, both liberal and technical, was the province of a university; the scope and limits of all learning were imposed from without by a dogmatic and omnipotent theology, and whatever knowledge lay beyond these limits was either proscribed as sinful, or its existence was denied.

Hence the human mind was not only bounded but crippled. Practice did not, indeed, follow theory to its rigid consequences. Schools of medicine, of civil law, even of natural science, grew up here and there, and flourished precariously under the jealous eyes of the Church. Art grew up of itself, without any systematic art-training. Architecture and engineering were in the hands of guilds, where knowledge was transmitted, in theory and practice, as a secret treasure from father to son or from master to apprentice. Painting and the sister arts wrought out a tradition of their own. Poetry insisted on making itself heard, but was discountenanced as heathen vanity or worse. The brilliant culture of Provence, which had gone out of Europe to the Arabs for a new and larger life, was crushed by armed force, and perished under the sword of the so-called Crusaders or in the fires of the Inquisition. Even at the end of the Middle Ages, and when the new world of the Renaissance was forming itself, Chaucer, the foremost of our own poets, ended by a formal and express disavowal of his own poetry, revoking and retracting it (all except legends of saints, and homilies, and books of morality and devotion) as vanity and sin. Physical science was equally suspect, and was subject, down to the time of Galileo and later, to equally jealous control and equally vindictive persecution.

This tyranny of theology lasted long enough to affect the modern universities likewise, down to a time which is within living memory. It was not broken either by the Reformation or by what is called the Revival of Learning. For the Reformation, as indeed its name implies if we consider its real meaning, only recast that tyranny in a new shape, "re-formed" it and imposed it afresh on the human mind; and the Revival of Learning was a partial, imperfect and agonizing struggle to regain that freedom of the intelligence on which all freedom and all progress ultimately depend. The pre-Revolutionary foundations in the American Colonies, like Harvard (the mother and head of American universities) and Yale (created in the first year of that eighteenth century which was the liberating age of human thought), were theological colleges, restricted by the tenets of Puritanism, and regarding all kinds of secular learning as subsidiary elements towards theological training. Fifty years after the foundation of Yale the first decisive step towards the liberation of knowledge was taken. The University of Pennsylvania, founded on lines laid down by Benjamin Franklin in 1751, led the way in the English-speaking world towards the conception of a seat of learning in which learning should be unrestricted by dogma and have no limits set to it other than the limits of human intelligence and capacity. That foundation, originated by men who were to be the creators of the American Commonwealth, was an achievement in the field of human thought which marks a new epoch, just as the foundation of the Republic a generation later marks an epoch in the political and social life of mankind. The step then gained has never been lost. More and more surely, as time went on, the declaration of intellectual independence made by those pioneers of the modern world became a profession of faith and a standard of conduct throughout the international commonwealth of learning. Progress was slow: it was not until 1871 that religious tests were removed from the ancient universities of Oxford and Cambridge; here, as elsewhere, the creators of the United States led the way, and the American Republic followed them in the advance towards a new conception and a new conduct of life. It became, in the full sense of the words, a New World.

That world existed at first, and for long, only as a sketch or outline: it drove its outposts forward through virgin forest or over empty prairie; the advancing tide, however swift its actual advance, required generations to fill up the channels laid for it and widen out into lakes and seas; the foundations were pushed on, here and there, at random, and the earliest superstructures built upon them were often slight and mean. It was not until after the Civil War that the American nation, secure in its unity and conscious of its greatness, began to organize its own higher education, and to realize the full culture of the human faculties as a function of its national life. Since then the growth, in all the States of the Union, of institutions of liberal and technical learning has been rapid and vast. Yet even so, it has hardly kept pace with the enormous growth of population, of civic organization, and of material resources. The new institution now being inaugurated at Houston is one among many such new foundations, and they will not be the last. The foundations are laid, but the structure towards which they are laid is only begun.

But while the number of American universities is steadily growing, the ideal of an American university is undergoing no less striking and fruitful an expansion. It is being recognized that a university, or any institution of university rank, must have a sphere of study and of influence as wide as the whole width of human activity. It can no longer confine itself to some special study; it can no longer be merely a theological seminary, or a school of letters, or a training-college of commerce, or a collection of laboratories and workshops. It must reinstate the medieval ideal of the *Universitas Studiorum*, but with a larger content than was known to the Middle Ages. Its function and scope must be universal. It must proclaim the unity of all knowledge, the kinship of the arts and sciences, the mutual interdependence of all study and research towards the conquest of nature and the complete civilization of man. To this task there are no bounds; beyond the widening frontiers of knowledge lie ever more and more unexplored territories. To the Republic of Learning no limits are set by the ocean. The growth of knowledge is the growth of power; the organization and communication of knowledge are the organization and communication of power; and that power is not merely a power over what is known, but a power and a will and an endless purpose to know more.

It is, then, matter of congratulation that the founders of this institution have determined that its studies shall not be confined to any single branch of knowledge, but that the technical and professional instruction which it will offer shall be liberalized by organic connection with art and letters. In the stately and ample surroundings which have been planned, with the large and varied equipment which is being provided, the Institute gives welcome promise of rising to the height of the opportunity presented to it. By a wise munificence, it will offer its education free to its students; it will lay no tax upon the acquisition of knowledge. By an equally wise breadth of view, it will base professional and technical training on a liberal general education, and will thus affirm the human side of science, commerce, and industry, no less than the scientific, commercial, and industrial value of art and letters— of "the so-called humanities," to quote a phrase from the authoritative statement of its Governing Board, which derive that name from a recognition of the fact that human life, at its broadest and fullest, is the subject-matter alike of all academic study and of all civic endeavour. It is proposed to assign no upper limit to the educational activity of the Institute; nor, indeed, is it right that any such limit should be fixed except that fixed by Nature herself—the limit of human activity and capacity. But its upward growth will be on broad foundations; its roots will draw life from a large and rich soil; and the hope may be expressed that its lateral radiating growth will, no less than its upward growth, be subject to no imposed limit. For only thus can its full natural expansion be achieved and its organic vitality secured.

Among the "humanities"—among those studies or pursuits in which the noblest instincts of human nature are fostered and its highest aspirations sustained—poetry takes a high, if not the highest, place. As language is the universal and necessary instrument of thought, and as thought is the source and motive power of all action, invention, and creation, so poetry is the organ of language and thought at their highest power, in their most intense and most vitalizing manifestation. In the life therefore of university students, and even in the studies which they pursue, poetry, not the poetry of the day or of the moment, but the whole integrated volume of the poetry of the nation, of the race, of the world, claims a place not by indulgence, but by right. It will not be irrelevant to the inception of a new university to consider more closely, first what poetry is, and then—a matter of no less moment and of a practical importance which will appear in the development of the discussion—what is the task or function of poetry in the modern world.

II

WHAT IS POETRY?

IN order to discuss anything rationally, we must first have a clear notion of what the thing is which we are discussing. Most misunderstandings, most false opinions, arise from mere confusion; and the heat of debate increases with the vagueness of definition. Even in the sphere of the physical sciences, where perpetual reference back to facts is implied in the nature of the case, and where these facts are visible, tangible, and ponderable, such confusion is not unknown. But the confusion is more apt to arise, and can spread further without detection, in matters where theory cannot be so readily, and has not to be so constantly, brought to the test of experience; where experience itself is fluctuating, and subject to the distorting influence not merely, as in physical science, of tradition and habit, but also of unreasoned instinct and variable emotion.

Only by the continuous effort of generations have the physical sciences been brought into the state in which their really scientific pursuit is secured; only by constantly applying them to practical problems can we test the truth of generalizations and the relevance of theories, and be sure that our knowledge is real knowledge, and bears relation—a real and helpful relation—to the actual world in which we find ourselves and with which we have to deal.

In what are called the humane studies—those of art and letters—the same twofold necessity exists: the necessity of a clear definition of terms, and the necessity of testing the value of any study or pursuit by laying it alongside of facts and seeing what relation it bears to the claims of life. Before considering, as it is my main object to do, the function and task of poetry in the actual modern world, whether as a subject of study, an art in practice, or (more largely) an element in civilization, it will be proper, and indeed necessary, to clear the ground by saying what poetry is.

In this as in so many other matters the instinctive tendency is to give to the question, "What is poetry?" the answer, "I know, so long as you do not ask me." And it is no doubt true that most people have some vague and general conception of what is meant by the word "poetry" floating in their minds. But their conception is so vague and indeterminate as to be of little use. That poetry is a kind of language, differing in its nature alike from the ordinary language of our daily intercourse and from the language used in books of science or philosophy or history, of treatises on politics or economics or religion, of memoirs or essays or narratives, would be generally admitted; but when we go beyond this and ask what is its specific nature, many would be unable to say more than that it is language arranged in lines of a certain arbitrary length, with the words so artificially ordered as to produce an agreeable effect upon the ear, and to excite a certain pleasure, comparable to that produced by music, in the senses of the reader. Beyond that, they would have to fall back on instances: poetry, they would say, is, in ancient literature, Homer and

Virgil; in our common English inheritance, Chaucer, Spenser, Milton; in more modern times, many authors on both sides of the Atlantic.

But what are we to think of these and other poets, not merely as men, not merely as writers, but as poets? What is that thing called "poetry" which they all produced, and what are we to think of it, as an art, as a way of occupying life and affecting the lives of others, as a subject to be studied or a craft to be exercised? When we come to this point we are faced at once with the confusion which arises from the absence of a clear notion of what is meant by poetry, and from the consequent absence of any firm common ground when we try to state and to appraise its function, its value, its relation to the task, the duty, the privilege of actual men and women here in the twentieth century. This confusion affects the eulogists and the detractors of poetry alike. Many wild words are spoken on both sides. It is needless to enlarge on this notorious fact. On the one side are the devotees of poetry, who regard it as something too lofty and sacred for definition, as something that stands outside of and apart from common people and their pursuits. On the other, in much larger numbers, are those who think of it as a rather trifling amusement, suitable for people who have nothing better to do; or even as something vicious and demoralizing, something that weakens the mind, destroys industry and accuracy, cultivates fancy and sentiment at the expense of intelligence, and is a stumbling-block in the way of the pursuit of truth. To them poetry is like alcoholic liquor, a dangerous servant and a destructive master. "One of the Fathers," says Bacon in his *Essay of Truth*, "called Poesy *vinum daemonum* (devils' wine), because it filleth the imagination with the shadow of a lie." The churches, and religious people generally, have always, if they did not go as far as Jerome or Augustine—it is uncertain to which of them Bacon refers—at all events regarded poetry with suspicion, and not been comfortable about it. And here they are, for once, in agreement with the rough common-sense of business men who care for religion as little as they care for poetry. It is easy to laugh at the mathematician who asked of Milton's *Paradise Lost*, "What does it prove?" But it is not so easy to ignore the man in the street who asks of poetry, not "What does it prove?" but "What sense is there in it?" It is not so easy to confute, before a careless public, the discontented man of letters who turns against his own art, and says of poetry, in the words of a contemporary of Shakespeare, that it is a thing "whereof there is no use in a man's whole life but to describe discontented thoughts and youthful desire." To such minds poetry is either a childish folly or a deliberate misapplication of human powers.

Against such an attitude we may set the many splendid tributes in which, while attempting to give a definition of poetry, the poets themselves have claimed for it qualities so marvellous, a value so great, that nothing else in life is so precious. Wordsworth calls poetry "the breath and finer spirit of all knowledge." Shelley calls it "the record of the best and happiest moments of the happiest and best minds." Matthew Arnold says that it is not only "the most perfect speech of man," but also "that in which he comes nearest to the truth." When poets commend poetry, their testimony may be taken by the outer world with some of the suspicion which attaches to people who cry up their own wares. Yet even after making all due allowance for this, the two attitudes of mind towards poetry are clearly inconsistent with each other. We may admit that there is truth in both, as there is truth somewhere at the basis of any widely and sincerely held opinion on matters which affect life. But if both are true, they are clearly not both true of the same thing and in the same sense. In order to reconcile them in any wider and more comprehensive truth, we must try to avoid on the one hand the glitter of rhetoric and sentiment, the "luminous mist" (in Coleridge's fine phrase) which imaginative artists are apt to wrap round their own art, and on the other hand the impatience of the practical and unimaginative man with anything that falls beyond the scope of his own daily experience, that uses terms with which he is not familiar and aims at objects which he has not learned to appreciate. And the best way towards arriving at common ground is to define our terms as clearly and simply as possible.

With this object, let us now proceed, not to praise or blame poetry (both are easy, and both are useless), but to explain what poetry is. I will first state the technical definition of poetry; from it, and keeping it in view, we may be able to frame a substantial or vital definition of it, to define it not merely as a technical term, but as an organic process or function. Like all other arts, poetry has both sides. Like music, painting, or architecture, it is a thing subject to laws which can be taught and learned, historically studied and practically applied. Like them, it is also not merely an art, but a fine art; that is to say, it is a form of creative human activity, bearing an intimate relation with the energies of human nature, and with the outlook of man upon the material and spiritual world.

Poetry is, formally and technically, patterned language. This is its bare and irreducible definition. Its specific quality, its *differentia* from other kinds of artistry exercised on the material of language, is that it works language into patterns and uses it not only for its common and universal purpose of expressing meaning,—not only for its heightened or artistic purpose of expressing meaning in such a way as to express it beautifully and thus satisfy the artistic sense,—but also, and expressly, so as to bring it within the scope, and make it subject to the laws, of that kind of decorative designing which we call pattern.

Some brief further explanation may here be added to make the point quite clear. When we are defining poetry and separating it formally from other kinds of spoken or written language, it is not enough to say that it is language which possesses design and has decorative value. All beautiful, dignified, and elevated language has that. The quality peculiar to poetry is something different. We may call it, as we choose, a decorative or a structural quality: for what lies at the root of all true art is, that in it structure and decoration are inseparable; each implies the other, and each exists, in any artistic sense, only by virtue of its essential relation to the other. Structure in the abstract, apart from the decorative quality through which it manifests itself to the senses and affects the imagination and the emotions, is matter of science, not of art. Decoration in the abstract, apart from the material in which it is wrought and its relation to the structure which it decorates, is meaningless. The synthesis of the two constitutes beauty; their vital union is the aim of art. Now the specific quality of poetry as distinguished from other kinds of literature is that in construction and decoration (its construction being decorative, and its decoration constructive) it follows the laws of pattern. The essence of pattern, as is well known to all pattern-designers, consists in its having what they term a repeat. Pattern is built up out of, or grows out of, a repeated unit; and the art and skill of the pattern-designer are shown by his success not merely in making the repeat as a matter of mechanism, but in so handling it that the whole field over which it extends has a beauty and a unity of its own, rising out of and yet distinct from the quality of the repeated unit. A row of equal dots is a pattern in its crudest and simplest form; these dots may be grouped, and the group repeated; these repeated groups may be themselves regrouped into a larger design, and that repeated; and so on. Not only so, but when the pattern is to be executed by hand and not by a machine, it may be treated flexibly and varied subtly; it may depart from exact repetition without ceasing to be a pattern so long as the repeat, in its main elements, continues to be felt. All really excellent patterns, patterns which are works of art, have something of this flexibility. It may extend so far that the repeat has to be sought for, is visible only to the trained eye, and affects other eyes with a pleasure which they feel but cannot analyse and do not fully understand.

This is well understood as regards the arts of painting and music. It is less well understood as regards the art of poetry; but it is true of poetry equally with the other arts of pattern. Poetry, according to a definition which in all probability comes to us from no less an authority than Milton, is the kind of language which "consists of rhythm in verses." Prose also has rhythm, and its rhythm may be of great and intricate beauty, but it is not "in verses"; its rhythm is not subject to the law of repeat. It is indeed the essence of prose that it has not a repeat; so much so that when it slips into a repeat it becomes bad prose, and affects us disagreeably. This is what its name means: "prose"—the Latin *prosa oratio* —means language which moves straight forward without a repeat in its rhythm. Similarly, "verse" (also a Latin word) simply means repeat.

The distinction then between prose and verse is fundamental. It is not quite the same as the distinction between prose and poetry; for while no prose is poetry (except in a very loose and figurative way of speaking, unhappily not seldom used), all verse is not poetry. All patterned language is verse, but to make it poetry the pattern must be skilfully designed and governed by the sense of beauty. Or, if we like, we may say that poetry and verse are the same, only then we must include bad poetry as well as good. It is simpler to say that bad poetry is not poetry at all. Milton again here supplies us with an illuminating phrase. In the *Paradise Lost* he speaks of "prose or numerous verse." Verse which is "numerous," in which the repeated unit and the way in which the repeat is managed are alike beautiful, is poetry.

The scope of pattern, in language as in all the other materials upon which human craftsmanship is exercised, is very wide. Its development varies from country to country, from age to age, from one school of artists to another; and even the same artist may use it very variously at different times and for different purposes. It suffers alternations of growth and decay: a period of healthy growth is succeeded by one of stagnation and disintegration, out of which again in time fresh growth arises. The condition of decorative art in any nation is, at any time, an index to the state of its civilization; for art is a function of, or an element in, the whole process of national life. Art in a sense exists for its own sake; but in a more important sense it exists for the sake of the human life in which it is a factor. Just as, amid great varieties and fluctuations of movement, there are traceable certain broad lines of national development, so it is with the decorative arts of a nation, and with poetry among these: there are certain normal or dominant types of pattern; on these each artist varies according to his own imagination and skill; and from the normal and central type extend outwards in all directions other types, continually in process of invention, cultivation, and change. Some of them are experiments which come to nothing; others strike root and become important enough to affect or alter the normal type of pattern. Thus the art of poetry is always renewing itself through fresh invention under the stimulus of individual genius, and always rebalancing itself through a slow but final current of judgment as to the success or failure of the new type. Instances may be found anywhere by even a cursory glance over contemporary poetry. But we shall be on clearer ground if we put aside living authors and look to the work of an earlier generation, which has already taken its place and can be looked at as a whole and from a distance. Among American poets of the last century we shall find the normal patterns of language, for instance, in the work of Longfellow, perhaps still the greatest, as he is the sweetest-voiced and sanest-minded, of them all. Notable divergences from normal pattern may be seen on the one hand in the lyrics of Poe, with whom curiousness of pattern was almost an obsession; on the other hand, in the singular and hitherto unique work of Whitman, in which the reaction against formalism of pattern went so far that it has been questioned whether any pattern, in the strict sense, is left at all: or in other words, whether the contents of *Leaves of Grass* are, or are not, poetry.

Poetry, then, according to its formal and technical definition, is patterned language, the material of words wrought by art into patterns; and it gives the pleasure, partly sensuous and partly intellectual, which all pattern gives through, and in proportion to, its decorative fitness and beauty. If we regard it not on its technical side, but in its substance and meaning, it has a corresponding definition: it is the art or process which makes patterns out of the subject-matter of language. That subject-matter is life. All poetry worthy of the name creates or reveals the pattern of some fragment or aspect of life; and the greatest poetry creates or reveals the pattern, the ordered beauty, of life as a whole.

As soon as we have grasped this truth firmly we shall understand the things which the poets have said about poetry. Life, as it presents itself to us while we pass through it, has no pattern, or at least none (except to some people of very simple and fervid religious belief) that is certain and intelligible. It is multiplex and bewildering; its laws are confused; it does not satisfy our hopes or our aspirations: sometimes it seems purposeless, often it seems, as Hamlet says, "out of joint." It makes no pattern; still less does it make a pattern of beauty. The high office, the unique function, of poetry is to compose this disorder into a pattern; to bring out, make visible, lift up as a light in darkness, the particular portion or aspect of life which it touches; and in the hands of the greatest poets, to do this with life as a whole. In the beautiful words of Shelley, which I may now quote with the hope that their significance can be understood, poetry "makes familiar things be as if they were not familiar." It shows us the confused, depressing texture of experience in a new and strange light under which we can realize it as part of the divine order. It lets us see life in its inherent beauty and value, and gives us strength to live.

Thus poetry is, in no mere rhetorical or sentimental sense, the highest human achievement. It is the culminating point of that wide combined effort or instinct which is at the base of all education, of all study, of all work; and this is, to realize the potentialities of life, to master the world and enter into our inheritance. To do this is, in the full sense, to live.

III

THE MODERN WORLD

THE present age is in a state of rapid flux. Not in one country only, nor among one social class only, but everywhere from top to bottom and from end to end, change is proceeding with unexampled speed. All movement, not only physical but intellectual and moral, has been vastly accelerated. The old barriers are everywhere breaking down, the old ideas and organizations disappearing, or in course of being fundamentally transformed. An enormous stock of hitherto latent

energy has been called violently into action, and to this process
it is not yet possible to assign any limit. We live, and our
children will live after us, among the wreckage of an old
order, and the girders and scaffolding of a new one which is
arising, amid dust, confusion, and seeming absence of any
mastering control or intelligible design, to replace the old.

The nineteenth century, which now lies so far behind us
that we can more or less look back upon it as on a past age
and receive from it a general total impression, was an age of
ideas, and of belief in ideas. Among its dominant ideas were
those of nationality and of enfranchisement in politics, of
organic continuity in history, of conquest of the physical
world in science. Such ideas, grasped, believed in, and practically applied, impressed upon the century a character of its
own, and one wholly different from that of any previous age.
They were all summed up and included, together with many
others of hardly less significance, in the governing idea of
progress. Progress was necessarily accompanied by change;
but change was sought not for its own sake, but for the sake
of giving effect to the ideas which lay behind it as a motive
force. Change was realized as development: this was the
achievement of science. Development was assumed to be
progress, and was hailed as such: this was the essence of
liberalism. It was an age of unbounded hope for the future
and of active belief in the work of the present.

A generation ago, a change began to pass over the human
spirit. The reflex action of the new ideas cut them away
from the base out of which they had sprung. For ideas, like
other things, are subject to the law of development, and
pass through an orbit of their own. The revolution of the
nineteenth century has, like other revolutions, "devoured its
own children." Its ideas have partly dwindled, partly failed,
partly so altered and expanded that they can no longer be
recognized for what they were. The law of development
has, in the phrase of engineers, "taken charge." In discover-
ing it, we have discovered our master. It is a law not of our
making, and but little under our control. Before its march
all the old traditions, and all the moral or customary sanctions
which attached themselves to these, crumble away or go

C

off in smoke. It is a power not only invincible, but incalculable. We may still talk of progress; but many of us have in our hearts ceased to believe in it; or if we do believe in it, it is a different thing in which we believe from that progress which quickened the impulses and inspired the actions of our predecessors. Progress meant to them betterment. It meant the coming of mankind, with certainty and with increasing rapidity, into their inheritance; and that inheritance was assumed, or believed, or as men thought, proved, to be a goodly inheritance, to include in it all good. The inheritance which we now see lying before us seems rather a burden than an enfranchisement. It is an "importunate and heavy load." Long ago, the greatest of the Hebrew prophets cried out sorrowfully to the Power which ruled above, "Thou hast multiplied the people, and hast not increased the joy." Some such feeling now weighs upon the present age. The Power goes on its own inflexible, sinister way, and forces us on before it. We find it more and more difficult to believe that it works for good; for we do not see it doing so. There is a wide-spread belief that progress, in the old sense of the word, does not exist.

The denial of progress, as a ruling law of life, has also been a doctrine held in past ages. But they differed from the present age in this, that they carried out their doctrine in practice. They were conservative. They tried, with all the power they had, to fix things as they were, lest a worse thing should come upon them. This was the whole effort of the Middle Ages. It was the effort of the conservative or reactionary element in society which strove, persistently but in the end helplessly, against the intellectual revolution of the eighteenth century, the industrial revolution which succeeded it, and the political, scientific, and social revolutions which have carried on the process down to our own day. But conservatism in the old sense has also ceased to exist as a real and effective doctrine. Change has been realized as an invincible force; the desire for change has become a fixed instinct; and to this, rather than to any reasoned belief or any assured hope, is due the intense restlessness of the modern world.

The solvent effect of many forces has co-operated to bring

this state of things about. Intercommunication in space has reached such a pitch of ease and regularity that the communities of mankind are no longer cut off from one another; what affects one, almost at once begins to affect all, and an impulse towards change arising anywhere from fresh ideas or altered circumstances is propagated, as it were by waves travelling in all directions through an elastic medium, over the whole world. An immensely increased knowledge of the past has come to men from the compilation of records and the organization of research; and the historical method (perhaps the greatest single invention of modern times) has interconnected all that knowledge so as to make it breed and multiply through mutual fertilization. Knowledge and understanding of so many past changes has brought about an attitude of mind in which nothing is seen to be unchangeable, in which no change seems impossible, in which life itself appears to consist of change. The development of applied science and the triumph of machinery have opened up a boundless prospect of the degree to which this inherent law of change may be utilized, may be turned by mankind to planned ends and foreseen purposes. Together with all these solvent influences is to be reckoned another, negative indeed, yet in its effect perhaps the most potent of all. This is the disappearance of religion, in the older and original sense of the word. For religion as it was understood in earlier ages was a system of enactments and prohibitions based on undefined fear and sanctioned by terrible penalties; once established, it was the strongest of all conservative forces, because exercising the highest and widest controlling power over the thought as well as the actions of men.

The joint result of all these solvent influences in their accumulated force is a movement of change so rapid and so widespread that all the old framework of life tends to disappear, and no pattern of life is left. The course of change points everywhere, which is the same thing as pointing nowhere. The compasses by which life was directed have been demagnetized. It is an age of perplexity, an age of disillusionment. This is not like the old clearing up of thought (the *Aufklärung* of philosophic historians) which sought to dispel illusions that had gathered round and blurred a framework of certainty. It is disillusionment in another sense. Its light is a blind and formless glare in which all objects disappear. It issues in the feeling that what is to be discovered is infinite and cannot be discovered fully; that what is to be done is infinite and cannot be done effectively.

Against this relapse into chaos what is needed is a steadying influence; and this influence, while it may arise from different sources and act along many channels, is to be sought and found nowhere with more clearness and certainty than in poetry. For it is the function of poetry, as we have seen, to make patterns out of life; to discover by its imaginative vision, to make manifest by its creative and constructive power, the order and beauty, the truth and law, that underlie the flux of things. To the paralysing sense of disillusionment it opposes a revelation of essential truth; beneath the chaotic surface of life it apprehends ordered beauty. It re-creates the fabric of life; it renews the meaning and the motive of living.

It would be needless, in speaking to any educated audience, to multiply instances in which this function has actually been performed by great poets, or to point out how their quickening and reconstituting influence is not confined to their own fellow-countrymen in their own age, but retains or may even increase its effect in distant ages and among other civilizations. All the great poets of the past derive their greatness for us in the present from the fact that their effective force on life still survives. The religious poetry of the ancient Hebrew people, translated into other tongues and reinterpreted by new minds, remains a dominant power not merely among the widespread colonies of their own descendants, but among all the nations who have received it as part of the inheritance of Christianity. Homer, the poet who wrote the Iliad and the Odyssey, was the teacher and in some sense the creator (so the Greeks themselves claimed) of ancient Greece; but after ancient Greece had perished, and ever since, down to the present day, he has remained a powerful influence over the ideals, and thus over the conduct and action, of successive generations of mankind. Virgil, the prophet and interpreter through his poems of the Latin race and the Roman Empire, shares with the Roman statesmen, jurists, and administrators the glory of having formed and transmitted to posterity the plan of an ordered civilization reigning throughout an organized empire and imposing itself on the outer surrounding world. The great poets of England and the English-speaking nations have, on one side or another, achieved a task hardly less. Chaucer interpreted and summed up the expansion given to life by the earlier Renaissance; he initiated modern England. Spenser gave voice to the ideals and inspired the action of the Elizabethan age. Milton engraved upon the minds of his countrymen (and among those countrymen were the Fathers of the American Republic) the doctrine, the belief, the law of conduct, which were the strength of Puritanism and the basis of Republicanism. In more recent times the poetry of Byron and Shelley carried on the work and enforced the ideas which, through the French Revolution and the movement of which the French Revolution was the symbol and centre, transformed the civilization and life of Europe. The Brownings became, a generation later, the interpreters of that Liberalism which, in the social, political, and industrial world, was the chief motive force of the nineteenth century. In the middle years of that same century the group of American poets among whom Longfellow, Whittier, and Lowell are the most distinguished names, exercised a powerful influence over national life, and share with Lincoln and Grant, with soldiers and statesmen and men of action, the glory of creating and sustaining that faith, and that resolution among the people, which saved the Union and established a free and indissoluble Commonwealth.

Poets have not ceased; and there may be poets now alive whose work in the judgment of future generations will be comparable in the history of the world to that of their great predecessors. Whether this be so or not, the task and function of poetry remain the same; and thus the study of poetry remains an essential part of human culture, and its practice an essential element in human activity.

Among the great poets, as among all great artists, there is very wide differentiation of function. While they all, in virtue of being poets, create or embody patterns of life, these patterns are never twice the same; they are the creation of individual genius working on material which, being co-extensive with life itself, is of infinite complexity and variety. In the phrase of St. Paul, "there are divers interpretations, but one spirit." The interpretation is never twice the same; the material to be interpreted never presents itself to two artists alike. Hence the task of poetry is never completed; it is a concurrent and endless integration of the meaning of life; and while the poetry of the past is our priceless inheritance, the poetry of the present is our ceaseless need. Some poets have been, primarily and distinctively, prophets of the future; with others, their work has been to reillumine the past and make it alive to us, to make it an effective part of our own conscious life. Others, again, have brought form and beauty into the present, and shown us the pattern in the things that lie nearest to us. Thus Tennyson owed his vast influence and popularity to the fact that he was for long just abreast of his time; he was the voice, during half a century of his poetical production, of the actual spirit of his country, the thought and emotion and work of his age. Other poets as great have failed to obtain the same universal acceptance, because the patterns of life they created were of a life somewhat further apart from common experience: such poets may have to wait for their fame until after death, or may exercise their influence not so much on the world of their own time directly as on a smaller number of minds whom they inspire and fertilize, and through whom they become powerful germinal influences on a later generation. To elucidate and appreciate this complex stream of creation and its effect upon mankind is part of the study of poetry: but more than that, it is part of the study of civilization, part of the equipment required for understanding the world and being able to deal with it, to master its springs and to sway its course.

The state of flux which I began by noting as characteristic of this early twentieth century is perhaps nowhere so marked and so rapid as in the United States. From its beginnings, and now as much as ever, the American Republic has been the laboratory and testing-ground of the whole world. The founders of the Republic set themselves to make that continent to which the name of the New World had been applied since its discovery and colonization, a new world in the full sense; and this has remained more or less, in principle at least, the guiding doctrine of their successors. But in the framing of a pattern for this new world, poetry and the poets (except, as I mentioned, in the course of the great struggle which established the freedom and unity of the nation) have borne little part. The creators of the United States were neither poets nor much influenced in their thought and action by poetry. Washington, Franklin, Hamilton, all had a certain amount of imaginative or creative genius; but they had minds of the prosaic, not the poetical order. The poetry of Puritanism had, a century before their time, put forth its first and last flower in Milton; unless we say that, half a century later still, the thin and austere but exquisite poetry of Emerson was a last autumnal flowerage from the same stem. There are many modern American poets, but no one among them has been recognized by the world as belonging to the first rank, or appears to be a moulding and formative influence over the national life. Of the two names whom many would hold to be the foremost among American poets, Poe was a stray exotic, and Whitman a splendid anomaly. Perhaps the national life is more confused, certainly the national history is poorer, through the comparative absence of poetry—of a national and great poetry—as one of its constructive and enriching elements. And in the solution of the vast problems which to-day confront the Republic, those patterns of life given by the poets, whether native or foreign, cannot be neglected without grave loss. It is necessary to maintain, it is at once a privilege and a duty to urge, the study of poetry as a part of the public provision for the education of the people.

This new Institute, like most modern foundations for promoting higher education, devotes itself largely or mainly to technology and science. This is quite right; for these are studies of immediate utility and pressing importance. But did it confine itself to these, it would contract its own scope and diminish its own value. Technical processes are means and not ends in life; physical science itself is based ultimately on ideas: letters and art give it not merely its interpretation, but its impulse and inner meaning. Thus the study of the humanities is at once the basis and the crown of the study of the sciences; or rather, we may say, supplies these sciences with a motive and an informing spirit.

The humanities, the studies which deal directly with the vital and human elements in life, with thought, emotion, and imagination, culminate in poetry; and we may now proceed to consider somewhat more closely and more in detail the function and task of poetry in relation to actual life at the present day. The modern world, as I said, is in a state of rapid flux and transformation. Among a thousand elements or forces which go to make its movement, one or another may be singled out as of special prominence. But there would be general agreement with any one who called the present age eminently an age of the extension and dominance of science; or who called it, no less eminently, an age of business conducted on a vast scale, at high tension, with exceeding complexity; or who, once more, called it the age of expanding and socialized democracy. Let us proceed to regard the function of poetry in relation to these three great distinguishing features of the actual world.

IV

POETRY AND SCIENCE

SCIENCE, as the term is now understood and as the study denoted by the word is now pursued, is a birth of the modern world. Its growth was coincident with the earlier development of the United States, where its practical application has expanded to keep pace with the ever-increasing demands of a national growth more swift and complex than has elsewhere been known. Within the last two or three generations it has also taken its place as an important, and even an indispensable, part of higher education. Technical institutes have sprung up on all sides in response to public demand. The study of science has been taken up by the older universities,

and is the main pursuit in most universities of modern foundation. Even higher claims are made for it. Its exponents speak
of it not only as having won an assured place in the front rank
of human studies, but as occupying in that rank a predominant,
if not, as some of them venture to assert, a practically exclusive
place. A note of triumph is sounded in these utterances. The
Royal Society of England has lately been celebrating, with
splendid ceremonies and before audiences containing many
of the foremost names of the present age, the two hundred
and fiftieth anniversary of its foundation. In connection with
these meetings, the importance and dignity of science were
asserted in these eloquent words:

"Our children are born into a time in which science has
already ceased to be a plaything; it has become, or is fast
becoming, the dominant factor in human affairs; it will deter-
mine who shall hold the supremacy among nations."

So far, the note is one of exultation: yet the satisfaction
of those who urge the claims of science is not complete.
They complain that science is not yet studied as it should
be; that other studies, whose value is inferior and whose
day is over, are allowed to encroach on a field and share an
authority which ought to belong to science alone. "It has as
yet," the writer from whom I have just quoted goes on, "no
adequate place in the intellectual equipment or in the education
of those who aspire to be the governing classes of the country."

This sentence is significant in more than one way. Whether
or not there are to be governing classes in the country—
be that country England, of which the words were spoken,
or America, to which they likewise apply—is exactly the
problem which lies for solution before modern democracy.
But however this may be, whether the nations will hand over
their government to a trained class, or with less prospect of
success to an untrained class, or whether, according to the
ideal impressed upon the United States by the founders of
the Republic, the governing power shall comprise all classes
and be the whole organized body of a self-governing nation
in which classes are obliterated, the claim is in either case made
that science in its modern sense is to be the staple of their
intellectual equipment.

Part of this claim has been already conceded. Immense endowments are lavished on scientific research and study. The axis of education has been sensibly shifted. Science has taken its place as an integral part of school and university education. The scientific methods of observation, record, and experiment have been introduced into other studies, and the scientific spirit, developed through the pursuit of the sciences, has become a general instrument of human culture. Unhappily, however, this great and beneficent change has not taken place smoothly, or without grave conflicts and violent misunderstandings. Partly from exaggerated claims made by enthusiasts for the new learning, and still more largely from a narrow and obstinate conservatism among the supporters of the old, friction has ensued which is as needless as it is prejudicial. The idea has grown up that science is in some way opposed to art and letters. The unity of all knowledge, the co-ordination and mutual support of all human effort, has been lost sight of on both sides in this controversy. On one side were vested interests, old traditions, the jealousy with which innovations are apt to be regarded by those whose minds have been set in a particular pattern, and who cannot shift their perspective to the changes which the course of time brings about. On the other side were a revolt against the domination of these interests and traditions, a rejection of the stagnation involved in mere conservatism, and a necessary assertion of new needs and new methods of meeting them. But together with these came also an impatience of the past, an outlook narrowed by its own eagerness, and a recurrence of the belief that the path of progress lies in one, and in only one, direction. The fancied opposition of science to art and letters, and more particularly to poetry, is injurious to the general interest of mankind, to which all more special interests are subordinate. In a national life which executes its functions fully, science and poetry will not be in conflict, but in co-operation. Each corresponds to a need of life; in the full and harmonious development of life each reinforces the other; and in any sound system of national education both have their place, their proper and indispensable function.

We may regard this co-operation from either point of view: that which has primary regard to what poetry gains from science, and that which looks, conversely, at what science gains from poetry. The creative instinct, the imaginative impulse, which find expression in poetry, are powerfully reinforced by the discoveries of science and by the growth of the scientific spirit. For that spirit affects the whole field of mental activity. The discoveries of science present the creative imagination with an ampler, richer, and more wonderful world; the spirit in which they are made and the methods by which they are pursued give a greater insight into that world. The scientific imagination is akin, though it works in a different field, to the poetic imagination. Both are creative energies; both work towards bringing out the organic laws of truth or of beauty which underlie the structure of man and of the universe in which man finds himself. The poetic imagination is, or ought to be, kindled by the work of science. The scientific imagination is, or ought to be, kindled by the work of poetry.

If we look to history, instances will at once occur where this conjunction has actually taken place. Ancient Greece invented science and perfected the art of poetry; and the development of Athenian poetry into what became, and still remains, the delight and wonder of the world, was coincident with the first growth, among the same race and in the same civilization, of scientific inquiry, that is to say, of the search into the meaning and connection of things. The physical sciences were no doubt then still in their infancy: but the impulse towards them had been created and went side by side with the more patent and widespread impulse towards the scientific study of language and the operations of the human mind.

So too, at Rome, the great poem of Lucretius, in which Latin poetry for the first time reached its full stature, was inspired by the Epicurean philosophy; and that philosophy was not only a system of ethics and a rule of life, but was—and was thereby distinguished from other philosophies—a systematic and brilliant attempt to solve the laws of nature and apply scientific principles to the construction and working of the physical universe. This scientific ardour was fixed by Lucretius as a poetic ideal. It was transmitted by him to his great successor in poetry. Virgil, in the celebrated passage where he gives utterance to his own ideal of life, prays that the Muses whose servant he is may before all else instruct him, not in the beauties of what is called a poet's world, river and woodland and a pastoral Arcadia, but in the "causes of things," the structure and law of the universe. Beyond poetry and beneath it lay the magnificent revelations of science; and only through the mastery of science could man enter into his inheritance, conquer fate, and dispel fear.

Once more, at the Renaissance, poetry and science found themselves working in close union. Each had a new birth; each gave the other mutual stimulus. Milton, in whom English poetry culminated, and who represents, for us as for his own time, the classic standard in poetical art, was a profound student of two sciences which in his age were making immense advances—those of music and astronomy. His scientific knowledge enriches and gives fibre to his whole poetry. In the *Paradise Lost* he mentions only one of his contemporaries by name; and that one, it is significant to notice, is not a man of letters, but the most eminent man of science of that generation—the physicist and astronomer Galileo. Had he lived two hundred years later, we may guess that the name he would have chosen for this proud eminence would have been that of Darwin. Christ's College in the University of Cambridge, where both Milton and Darwin received their education, has lately been celebrating the memory of both. In that double celebration we may see vividly not only the continuity and interconnection of learning, but the kinship of poetry with science, and the ideal of a university.

The expansion of science in more modern times has been concurrent with a similar expansion of poetry. The difficulty which both poetry and science have now to face lies just in this immense expansion of their field. Material accumulates faster than it can be dealt with. It is the day of the specialist both in science and in the art of letters. Against the narrowing effect of over-specialization in his own particular field, the only safeguard is that width of outlook which is gained by grasping life as a whole, by mastering its pattern, as that pattern is discovered by the investigation of men of science, and is re-created or reinterpreted by the poets.

What poetry gains from science is strength and substance, a closer contact with the truth of things, and the power given by the use of a trained intellect. What science gains from poetry is something more impalpable, but not less important; it is what a French scientist calls *élan vital*; it is the impelling and organizing force of ideas and imagination. Without ideas, pure science is little more than a record of facts. Without imagination, applied science is sterile. Invention is the application of imagination to material things. The earliest scientific theories were expressed in the imaginative forms of poetry: the latest are the application, to enormous masses of facts gathered through observation and experiment, of what may be almost called a creative insight, akin to, and based on, that imaginative power which is the essence of poetical creation, and which is fostered by the study of poetry. For by studying poetry we become partakers, to some extent and according to our powers, of the genius of the poets; we develop our own power of creative imagination. Now this creative imagination is not a separate faculty, shut off from the rest of our faculties. If it is treated as such, the results are disastrous: much of the suspicion and dislike with which poetry has been regarded among men of science is the natural result of a claim arrogated by men of letters, or by people brought up in the tradition of a time before science was recognized as a part of human culture and before scientific method had been applied to all the processes of life, that art and letters were the only sphere in which the imagination can work. But it remains true that it is normally through these that it is first kindled. It remains true that the study of science is most effectively pursued by those who approach it with an intelligence made sensitive, an imagination quickened, by the patterns of life created by poets and the pattern-making power which the study of poetry develops.

If there are defects in the present system of American education, they are due, according to the judgment of many

thoughtful observers, to the fact that it hurries towards
results without the wide preliminary training which develops
the powers of the mind on all their sides. So far as this is
the case, it condemns men to work with inferior tools, with
an inadequate mental equipment. The result is like that of
an engine racing: the mind is not in gear with the whole
system of its surroundings, and much of its work is wasted.
Energy and capacity are there in full measure; but the capacity
has not the proper field to deploy itself in; the energy is forced
to run in contracted channels, or, beyond these, to run to
waste. Let me quote here the striking words used recently by
a distinguished man of science and one of the most zealous
advocates for giving science a primary place in national
education.

"Several Americans have told me," says Mr. A. E. Shipley,
"that comparatively few things are actually invented in
America, that most inventions come from abroad, but are
eagerly taken up and exploited in the States. Where the
American really shines is not as an inventor, but as a manufac-
turer. It is a striking fact that originality is rare in America,
and I think it must be accounted for by the educational system.
It stifles originality."

This is a grave charge; but so far as the defect actually
exists it should be realized, and so far as it is realized it can
be remedied. We need to lay stress—and stress is being effectively laid by nearly all educationalists—on the necessity
and value of scientific training for those who are destined to
pursue art and literature. We need to lay stress likewise—
and this need should not be neglected or postponed—on the
necessity and value of literary and artistic training for those
who are destined to pursue science. But to put it so is to state
the case inadequately. For it is only a minority in an educated
nation who will do either, whose life will be devoted wholly
either to literary and artistic, or to scientific pursuits. Not
only for these two limited classes, but for the whole of the
nation of the future, the ideal which rises before us is that
of an education developing all the faculties in harmony; of a
nation brought into touch with the facts of nature and her
laws, and into touch no less with the best of what has been

thought and felt by mankind, and with its noblest and most beautiful expression. And this last is given us by poetry. Nature, as Bacon said, is conquered by obedience; and science teaches us the laws to be obeyed and the mastery over nature which may be achieved by this obedience. Life is grasped and ordered by imaginative insight; and poetry teaches us the pattern of that order, and creates in us a new meaning, a new beauty and value, for the world and for ourselves.

V

POETRY AND BUSINESS

ONLY a few dedicate their life to the pursuit of science, only a few to the pursuit of art and letters. But we have all, in a greater or less degree, to do business. In it we have, directly or indirectly, our means of subsistence and our current occupation. Business is the substructure of life. A scientific community only means a community in which certain persons (comparatively a few) work systematically at science. They record their inventions or discoveries; they communicate the results of their research and the stimulus of their enthusiasm to others; and thus a certain secondary scientific knowledge, a certain appreciation of the scientific spirit and a large power of using scientific results, reaches through the mass of the people and colours the national life. A literary and artistic community only means a community in which certain persons (these also comparatively a few) do creative work in art and letters, and in the main body of which there is a certain appreciation of that work, and through it of the art and thought of other centuries and ages likewise. But a business community means one in which the whole mass and body of the nation, with insignificant exceptions, is engaged in business as its daily function, in which business is the staple of the national activity.

The United States are the greatest business community in the world. Industry and commerce have been, from the earliest days of the Republic, the chief pursuits of the nation, those to which it has applied itself constantly and eagerly, upon which it has grown and thriven. On them the whole social fabric has been built up. With the vast increase of wealth due to expanding population and increased power of handling or creating material resources, the energy of business has kept increasing likewise, and its claims on life have become more and more imperious. A sort of fury of industry set in with the extension of the nation over the Middle and Western States, and just at the same time the great discoveries of applied science began to be made which have increased a hundredfold the control of man over nature. After the Civil War the reunited nation plunged into the business of material development on a scale and with a passion until then unknown in history. The business to be done multiplied faster than the hands who were there to do it. Everything became speeded up. Business encroached on all other national activities, and threatened to overwhelm the whole of life. Against this over-encroachment the national conscience is now beginning to rise up, and to reassert the claims of a smoother, less hurried, less perplexed life, not loaded down and breathless under the weight of its own machinery, but using that machinery towards ampler ends— as its master, not its slave.

Poetry and business may seem to have little to do with each other; or their relation, so far as any exists, to be one of mutual dislike and antagonism. Business methods are not the methods of art. The man of business is apt to regard poetry with contempt; and his contempt is fully reciprocated by many followers of poetry. Yet if both are necessary elements in civilized life, there must be some understanding to be come to between them, some harmony attainable. No poet can afford to neglect the machinery of industry; for by means of it he, like all other men, lives. But neither can the man of business afford (if he knew it) to neglect poetry; for in it the life which he, like all other men, lives, receives its meaning and interpretation. Business is a means, not an end. Its uses are necessary and great; but they require to be adjusted to ends beyond itself, beyond business for its own sake, if the life of the business man is to be one in which the full human capacities can be worthily employed. If his life is not touched and uplifted by imagination, he is the slave of business, and not its master.

For some, indeed,—and more perhaps in America than elsewhere,—business is more than an occupation: it is an art, and its exercise has a quality which might almost be called creative. The born man of business loves it for its own sake; and love implies some sort of ideal, some sort of exercise of the imaginative as well as of the practical faculties. Or we may rather say that the imaginative faculty, checked elsewhere, and not finding its natural outlet, forces itself into the one channel left open for it, and to some extent informs the life of business with ideals of its own, not to be scorned or denied, however short they may come of the higher and larger ideal. Without some such imaginative touch upon it,—and the touch is at best imperfect and rare,—how grey and joyless the purely business life is; how purposeless it seems in moments of serious reflection; how prosaic a world it offers! It keeps the world going, but at what a waste of the energies engaged on that laborious task! Let me quote what was said, sixty years ago, by an able man of business, a master of the theory and practice of finance. "By dull care," he wrote, "by stupid industry, a certain social fabric somehow exists. People contrive to go out to their work, and to find work to employ them; body and soul are kept together. And this is what mankind have to show for their six thousand years of toil and trouble!" These words of Bagehot are as true now as they were then. The human race want more than to keep body and soul together: they want, and claim, not merely the continuance, but the fruition of life. Machinery to keep the world going is necessary; but it is not necessary, it is not right, that it should be kept going by turning masses of the nation into mere parts of the machine. For this would indeed be, in the noble line of a Latin poet, *propter vitam vivendi perdere causas*, "for the sake of life to throw away all that makes life worth living." It was not for this that man was created. It was not for this that the rights of man were asserted. To be enslaved to business is no less servitude than to be branded with the name and work at the caprice of a slave-owner. And as

D

with the chattel slavery abolished by the Republic half a century ago, so with this subtler but equally real slavery to business (whether forced on the individual by circumstances or adopted by him of his own will under the illusion that it will bring him the real wealth of life), the evil effects spread far beyond the slaves themselves: they contract, degrade, and vitiate the whole life of a nation.

In common speech, as in popular thought, business is opposed to pleasure. This is highly significant. So far as the opposition represents a fact—and if it does not represent a fact, how are we to explain its prevalence, its being taken everywhere for granted?—it means that the unity of life has been lost. Business that does not bring pleasure with it, and in it, is only drudgery. It sustains life, but the life which it sustains is thin and barren. It accumulates wealth, but the value of wealth depends on the use made of it, and national, like private, riches are but the substructure of national well-being: they are the means of living, not the object of life. To bring business and pleasure into their true relation, business must be elevated from a mechanism into an art. This is not done by legislation: it is done by the self-realization of the human spirit. Towards this self-realization poetry works; and therefore a nation needs poetry.

Business, or industry, has two sides—production and organization. In order to elevate it into an art it must be carried on with pleasure and for the sake of pleasure. For this is the definition of art: it is production with pleasure and for the sake of producing. The pleasure of production is given by the pattern or ideal in the mind of the producer. And similarly, the pleasure of organization is given by the pattern or ideal in the mind of the organizer. Now the function of poetry, as we have seen, is to create patterns or ideals of life; and the study of poetry means the reception into the mind of these patterns of life created by the poets, and their assimilation by the sympathetic instinct which they awaken. Thus received and assimilated, they fertilize life and make it fruitful; they make industry into a conscious pleasure. The beauty and the joy of life which they embody become part of our own life. Our industry becomes truly creative; our business is not carried on as a burden, but exercised as an art. Work and enjoyment are no longer contrary forces tearing our life asunder between them. Poetry, through the patterns of life created by the great poets, will raise us above our own lives, give us spiritual control over them, make the conduct of them no mere mechanical keeping of things going from day to day, but the daily exercise of faculties through which we are partakers in a full humanity.

Poets are often called dreamers, and some poets have been such. For the making of poetry is, like the other arts, also an industry; and, like other industries, it can be pursued mechanically: the poet may become absorbed in the workmanship of his art, and practise it, as the business man may practise his business, from mere habit, when he has lost the vital energy of creation. Or, like other ways of life, it can be pursued with too much absorption; and, cutting itself away from the deep roots of thought, emotion, and experience, it may become a tissue of fantasies where the creative or imaginative powers have been working in a vacuum, and the patterns of life which they produce dissolve in the very act of forming themselves; as in some witch's weaving, "the web, reeled off, curls and goes out like steam." Nor is the study of poetry free from the same danger. Those who neglect business, which is the foundation of life, and conduct, which in the famous phrase is three-fourths of life, for the mere study of poetry as an art or a relaxation, may still find in that study both pleasure and occupation; but when thus cut off from what should be its foundation and substance, such study degenerates: it is apt to turn into the assiduity of the pedant or into the busy idleness of the dilettante. For those who content themselves with it—and all the more if by it they drug themselves into unconcern with activity and duty—the censure of the practical man of business is justified, and his contempt intelligible. They discredit the study of poetry by studying it wrongly. Not one of the least important functions which an institution of higher education fulfils is to direct and organize this study so as to make it really fertile, and to combine it with other studies in the scope of a training at once liberal and practical. The product of such institutions, so far as they succeed in doing what they set out to do, will be men and women nurtured among the ideals of thought and art, made sensitive to beauty, quickened by sympathetic intelligence, yet not so the less competent, but the more, to take their share in the business of the world, in commerce or finance or industry. A generation so equipped for life, and sent into it with the whole range of their faculties so developed, will not only keep the world going, but will raise the whole national life to a higher plane. They will be in the highest sense good citizens; and in the goodness of its citizens lie the excellence and the true greatness of the state.

The ideals of citizenship include in them nearly all the lesser or more partial ideals aimed at through the specialization of faculty on particular pursuits. By their wider scope and larger outlook they connect and balance these others. It is the privilege, as it is the duty, of a community which through the labour of past generations has conquered and cleared a dwelling-place for itself, to set in order and beautify its house. The pursuit of riches, of material comfort, even of greatness, is with the nation, as with the individual, a pursuit upon which the whole of life should not be spent. Until now the Republic has had her hands full with a great, necessary, and engrossing task—that of creating a nation, of organizing a commonwealth, of bringing the resources of a continent under her control and asserting her place and dignity in the world. Upon that vast structure the spirit of beauty must be breathed, into it the patterns of noble thought, action, and emotion must be brought, to make the Republic of the future fulfil the plan of its founders, and justify the vast labour that past generations have lavished on building it up into material stability.

VI

POETRY AND DEMOCRACY

THE suspicion or dislike with which poetry is regarded by practical people, however unjust or exaggerated, has its reasons, and has existed in all ages and under all organizations of society. But in a democracy poetry lies under another special charge, which if made good against it would be fatal. It is regarded as the amusement of a leisured class, as something savouring of an aristocratic society. Art and letters as a whole share in this charge, but it falls on poetry with special force. Some kinds of literature have an obvious popular interest and make an obvious appeal to the mass of the nation. Some of the fine arts are applied directly, like architecture, to the public service, or directly affect, like music, the sensibility of massed audiences. Others are excused, rather than approved, because they employ labour, encourage special industries, and produce tangible material products. This is not the case with poetry. It stands or falls on its own merits, in its own inherent virtue.

But poetry is a function of life; and where life is organized under democratic standards poetry is, or should be, a function of the democratized nation. Much of the poetry of the past has been produced by and for a small cultured class. In aristocratic societies such a class was the pivot and guiding force of the nation; in it the imaginative ideals and the creative instincts of the whole people were concentrated, or, so far as they existed elsewhere, were used by it for its own purposes. The rest of the nation was but the soil out of which that flower grew, or the fuel consumed to give the ruling class sustenance, ease, and material force ready to its hand. The public conscience now demands that there shall be no ruling class, but that all shall be fitted to rule. The aristocracy of intellect is subject to the same vices, and falls under the same condemnation, as the old aristocracy of birth, or the cruder modern aristocracy of riches. The ideal of democracy—far, indeed, yet, from being realized, but felt everywhere, alike by its opponents and its followers, as a pressure steadily moving mankind in a particular direction—is that culture, like wealth and leisure, should be diffused through the whole nation. It abolishes the distinction between active and passive citizens, between a governing caste and a governed people. That is its political aspect. But its larger and nobler ideal is that of a community in which not only the task and responsibility of setting its own house in order and swaying its own destinies, but the whole conduct and development of its own culture, shall be universally shared; in which not only government, but life in its full compass, shall be conducted by the people for the people; in which the human race shall be joint inheritors of the fruits of the human spirit.

Only once, and among a single people, has this ideal been partially realized in the past. The democracy of Athens set no less an aim before itself, and for a brilliant moment seemed to have attained it. Poetry and art reached their climax there together with democratic government. It was the boast of Athens that culture no less than political power was shared by all her citizens. Poets and artists drew from that national atmosphere the creative and imaginative power which they embodied in their work, and returned to the nation in visible and immortal shapes the patterns of life with which the nation had inspired them. But the Athenian democracy rested on insecure foundations. Like so many bright things, it came quickly to confusion, leaving behind it only a memory and an ideal to inspire all future ages. Many centuries had to elapse before the ideal of a civilized democracy was again raised as a standard before mankind by the founders of the American Republic.

The crimes and follies of the Middle Ages, it has been well said, were those of a complex bureaucracy in a half-civilized state. It is towards the end of the Middle Ages that we find the beginnings of national self-consciousness, and, with it, of democratic poetry, embodying patterns of national life. Nor was this all. As the inchoate or embryonic democracy began to be conscious of itself, it began also to be conscious of art, even when that art was the art produced among and for a limited class. As it began to be civilized, it began to have sympathy with the products of civilization, and to take, if not yet to assert, some share in them. The ideal world of romance and chivalry opened out before it as something in which it could find patterns of life for itself. A common and universal religion, which in theory at least, recognized no distinction between classes, between riches and poverty, between prince and people, gave a wide popular basis to all the arts which were employed in its service. Education began to leaven the community. Poetry sought and found a wider audience. Shakespeare produced his plays not for a literary class nor for a court circle, but for the populace of London who flocked to see and hear them. His own sympathies with the people have been doubted or denied; he seems, in the mouths of his characters, to speak of them with something like contempt; which was in fact exactly what they wished and what they enjoyed. But he gave them a national drama. Even the epic, that stately form of poetry which has thriven in the courts of princes and deals with the high actions and passions of the great, became in a wider sense national. The verses of Ariosto and Tasso, court poetry written for a highly educated aristocratic circle, were sung by Venetian gondoliers and Lombard vine-dressers, as those of Pindar had been sung in ancient Greece by fishermen, and as those of Virgil are found scrawled on street walls in Pompeii. In England, Milton, a poet of profound learning and extraordinary technical skill, was read and appreciated not only by scholars or artists, but widely among a people whose study of the Bible had introduced them to literature and taught them in some measure to appreciate poetry. His genius penetrated and inspired the Puritan democracy; and though his own republicanism was of a severely aristocratic type, he may be called in some sense the source of republican poetry. For, once poetry had taken to do with the fate and destiny of mankind itself, it had to concern itself with the life and labour of the people as the main factor in human affairs. It found the reflection of the kingdom of God in the commonwealth of mankind. The freedom of God's ransomed drew with it as its consequence a freedom which was of this world. The equality of men before God bore with it their equality of rights and dignity here. The brotherhood of all God's children led on to the doctrine of a true fraternity, not only religious but political and social likewise, linking together all members of the human race.

The eighteenth century, that great germinal age of the human spirit, the age in which not only the American Commonwealth but the modern world was created, was one in which poetry held itself back. It was waiting for the shaping of the new structure of life: the task lay before it of fashioning that structure into new imaginative patterns, and giving it thereby organic form and vital interpretation. Towards the end of the century this preliminary work was well on foot: the new world was taking substance, and lay ready for the transforming touch of the poets. The American Revolution had created the Republic. The French Revolution had shattered the old régime and its tradition in Europe. The Industrial Revolution was transforming the whole mechanism and texture of civilized life. In both continents a new world had begun. It was the world of the Rights of Man, of the *carrière ouverte*, of the sovereignty of the People; and into this world poetry let itself loose, to create, to interpret, to vivify. The idea of democracy had arisen among the thinkers and been translated into action by the statesmen; the patterns of a democratic world began to be wrought out by the poets.

Among the great English poets of that age, the greatest, in the combined mass and excellence of his work, is generally accounted to be Wordsworth. He divined the new age, but did not enter into it. His early democratic enthusiasm, chilled by the terrors of the French Revolution, became converted first into despair, and then into a search, in the recesses of his own mind, for ideals of life independent of external things. Yet he was the first, after Burns,—and Burns was then still only the poet of a small nation, not of the English-speaking race,—to link poetry with the requirements of nascent democracy. In his *Lyrical Ballads*, as in the poems which succeeded them during his greatest period, he set himself expressly and deliberately to write poetry in the language of the people, and to seek the material out of which poetry was to be shaped in the common thoughts and passions and experiences of mankind.

Hardly less was the share borne in the democratization of poetry by other great poets of that great period. Byron, himself an aristocrat by birth, believed in democracy; by his appeal to the elemental human passions he brought the impact of poetry on the larger world which was prepared to receive it. Shelley reared before the eyes of that larger world the glittering fabric of an imaginatively reconstructed universe in which, freed from tyranny and superstition, from selfishness and apathy, the human race might develop its noblest qualities, and life be one long ecstasy of joy. Even those who regard Byron as a beautiful fiend, and Shelley as an ineffectual angel, must admit the truth of the striking words used of them by Tennyson, that these two poets, "however mistaken they may be, did yet give the world another heart and new pulses."

Even more striking and significant is the attitude towards an anticipated democracy, and the part to be played in it by poetry, which was taken by Keats. He was the youngest of that great group of revolutionary poets, the most gifted and the most splendid in his wonderful promise and unfinished achievement. Beyond all those others, with a width and foresight of vision all his own, he pointed and urged poetry forward. The horizon to which he saw is still distant and unreached. That "joy in widest commonalty spread," of which Wordsworth had profound glimpses, and which Shelley saw, as it were, through an iridescent burning mist, lay before the eyes of Keats, clearly, definitely, attainably. The world to which he looked forward was one in which, as he says, "every human being might become great, and humanity, instead of being a wide heath of furze and briars, with here and there a remote oak or pine, would become a grand democracy of forest trees." In that image he embodies for us the ideal of democracy in the highest and amplest form. And of this democratic ideal, poetry, because coextensive with human life, will be the informing spirit.

Democracy, we are often told, is on its trial. The brilliant promises of its youth have not been realized. It has not transformed human nature. It has not done away with the vices of older civilizations, and it has developed new faults of its own. It is, among many of those who do not expressly reject it, accepted wearily as a necessity rather than embraced eagerly as a faith. Citizenship has with them become a burden, not an inspiration. Freedom and equality have sunk into mere formulary names, giving neither light nor heat, having little to do with the actual conduct and motives of life. Material progress goes on mechanically; the higher progress, the fuller self-realization of mankind, is doubted or denied. Once more, as Wordsworth complained a century ago, false gods have been enthroned in the temple of the human spirit.

> The wealthiest man among us is the best;
> No grandeur now in nature or in book
> Delights us: rapine, avarice, expense,
> This is idolatry, and these we adore:
> Plain living and high thinking are no more.

So Wordsworth wrote then; and we must remember, if we are inclined to be despondent over the present case of democracy, that our dissatisfaction is no new thing, and that the mere fact of our being dissatisfied shows that we have not lost sight of higher ideals, and have the impulse in us, if we can direct and sustain it, to resume our progress towards them.

Poetry is also on its trial. The patterns of life it offers to us, the interpretation of life with which it presents us, seem to many unreal and remote. It speaks a strange language, thin and ghostly to the ears that are not attuned to it; it often holds itself aloof from, or mingles but passingly with, the main current and texture of occupations and endeavours, of private pursuits or public interests.

Each alike suffers from the divorce that is between them. A democracy which excludes or ignores poetry cuts itself off from one of the main sources of vital strength and national greatness. A poetry which is out of sympathy with democracy is thereby out of touch with actual life. But the future that lies before both is splendid, if both will work in harmony, if national life is inspired and sustained by poetry, and poetry takes nothing less than that life for its province, gives it a heightened meaning, brings out from it the latent patterns of beauty after which it blindly but unceasingly aspires. Poetry, as Dryden said of it, is articulate music: the music to which life moves, and in which it finds its discords resolved.

Such is the task and function of the poets. But the study of poetry is not for poets alone, any more than the study of colour and form is confined to painters, or the study of music to composers. The appeal of art is universal. The inheritance of the present age is not merely the present, but the whole past as well. Of that inheritance, the great poetry of the world, from Homer downwards, is the most precious portion. It preserves for us, still alive and still having power to move and kindle, the best of what mankind has thought and felt, the most perfect forms into which it has cast its vision and reflection, its emotion and aspiration. And thus the study of poetry is part of democratic education; and the poetry of democracy, kindled by that study and appealing to a nation educated in it, will be the articulate music of national life.

WHAT IS THE GOOD OF GREEK?

[*A Public Lecture given at Melbourne by the invitation of the University,
22 June, 1923*]

I MAY be allowed, on my first appearance before a
Melbourne audience, to express my sense of the warmth
of welcome which I have received not only from the University by whose invitation I am here, but more largely from the
great capital of a great State, and from many of her most
distinguished citizens. My gratitude is free from any of the
embarrassment that might arise if this reception were a personal
tribute. I recognize and acknowledge it as an expression of
the kinship of the Universities of the Empire as joint members
of the Commonwealth of Learning. And the presence of the
Lieutenant-Governor in the Chair emphasizes the link between
the University and the State. It is a mark of recognition that
higher education and large humane culture are, no less than
material prosperity or diffused comfort, matters of national
concern: of determination that those "higher walks" to which
Sir William Irvine has felicitously referred shall not be
inaccessible to the citizens of a modern democratic
Commonwealth.

If the subject chosen for this address may have seemed to
any of those here, when it was announced, one of only sectional
interest and irrelevant to a larger issue and a wider audience,
I would ask them to suspend that judgment. For I hope to
persuade you, if you need persuading, that it is neither.

I have put it in the form of a question. It is a question often
asked in sarcasm or in scepticism, and even oftener in the
mere carelessness that does not expect or wait for an answer.
But it also may be, and is, asked in a spirit of serious inquiry.
It is in this spirit that I ask you to consider it with me. The
answer to be given is important; it deserves our best thought
towards getting at the real truth of the matter. For on the
nature of the answer, and the conviction or failure of conviction which it carries, depends our attitude as citizens of a

responsible self-governing community towards the aim and sphere of national education in its widest sense. This is so in three respects: first, towards Greek as a language and a literature embodying a special manifestation of the human spirit; next, towards that Greek civilization out of which and under whose influence our own civilization, as a matter of traceable and demonstrable historic fact, arose; and lastly, towards the whole group of humanistic studies of which Greek is one; to the studies, that is to say, which are not concerned, or are not concerned directly, with the laws and processes of the physical world, but with life, thought, and conduct, with human nature as it is, as it has been, and as it may become.

Times change; fashions vary; beliefs alter. In Scotland fifty years ago, when I was a schoolboy there, the question we are considering was seldom if ever asked. The value of Greek was taken for granted. Partly, this was a matter of old tradition in a proud and conservative race. Partly, it was due to the rooted belief in education, the national respect for learning for its own sake. Partly, it was the result of a more intangible prestige, towards which these and other elements combined. Education was prized, no doubt, for its results in market value. But it was prized higher, and more widely, for itself. It was recognized as enabling human beings, not perhaps to be successful in the ordinary sense, but to realize their moral powers and intellectual capacities; thus giving its possessors self-respect and entitling them to respect from others, furnishing them with a surer hold on life, with sources of lasting strength and inward happiness.

In education as thus viewed, as given and received in this spirit, the classics, and Greek in particular, held a prominent and an unchallenged place. With most pupils, the classical teaching received did not go beyond the elements; and it was, of course, only a small minority of the population who received even that. But to be entered on Latin was a source of great satisfaction; it was a distinction and a privilege. To be entered on Greek was a higher and rarer distinction still. Greek was regarded not as a useless luxury or an idle accomplishment, but as a prize for the aptest and most forward, who were a little envied, and a good deal looked up to, by their less fortunate schoolfellows. Nor was it a privilege in the lower sense of the term, the appanage of superior birth or wealth or social standing. That age was in a way more democratic than the present, because it was so by a common instinct rather than by contentious theory or abstract dogma. There were classes, and they were clearly defined; but they were organic. The artificial growth of class-consciousness was yet to come. Class-consciousness, and the sectionalism which it implies, are the antithesis of democracy, and they only hamper the life of a nation.

Such was the educational practice—it was rather practice or habit than theory—which produced a corresponding type of citizen: hard workers, clear reasoners, with developed capacities for acting and producing and thinking; with intelligence and character; people to whom life was a serious thing, and learning was perhaps the most precious thing in life.

Now we are in a new world. Nothing stands still. What we have to regard here is not the Scotland of fifty years ago, but the Australia of to-day. The industrial and political revolutions of the last century have been followed or accompanied by a cultural revolution no less profound. Great new fields of knowledge have been opened. There has been an immense specialization of industry in the intellectual field. One of the most marked results of this revolution was that competition rather than co-operation of studies became prevalent. A multitude of options replaced the old unity of education; and vocational training was held of more account than the formation of a wide solid basis of intelligence and character. Education, or what went by that name, was given and received not for its own sake, not for its human and humanizing value, but for its material profit, its immediate value in the market. As cause and as consequence, there came a marked loss of belief in learning as an end in itself, as an inward possession. With loss of belief in it there naturally came loss of respect for it in others, perhaps too of the self-respect it created in its possessors, and of the sense of human dignity which it once had given.

So it was that Latin and Greek came to be thought of, and then openly spoken of, as dead languages. Latin was kept, as it were on sufferance, for certain direct and indispensable uses. Greek tended more and more to be discarded as useless. The results of this were not immediately obvious, still less were they immediately fatal. We have been until lately living on the intellectual and moral capital inherited by us. But we have been and are using it up fast. That form of wealth, like others, becomes exhausted if it is not kept steadily replenished.

The object of the most clear-sighted thinkers and administrators is to reinstate, while there is still time, the ideal of humanism. That ideal is to realize human possibilities and rise to them; to grasp and assimilate the fundamental truths of life; to get in touch, by methods which call for perpetual readjustment, but on lines which remain steadily the same, with the human spirit and the human environment; with the spectacle of the world in which we find ourselves, with the laws and processes of nature, and with the history, thought, and action of mankind.

Now the use of Greek is this, that it lies at the base of humanism. It was through the Greek genius that man became fully human; and without Greek the humanistic mastery of life remains incomplete. And there is this further point to be added—it is of scarcely inferior importance—that the Greek achievement, more particularly in literature, both prose and poetry, is unequalled in quality. In the great Greek writers there is an excellence never reached before or since. They supply us, and this is as true now as it ever was, not only with an unfailing source of the highest human pleasure, but with a permanent model and standard for our own utmost effort.

Greek is not a quack specific. It can be badly taught and badly learned. It can be so handled (as all the best things can) that it becomes useless or worse than useless. But, even after all allowance is made for this, it is a gate opening into an enlarged and ennobled life. Education without Greek may be, and often is, very good; but with Greek it is better. In this, as in other things, the hope may be cherished that this Commonwealth will not be content with anything short of the best. No democratic nation can fulfil the height of its mission unless it develops the highest possible level of culture throughout the community. No nation conscious of its own greatness and realizing in what national greatness consists can afford to do without the highly cultured citizen who is of vital power in civic or State affairs, or the trained scholar whose function it is to keep up the quality and standard of culture.

Here a word must be said on the doctrine of substitutes. It is often asserted or suggested that the value of Greek may be got in other ways; that through translations of the Greek classics, and through modern books about Greek history, Greek civilization, Greek letters, thought, and art, we can acquire all that is really useful or enlightening for us, without the labour of learning the Greek language. This is a complete fallacy. However it may be in other matters, in things of the mind there is no such thing as "getting ninepence for fourpence." Substitutes are futile: short-cuts lead nowhere. The way can only be entered through the gate. "I hope all will be well," says that brisk lad, Ignorance, in the *Pilgrim's Progress*, "and as for the gate that you talk of, all the world knows that that is a great way off of our Country. I cannot think that any man in all our parts doth so much as know the way to it; nor need they matter whether they do or no, since we have, as you see, a fine pleasant green lane, that comes down from our Country the next way into it." "It pities me much for this poor man," Christian observes to Hopeful; "it will certainly go ill with him at last." And so it did.

Translations from the Greek have their use and their value; but they can in no sense replace the originals. This cannot be put more briefly or pointedly than in the words of a distinguished scholar and translator, Professor Gilbert Murray; they may carry the more weight here because he is himself Australian-born: "When we translate it, the glory is gone." That is true of all the Greek classics, but eminently true of the greatest glory of Greek, its poetry. It is of the essence of poetry that it cannot be translated. The attempt is continually made, because the lure is irresistible. New translations go on being made, simply because each, when it is made, is and is felt to be unsatisfying, misses the vital essence.

So too with books or lectures about Greek literature, Greek thought or speculation, Greek political theory and practice. To those who have entered through the gate they may be and often are of the greatest value. To those who have not, they may by luck be stimulating, but are mostly either useless or misleading.

During the Middle Ages, Greek was lost to Europe. Its re-discovery in the fifteenth century was equal in importance to the discovery of America; both were new worlds. There followed on their discovery, and largely as a consequence of it, a great liberation and expansion of the human mind. In course of time that movement, as happens to all movements of the human spirit, stagnated. Greek studies became professionalized, and Greek itself seemed to be losing some of its virtue. It did not; it was only biding its time. The new world-movement of the last generation has included what is nothing short of a new discovery of Greek. It is only possible here to mention in passing the enormous effect, not only on thought but on practice, of Plato's *Republic*, of the drama of Euripides, of all those historical or philosophical or imaginative writings which show us the Greek mind in speculation and in action. There is no ethical or political or social problem of our own day which the Greek mind did not raise, and of which, whether with success or with failure, it did not attempt a logical solution. One may say with conviction that the Greekless mind is as imperfectly equipped for citizenship as it is for appreciation of literary and artistic excellence.

This is beginning to be realized; but only just in time. For Greek had already dwindled away in schools; and as a natural or even necessary consequence, became very largely crowded out in the Universities. There has been a lamentable falling-off both in the provision for teaching Greek and in the numbers of pupils learning it. This is what can be, as it ought to be, remedied; it will be, if the public consciousness is aroused. In Scotland, once a home of Greek study, the Education Department announced, some years ago, that industrial communities saw no use in Greek. This would hardly be said now by the responsible authorities; nor, if it were, would it be accepted by an intelligent democracy. It is an industrial community which has special need of a high civilization.

It is time now to say something about that Greek literature for the sake of which it is that we learn Greek. But first it

E

should be noted that the Greek language itself is an unequalled instrument for delicacy, accuracy, and beauty. It was applied to many purposes by writers of all sorts; the stream of time has brought down to us large quantities of rubbish as well as the gold. But the language itself, even when used, as it often was, to little purpose, gives a new insight into the mechanism of expression.

The Greek genius created that language, and in it and by means of it created all the main types of literature, both in prose and poetry, and brought nearly all of them to perfection. Further, in the hands of its great masters, it gave expression in them, once for all, to the primal and essential interests of humanity.

Those who do not know Greek must of course take this on trust; they can only prove it for themselves by learning Greek. And even those who have learned Greek cannot realize its value until they have had experience of life. There is a well-known passage in Macaulay's Diary where, after reading Thucydides (perhaps for the tenth or twentieth time) when he was himself a practised statesman and an accomplished historian, he adds, as comment on his amazed admiration, "Young men, whatever their genius may be, are no judges." It would be easy, but unprofitable, to multiply testimonies. But two more may be cited, as coming from men whose integrity of mind cannot be doubted, who took no doctrines on trust or in indolent acquiescence, and who held no brief for the Classics. Wordsworth calls Herodotus "the most interesting and instructive book, next to the Bible, that has ever been written." Mill pays homage to the Greeks as "the beginners of everything, who made the indispensable first steps which are the foundation of all the rest."

Herodotus, no doubt, remains both interesting and instructive in what is left of him in a translation. But the difference! the light and colour, the pulse of life, the live voice, have all gone out of it. What Mill had more particularly in mind was the sphere in which his own chief interest lay, that of politics, economics, and social science. Here also translations are quite ineffective substitutes. I have already mentioned the immense influence of Plato, the first and most advanced of Socialists,

on modern social theory and practice, both among the Labour
Party and in the general trend of popular thought. But
that influence acts mainly at second or third hand; and in
second-hand knowledge there is a very subtle danger. As
diluted or distorted, whether by translation in the ordinary
sense, or by the still more perilous translation of substance,
which whether consciously or unconsciously is made by all
who attempt to popularize the unknown, Greek can become,
as the case may be, a narcotic, or an intoxicant, or a high
explosive. There is only one security against this danger; and
that is, to know Greek.

Another point may be made here. The Greek masterpieces
teach us the lesson, never more needed than now, of humility.
They make us feel that we have to go to school to the Greeks.
Goethe said of himself in the art of which he was so great a
master, "Beside the Greek poets I am absolutely nothing."
In a confused Babel of tongues, in the torrent of cleverness
which spouts and foams round us in endless volume from
journalists, novelists, poets, propagandists, it is through Greek
that we can keep our feet on solid ground; can realize the virtue
of direct truth to nature, of economy in language, of simplicity.
Crystalline simplicity—what tells and what lasts—is the final
quality of Greek work whether in prose or in poetry. In
translations, even the best, it evaporates or becomes turbid.
This is just why I will now ask you to consider a few instances
from Greek prose-writers and poets.

Let us take first the account given by Herodotus of
Marathon, the battle which even now can hardly be named
without a lifting of the heart, which determined the whole
course of European civilization, and fixed for a thousand
years the Western limit of the Asiatic races. This is how
Herodotus, in a few simple sentences, tells the story; I translate
his Greek as literally, word for word, as I can.

Then the Athenians were let go, and charged the barbarians
at a run. Between the two armies was a mile or rather more.
The Persians, seeing them coming on at a run, prepared to receive
them, imputing to the Athenians nothing short of disastrous
insanity when they saw them few, and even so coming on at a

run, with no force of cavalry or archers. So the barbarians thought. But the Athenians, when they engaged the barbarians in close order, fought worthily of account. The first of all Greeks within our knowledge they charged an enemy at a run; the first they stood the sight of the Median uniform and the men who wore it; until then the very name of the Medians was a terror to Greeks to hear. The fighting at Marathon lasted a long time. In the centre of the line the barbarians had the advantage, where the Persians themselves and the Sacians were posted; there the barbarians had the advantage, broke the line, and began to pursue inland. But on each wing the Athenians and Plateans won. As they won, they left the routed forces of the barbarians to flee, and bringing both wings together, engaged those who had broken their centre; and the Athenians won, and pursued the fleeing Persians, cutting them down, until they reached the sea.

That is all. In this or in any English it is bald. That is just my point. In the Greek, the simplicity is charged with emotion that makes every word tell; and it cannot be read, for the first or for the hundredth time, without a thrill of exaltation and awe.

Turn now from Herodotus, "the father of history," to Thucydides, the earliest and still the greatest of scientific historians, and look at the two or three tense vivid pages giving the account of the destruction of the great Athenian army in Sicily. "The modern historian," as Grote observes when he reaches this episode in his *History of Greece*, "strives in vain to convey the impression of it which appears in the condensed and burning phrases of Thucydides." "There is no prose composition in the world which I place so high; it is the *ne plus ultra* of human art": so Macaulay writes of it, citing with delighted approval the comment made on it by the poet Gray, "Is it or is it not the finest thing you ever read in your life?" We can realize it now even better than they, when we think of Gallipoli. At Syracuse there were a hundred and ten Athenian warships and about forty thousand troops, the flower of Athens: and this was out of a total population, slaves included, of only half a million. Imagine, if you can bear to imagine it, the total loss both of the fleet—for not one Athenian ship was saved—and of the whole army landed on the peninsula; and then listen, so far as it can be put into English, to the Greek historian's description of the final scene in a disaster even more awful and irretrievable.

All the day before, the wreck of the army had been struggling through scrubbed hills under a blazing sun without food or water or equipment, the enemy on three sides mowing them down at close range. At night they had to halt; some three hundred men broke through and went wandering through the darkness, only to be caught and cut down by cavalry the next day.

When day broke, Nicias began to move the army on; the Syracusans and their allies pressing them in the same way from all sides, shooting them down. The Athenians kept pressing on towards the Asinarus river, forced by the attack from all sides of the whole swarm of the enemy, including numerous cavalry, and thinking that it would be a trifle easier for them if they could get across the river, and at the same time by their distress and their fierce craving to drink. When they reach it, they tumble in, no longer in any order, but every one eager to get across first. The enemy, hard on their backs, made crossing difficult now; for, forced as they were to move in a crowd, they kept falling on one another and trampling one another down; some perished at once on their own spears and packs, others stumbled and kept falling in heaps. From both sides of the river—it ran between cliffs there—the Syracusans kept shooting the Athenians from above, and for the most part while they were drinking greedily and all bunched in confusion in the hollow ravine; while the Peloponnesians got down after them and made a great slaughter of them in the river. The water was spoiled at once, but was drunk as greedily as ever, mud and all, full of blood, and fought for by the crowd. At last, when the dead bodies were now lying in heaps on one another in the river, and the army destroyed, partly in the river-bed, and any that struggled through, by the cavalry, Nicias surrenders to Gylippus, putting more reliance on him than on the Syracusans; telling him and his Lacedaemonians to do as they choose with him, but to stop the murder of his men. Then Gylippus gave the order to take prisoners."

A little later, the two Athenian generals, Nicias and Demosthenes, were killed by the Syracusans, "against the wish of Gylippus"; not that he was any more humane or chivalrous than they, but because he had looked forward to the glory of parading them as prisoners at Sparta. The surviving wreckage of the army was driven into the quarries of Syracuse, where, with no food but a little flour and water, no shelter, no medical attendance, packed close and dying like flies, first in the fierce autumn heat and then in the freezing nights of early winter, amid the "intolerable stench" of wounds and corpses, "suffering all that was possible to suffer in such a place," they were herded miserably for more than two months and the wretched survivors then sold for slaves. "Such," is the unimpassioned comment of Thucydides, "was the total destruction, fleet and army and everything, and few out of many returned home."

The story of Anzac has been not unworthily told, but not told like this; nor could it have been told so well as it has been, if those who have recorded it had not themselves inherited something of the Greek tradition, with its economy of language, its lucid simplicity, its exact truth. Two thousand years hence, will it be a story that the inheritors of our civilization will be able to see as though it were passing before their own eyes?

Or once more, take the closing passage of Plato's *Phaedo*, with its record, in which consummate art and incomparable beauty of language are used with the amazing Greek simplicity, of the last moments of Socrates.

He uncovered his face, for he had covered himself up, and said (they were his last words), "Crito, I owe a cock to Asclepius; will you remember to pay the debt?" "The debt shall be paid," said Crito; "is there anything else?" There was no answer to his question; but in a minute or two a movement was heard, and the attendants uncovered him; his eyes were set, and Crito closed his eyes and mouth.

Such was the end, Echecrates, of our friend, whom I may truly call the wisest and justest and best of all the men whom I have ever known.

The quietness can be felt; the voice that does not need to shout in order to be heard. But no less here than in the other passages, the English can give but a faint idea of the lucid precision and effortless power of the Greek. This is still more

so if we turn from prose to poetry, in which form and substance are wholly inseparable. Any instances from poetry had
better, therefore, be of the briefest.

For one instance, I ask you to take the last line of the *Iliad*,
"So these held funeral for Hector the knight," and the comment made on it by one of its translators who was himself a
poet. "I cannot take my leave of this noble poem," are
Cowper's words, "without expressing how much I am struck
with this plain conclusion of it. I recollect nothing among
the works of mere man that exemplifies so strongly the true
style of great antiquity." "The true style": that is a phrase
worth remembering and taking to heart. For *le style*, in the
famous adage of Buffon, *c'est l'homme même*; and when we
speak of the true style we mean the perfect expression of the
true greatness of man.

For another, one might cite what is perhaps the noblest
utterance ever placed in human lips, the couplet written by
Simonides for the memorial-stone set up over the three
hundred Spartans who died at Thermopylae: *Passer-by, tell the
Lacedaemonians that we lie here obeying their orders.* So we may
attempt to render it; but this or any other rendering loses not
only the beauty, but half the meaning, of the original. The
word translated "passer-by" means that, but it also means
"stranger," and it also means "friend." The word translated
"lie" means that, but it also means "fell." The phrase
rendered "obeying their orders" is many-faceted; it means
that, but it means likewise "accepting their laws" and "having
faith in their word."

For another still, we might take one of the fragments of
Sappho, that incomparable lyrist who was to the Greeks
simply "the poetess" as Homer was "the poet": the seven
incredibly simple words for instance, of which the English
shadow is "I loved you once, Atthis, long ago," and which
give, as no other poet has given, the nightingale-note with its
liquid piercing sweetness.

Or if time allowed, I could speak of those many intense
and poignant lines in Sophocles (the most consummate of
all dramatists) that are not led up to and are not stressed,
but simply are there as if they happened—lines in which

language becomes transfigured and almost more than human. But of these one may gather some idea from lines in Shakespeare which have the same terrible and piercing simplicity, like Macduff's words in *Macbeth*,

> I cannot but remember such things were,

or Edgar's in *King Lear*,

> Men must endure
> Their going hence, even as their coming hither.

In such lines, more than ever, the actual form, the music and cadence of the language, are of the essence of what the words express. Translation spoils them; commentary only blurs them. The fact then is this: if we would make Greek poetry a possession and an inspiration of our own (and there is no possession more precious, no inspiration more powerful) we must know Greek. There is no other way.

It is further to be borne in mind that Greek is at the foundation not only of literature and art and thought, not only of the physical and social sciences, but of the Christian religion. It was in fact, in Europe from the sixteenth century onward, taught and learned primarily as the necessary equipment of clerics and theologians. St. Paul is in this sense one of the most important Greek classics. No less are the Gospels; for while they are based on Aramaic documents or oral traditions, these are lost, and we cannot, except imperfectly and conjecturally, get behind the Greek Gospels. With St. Paul as with Plato, with St. Luke as with Herodotus, the English rendering inevitably loses something of the original, by distortion or variation or subtle changes of implication or emphasis. Both the Authorized and the Revised Versions, and any other that can be made, are necessarily imperfect. I need not enlarge on this; it is only necessary to note that Greek is indispensable for an educated ministry, and that it cannot be satisfactorily acquired in Universities or theological Colleges without school-grounding. Colleges must be fed with prepared material if they are to do their own work effectively. It is the bedrock principle of national education that it should be a single organism, of which every part performs its own function. In that organism, the Universities have their function, the schools theirs. There must be continuity, but not confusion. To set a University to do the work of a secondary school is as wasteful as it would be to set a secondary school to do the work of a University. This applies to Greek as it does to English or to history or to science.

It has been noted by a thoughtful observer, as the great weakness of American civilization, that there is no aspiration, in cities or communities, to intellectual leadership; that the rivalry which is a powerful and need not be an ignoble stimulus to progress extends only to growth of numbers, or material wealth, or industrial output. Is this true of Australia also? or of Melbourne? I hope not: but the question must be asked expressly and answered honestly. A White Australia worthy of the name must be white not only racially but culturally; it must preserve and heighten its standards. People here as in Great Britain talk, hopefully or despairingly as the case may be, about the prospect of saving Greek. They have done so for long. It is nearly fifty years since Jowett wrote of Oxford and Cambridge: "I hope we shall save Greek in the Universities." The Universities cannot save either Greek or anything else, unless they have national consciousness behind them; unless there is in the body of the nation the will to live a high life, love and respect for knowledge, belief in the discipline and elevating power of learning, a sense of the human ideal as it was created in Greece.

That ideal hinges on three words; truth, beauty, freedom. We have still to go back to Greece to learn savingly the lesson that these three are one and inseparable; that truth without beauty and freedom is a withering up of vitality; that beauty without truth and freedom is poisonous; that freedom without truth and beauty leads straight to anarchy and dissolution. Or, to put it in other words, it is only truth and beauty that make man free; it is only truth and freedom that make life beautiful; it is only beauty and freedom that make truth live.

I have shown, as I hope, that Greek is not an idle luxury. The heavier charge is that it is, or may be, an intoxicant. But that is true, as I have also endeavoured to indicate, of its dilutions and misinterpretations rather than of itself. Itself it is indeed a powerful stimulant, but also a disciplining and controlling power.

Still one objection may be raised, and it is perhaps the commonest: what is the good of a little Greek? When science was introduced into our schools, it was decried by reactionary conservatives as smattering. It has lived through that outcry and established itself. Now the tables are turned, and contempt is poured as freely (and as foolishly) on "a smattering of Greek and Latin." But smattering is a different thing from grounding. No one says that to learn the multiplication table is to get a smattering of arithmetic. To the question, What is the good of a little Greek? it would be sufficient answer that virtue goes out from even a little of it. It is wonderful how soon we can get into touch with the essence of the Greek spirit even by touching a corner of it, the hem of its garment. We forget it all afterwards. Perhaps; but it has made us different. But the question itself, if we think a little more deeply, is futile. What is the good, one might as well ask, of a little of anything? of a little food? or of a little joy? or, if we come to that, of a little life? Life, with its splendour and its awful brevity, is given us not to be left empty, but to be filled. Even a very little Greek—but need it be always so very little?—helps towards this, whether we regard it as an instrument, or an equipment, or an organic energy assimilated by us and becoming part of us. It enables us to enter more fully into the human inheritance.

I have touched on what Greek literature means, but said nothing of Greek art; nor does the occasion permit of our entering now on another field of equally fascinating interest: what we owe, not only historically and as a debt of the past, but in actual research of the present day, to the work of Greek masters in the mathematical and physical sciences, and in the whole group of studies which circle round the medical profession and the mistress-art of healing. It must suffice if I have shown, as has been my aim, that Greek is an invaluable element in civilized life. If that be established, it follows without argument that it is an irreplaceable element in the education of a civilized State.

What is civilization? The word, like so many in our language (sixty per cent, it has been calculated), is Latin; and the thing is in its substantial structure a Latin achievement. But to the Romans, as to us, vital force came from Greece. They gained, as we do, experience, ideals, power of expression, sense of the dignity of human nature, from the products of the Greek genius. From the same source they drew their maxims on the relation of the individual to the community, and the relation of both individual and community to the physical world in which they live, and to the spiritual world which is the highest reality.

There is an old story, familiar no doubt to many here, of the question which I took for the title of this address being asked of a Dean of Christ Church a century ago or more, and of his reply that knowledge of Greek not only enabled those who possessed it to feel conscious superiority over others, but also led to positions of great dignity and emolument. The latter of these motives cannot be offered now; but there remains as a reward the dignity of human nature, and the spiritual emolument which cannot depreciate, cannot be lost or confiscated. For the former, the claim which holds good is that Greek makes us consciously superior not to others, but to ourselves. The good of Greek, in the last resort, is that it gives, in a way that nothing else quite does, the highest kind of joy; and such joys are not so common that we can afford to cast them away.

A LESSON ON AN ODE OF HORACE

[A Lecture in a Course for Teachers of the Classics, given at Oxford, 1920]

CLASSICAL scholarship makes great demands on the intelligence; and the teaching of Latin is a fine and laborious art. For its effective exercise two requirements must be fulfilled; first; that the teacher have accurate knowledge of what he teaches; secondly, that he can convey into his teaching a sense of the human value of what is being read. Of these, the former takes priority. Clear thinking, which means the accurate use and appreciation of language, is the foundation of all studies, and Latin if properly taught is an unsurpassed, perhaps even an unequalled instrument for this purpose. But education should not only discipline the intelligence; it should develop the imagination: for imagination is not fanciful, but the contrary; it is the seeing of things in their reality through training of the perceptive and creative powers. A good teacher must have both, the accurate knowledge and the finer perception, from the first, and must exercise both from the first. It has been truly said that scholarship, as a craft and a spirit, is most important in the teaching of beginners.

The lesson on a Latin text, such as may be found set out in the notes to any modern school edition, is a matter partly of linguistic and grammatical drill, partly of summarizing facts, historical and other, more or less relevant to the author or the book being read. Some of this is necessary, and a good deal more is useful; but in any case it should not be all. It is worth considering whether minute formal study might be concentrated on portions of the text which are of less artistic and imaginative value, and the finer passages (particularly in poetry) dealt with in a larger and freer, though not a less searching way. To classical teachers, the classics, or some of them, ought to be a vital force at the back of their work. Their vital quality should not be obtruded. To try to hammer it into a class is fatal. Even to talk much about it is dangerous.

It must be disengaged through the teacher's personality. But as soon as pupils have acquired the elements of Latin by strict and even severe linguistic drill, they may be given a taste now and then from the more generous cup. This must not be done mechanically; it need not, indeed it should not, be done even systematically, but rather as by one who now and then imparts a secret. Thus they will come to believe, and through believing will come later to know for themselves, the value of the classics. But this can hardly be expected to happen unless the teacher himself knows and believes it.

What is given in this way must not be watered down to what the teacher supposes to be the pupils' capacity. It must not be mashed into a pulp for them. It does not matter so much whether they understand—understanding will come later—if their intelligence is excited. A little given, and given pure, may in many, and in some it will, germinate and be a live force. One cannot tell how a young imagination will work, or to what it will respond: let it be given a chance. Napoleon's saying, *La jeunesse a de l'imagination pour saisir toutes les grandes choses*, might well be written up in gold in all schools, and ought to be engraved in the minds of all teachers.

What I shall attempt to do now is to apply this method of handling to a concrete instance, taking one of Horace's Odes as a text, and addressing myself primarily and directly to those who are actually engaged in teaching Latin, though with a wider reference to students and lovers of the classics generally. The Ode chosen is one from the first three Books, which, it may be desirable to say, are not only a single volume but a single body of poetry. The volume is not a structural whole with beginning, middle and end. Its arrangement is skilful, but systematically unsystematic. One does not lose anything material by reading its contents in any order. In this respect it is not unlike the Book of Psalms, and indeed has been described, not unjustly, as a Secular Psalter.

Beyond this, I shall take for granted all that may be said about Horace, and about the Odes generally, only adding that while full appreciation of them is the last reward of trained scholarship, the last gift of long experience of life, they can be at an early age begun, learned by heart, much enjoyed and in some

measure at least appreciated: that no translation can replace
them or even convey much idea of what they are like; that
they go straight to the centre of things and present attainable
ideals; and that they are, throughout, a lesson in the use of
language so as to get the greatest effect out of the simplest
words. I shall take this single Ode, and ask you to weigh and
test it with me as a poem and not as a mere exercise. For this
purpose, a short Ode must be taken; and to make it a crucial
instance, it should not be one of the great Imperial Odes, nor
one of those, in their way equally great, which embody the
poet's profoundest thought: but, as nearly as may be, a
specimen of the "light Ode," one which at the first reading,
and afterwards if it has been read carelessly or unintelligently,
may seem trivial and unworthy of the high function of poetry.
In the mid-Victorian age, Conington, in the preface to his
verse-translation of the Odes, thought it necessary to offer a
sort of uneasy apology for Horace not being some one else.
"The Odes of Horace," he wrote, "will I think strike a reader
who comes back to them after reading other books as distinguished by a simplicity, monotony, and almost poverty of
sentiment, and as depending for the charm of their external
form not so much on novel and ingenious images as on musical
words aptly chosen and aptly combined. We are always hear-
ing of wine-jars and Thracian convivialities, of parsley-
wreaths and Syrian nard; the graver topics which it is the
poet's wisdom to forget are constantly typified by the terrors
of quivered Medes and painted Gelonians; there is the perpetual
antithesis between youth and age, there is the ever-recurring
image of green and withered trees, and it is only the attractiveness of the Latin, half real, half perhaps arising from association
and the romance of a language not one's own, that makes us
feel this lyrical commonplace more supportable than commonplace is usually found to be."

Let us see then how this lyrical commonplace on scrutiny
unfolds, expands, yields secret after secret, connects itself with
the whole of literature, opens out the marvel of language and
the rhythm of life. The only way to appreciate the Odes
fully is to know them by heart, to be saturated with them, and
then to let passage after passage, phrase after phrase, line after

line expand and germinate as memory recalls it, association touches it, imagination kindles it, experience verifies it. The importance of knowing the Odes—or some at least of them—by heart can hardly be over-estimated. Poetry so distilled, close-packed, stripped down, must be disengaged to yield its full effect. A line or phrase thus disengaged always thrills one with unsuspected depths of beauty and truth: it expands, takes colour, becomes alive.

Let us turn then to the Fifth Ode of Book I, and endeavour to approach it as though it were new to us and being read for the first time; dismissing the commentaries, ignoring the heading *Ad Pyrrham*, which is modern, and neglecting the modern punctuation. In any lesson of this kind attempted with a class, the poem or passage chosen should be read aloud very carefully at the beginning, and again at the end, with the most careful attention to rhythm and phrasing. The class may follow it in their books, but it would not be amiss to have it written out on a blackboard so that they may have it before their eyes the whole time. For this purpose I give the text of the Ode here, reducing punctuation, for reasons which will presently appear, to a minimum.

> Quis multa gracilis te puer in rosa
> perfusus liquidis urget odoribus
>   grato Pyrrha sub antro
>   cui flavam religas comam
>
> Simplex munditiis. Heu quoties fidem
> mutatosque deos flebit et aspera
>   nigris aequora ventis
>   emirabitur insolens
>
> Qui nunc te fruitur credulus aurea
> qui semper vacuam semper amabilem
>   sperat nescius aurae
>   fallacis. Miseri quibus
>
> Intentata nites me tabula sacer
> votiva paries indicat uvida
>   suspendisse potenti
>   vestimenta maris deo.

With the text thus before us, we are now in a position to examine its structure and content.

The metrical structure of the Ode consists of four stanzas, each self-contained, but interlinked by the phrasing. By the grammarians (as you will find in your annotated texts) this stanza is called the "Fifth Asclepiadean," and consists of two lines of choriambic trimeter acatalectic or Minor Asclepiadean, one of choriambic dimeter catalectic or Pherecratean, and one of choriambic dimeter acatalectic or Glyconian. This jargon is as useless for our purpose as it is hideous. What has to be done is to feel the rhythm, which is best effected through knowing the Ode by heart and repeating it over and over, "practising" it, both silently and aloud; and in particular, to grasp the choriambic basis which gives the stanza its peculiar rippling quality, in contrast with the smooth steady movement of Horace's favourite stanza, the Alcaic, with its weight and resonance. He uses the Alcaic in thirty-three out of the eighty-eight odes of Books I–III, this beautiful stanza only in six.

Syntactically however the Ode consists not of four, but of three, "periods" or "movements." The first and third of these are of four and a half lines each, the second, of seven lines. The subtle rhythmical relations involved by the fitting in, over-lapping, and interplay of the metrical and syntactical structures are a matter for artistic feeling rather than for mathematical calculation.

Of the first importance is the phrasing. It plays across the metre, giving a constant delicate variation. It is the technical secret of poetry, consummated for Latin by Virgil and Horace, and for English by Milton. It will reveal itself more fully as a poem is known by heart and its phrases are allowed to ring and repeat themselves in the head: new delicacies will appear, and we shall come to understand what Dryden meant by calling poetry "articulate music." Poetry must appeal to the ear and not to the eye only if it is to exercise its proper virtue.

The substance of this Ode is in structure very simple. It consists of three "periods" or "movements," corresponding to its three syntactical periods. They are

(1) Who is your young lover?
(2) What disenchantment awaits him!

(3) I have passed through that experience myself and am thankful.

But in the development of these, one must study the detail: the distilled and concentrated art, the exquisite order of words and syllables, the parsimony of language, the economy of epithet; the way in which words take a new colour from their setting (in separation as well as in juxtaposition) so that each word fulfils a multiplied function and is raised to a new power, and the skill with which each word comes in so as to add to the cumulative effect. Notice as one instance, how with a single exception a noun and its epithet are never placed together. This is a matter in which the inflected Latin has the advantage over English or any uninflected language. We can only partially get the same or rather a similar effect, chiefly by using Milton's favourite device of placing the epithet after its noun. Phrases of his like *the road of heaven star-pav'd* are about our utmost limit as compared with *aspera nigris aequora ventis* or *tabula sacer votiva paries*.

Let us now take some points as they come in this Ode, as a sort of running commentary of a sort which will not be found in school-editions of Horace; and first, get the picture— Horace's pictures are always clear and precise—for if we miss that, we miss everything.

The notion, to which the inappropriate heading *Ad Pyrrham* in modern texts has largely contributed, that the Ode is a personal address to a former mistress of the poet's own, must be discarded at once. The picture, the *chose vue*, is a couple in a rose-arbour, just seen; a slim boy with his arms clasped tight round a girl, who sits knotting back her hair. Observe the individual touches. The first four words, *quis multa gracilis te*, are one of Horace's characteristic and masterly openings; they all look forward, conveying by themselves nothing beyond expectation; they are going to be developed and resolved. *Gracilis* has a double implication; it gives the note of contrast not only with the more opulent contours of the girl, but with Horace's own change from the young days when he, too, "was not an eagle's talon in the waist." *Multa in rosa* does not mean "on a bed of rose-leaves"—such enormities of actual or imagined later imperial luxury have nothing to do

F

with the scene—it simply means what it says, "amid clustering roses": and the *antrum* is an arbour or grotto—either word will do well enough, and the thing itself may be seen in any English park or public garden—over which, in the Italian spring as in the English summer, the thickly clustered roses break into a foam of blossom. The boy belongs to the *jeunesse dorée*, is heavily scented, and got up accordingly: in contrast to his slim dark handsomeness is the blonde girl, *Pyrrha*, that is to say, with a fair complexion and hair of warm yellow. In visualizing the *flava coma* which has been dishevelled in his embrace and which she is now tying back into a simple knot, it is to be noticed that *flavus* is used of the colour of honey by Lucretius, of the colour of ripe wheat by Virgil, and that the colour-sense of both these poets is faultless. The simplicity of her dress is of a piece with that of her coiffure; she is not bedizened or jewelled or scented, but gives the effect of being beautifully clean. *Munditiae* is a prose word of daily household use, exactly equivalent to our "cleaning up": it is reset and given a new value. Here, as elsewhere, George Herbert gives, more than any other English poet, the complement or converse of the Horation touch, transferred from the physical to the spiritual sphere: *How fresh, O Lord, how sweet and clean are thy returns!*

Such was the picture flashed for half a minute on Horace's eye as he passed it, perhaps in Maecenas' gardens on the Esquiline, the same picture as may be seen anywhere, in any summer dusk. It remained with him, and germinated. That chance sight of a moment summoned up thoughts, memories, a wistful reflex of emotions: the envy of advancing years for youth; the sense of transitoriness and disillusionment in those immature passions; and finally, the philosophic mind with its recognition of life's compensations and of life itself as a whole. All this is here crystallized, and the Ode is, in the full sense of the phrase, "a moment's monument."

In the central movement of the Ode (*heu quoties* down to *fallacis*) some points among others deserve special attention. Notice in it (1) the characteristic economy of language in *fidem mutatosque deos*, which is so contrived as to make the epithet colour both nouns and be equivalent to *fidem mutatam mutatosque deos*: (2) the weight of even rhythm in *aspera nigris aequora ventis*, as later and even more strikingly in *uvida suspendisse potenti vestimenta*, where the ripple of the metre spreads into a still pool: (3) the mass and edge of the sonorous *emirabitur*, a word which is not found elsewhere in classical Latin and seems to have been coined by Horace here: (4) the meaning of *aura*, which is not "wind" or "gale" as it is often rendered; it is much subtler, and has no English equivalent except the technical words "emanation" and "radiation." It covers whatever strikes out or radiates from an object on any of the senses, and as applied to a person, it is the *aura* of that person as technically used in psychical research: (5) the central position in the Ode of *insolens*. By neglect of formal punctuation we shall feel how it is the hinge linking forwards or backwards according to the way in which we interpret the phrasing. It uses all the force of its double meaning; "unaccustomed" to the strange experience of blackness and raging waves instead of sunshine on a sleeping sea, and "arrogant" or "immoderate" in the present possession of the golden fruit (*fruitur aurea*) which credulous youth fancies will be its own for ever.

So far, the roused emotion or reflection is sad, and almost cynical. Then comes the third movement, subsuming and resolving the preceding themes in understanding and acquiescence. "Poor children of men, for whom the unexplored world glitters as a Paradise! with tempest surely to come, and fortunate if, like me, you come out from it alive and safe, and can hang your drenched garments up with thanksgiving." The Ode is the poet's own votive tablet.

Life is stocked with germs of torpid life; but may I never wake
Those of mine whose resurrection could not be without earth-
        quake!
Rest all such, unraised for ever! Be this, sad yet sweet, the sole
Memory evoked from slumber; least part this: then what the
        whole?

This is the sort of reading that in addition to accurate verbal and grammatical study should be given to a classic, if its full value is to be appreciated. It is not, let me repeat, the com-

mentary which should be lavished (and still less, forced) on a
class, though the class may be allowed glimpses of it. But
in those who really appreciate Horace—or for that matter,
any classic, whether of poetry or of prose—their own appreciation will be a silent force behind all their teaching. It will tell
of itself: you need not preach over your liquor.

A word may be added here as to punctuation. Punctuation
is really a compressed explanatory commentary indicated by
conventional marks: it should follow, not prescribe, the
phrasing. In this Ode, the first two lines are a single prolonged
phrase. So are the last three and a half, except for the slightest
possible pause after *indicat*. But what about line 3? In modern
editions, it is generally if not always attached to lines 1 and 2,
with an interrogation mark after *antro*, and another after
munditiis. But the rhythmical as well as the rhetorical balance
seems rather to require the pause to be made at the end of
line 2, line 3 running continuously on into line 4. Is *cui* in
line 4 a fresh interrogative, or a relative pronoun? Here again
the rhythmical structure suggests the latter. Milton's celebrated
translation of the Ode leaves it curiously, perhaps purposely,
uncertain in which way he took it. Line 8 is best left un-
punctuated, and the interpretation of *insolens* left to individual
feeling.

As a reinforcement of these notes, an attempt may be made
to follow the Ode once more in a literal prose rendering. This
of course leaves out not only the beauty and music of its
wording and much of the delicate artifice of its arrangement,
the implications, the harmonics, the complex functions of
words and phrases; all, in fact, that makes the Ode, like all
poetry, untranslatable.

What slim boy steeped in liquid scents presses you amid clustered
roses, for whom under a pleasant arbour, Fair-hair, you knot back
these blonde tresses? Ah, how often shall he weep for faith and
gods estranged, and gaze aghast on seas rough with black winds,
witless, who now confidingly possesses you, his golden one, who,
ignorant of the delusive radiance, expects you always disengaged,
always loveable! Luckless they to whom you shine unexplored;
me a tablet on the holy wall records to have hung up my dripping
garments to the mighty God of the Sea.

It is not only prose which succumbs to the task of translating Horace. Three of the many attempts made with this Ode may repay special attention. One is the version of 1651 by Sir Richard Fanshawe, in the stanza best known as that of Marvell's famous *Ode to Cromwell*. It is a curious mixture of felicities and failures. The second, and the best hitherto, is well known. It is Milton's, and is probably of about the same date as Fanshawe's, though it first appeared in print among the additions made to Milton's volume of minor poems when it was reprinted in 1673. It seems likely, though there is no direct evidence, that Milton wrote it after seeing Fanshawe's, to show how the thing should be better done. The scrupulous, weighed and ordered, almost abstract language, the severe rhythms, the clarity of outline and faintness of colour, are more Horatian, one might say, than Horace himself. The third, and the least satisfactory, is Conington's (1863). Conington was an accomplished scholar, and his rendering is wonderfully exact. But after reading it, we have to ask ourselves, Is it poetry?

As with the wording of the Ode, so with its substance. The picture, the incident, is, you may say, trivial or even vulgar, whether long ago on the Esquiline or now at Hampstead. Quite so. Out of such things the stuff of life is woven. Horace has distilled from it an essence, has immortalized it. That is what poetry and poetry alone can do.

THE ITALY OF VIRGIL AND DANTE

[1921]

IT is matter of common consent that Dante is, not only the greatest of the poets produced by Italy since the age of Virgil, but also a national poet in the fullest and most vital sense. From the beginnings of the Risorgimento until now, he has been accepted and proclaimed as the poet and prophet of Italy. Writers and thinkers of all types ranging from Leopardi to Mazzini were at one in so regarding him. To this view, when once it had been firmly established and had spread through the common consciousness of the civilized world, is very largely due the extraordinary growth, both in extent and in depth, of the study of Dante during the last thirty or forty years. There were many contributory reasons for it: the general widening of the intellectual horizon; the development of the historical method as a new calculus for searching and interpreting the past; the revival of interest in the Medieval Empire and in the institutions or ideals of the Middle Ages; and, it may be added, a better appreciation both of poetry as an art and of art as not merely an expression but a function of life. But among all these and other reasons stands prominent this: that Dante was one, and one of the most important, of the intellectual and spiritual forces which went to create Italian unity and nationality, and to show the path for the mission of Italy as well as for her effective existence.

The purpose of the present paper is not to analyse this claim. It is rather to attempt some closer definition of it, and to mention some lines of thought which it suggests. To weigh it more fully would be a task at once intricate and immense. It will be sufficient, for the time, to indicate without pursuing them into detail, some of these lines of thought and their interconnection, and more particularly to observe, as perhaps has not hitherto been clearly enough done, the analogies in this respect between Dante and Dante's master. The more we study these, the more fertile will they appear in suggestion, the more potent in illumination, and this not as regards the two poets and their works only; for they bear directly on the question, no mere abstract one, how far Italian nationality and Italian unity are a new creation, and how far the recapture of an ancient ideal or even the renewal of an ancient achievement.

Questions which at once occur in our reading of Dante are, among others, these: First, what precise meaning is to be attached to the term Italy as he uses it? Secondly, in what sense was Dante, or in what sense did he feel himself to be, an Italian as distinct from a Florentine on the one hand and an Imperialist on the other? Thirdly, what influence was exercised on him by his conception of Italy, and what influence did he in turn exercise on that conception in other minds, in his own time and afterwards?

All these questions may be asked about Virgil likewise; and in exactly the same terms if "Mantuan" be substituted for "Florentine." With regard to all three, the parallel between Dante and Virgil is striking and highly significant, quite apart from the further and equally interesting study of the direct influence of Virgil on Dante in the whole matter. In so large a subject, all that can be done here is to sketch its outline and indicate some of the primary conclusions to be drawn from the inquiry. Further study would lead on to the still larger question of the relation of poetry to history. That has two sides. It involves the extent to which political and civic institutions or ideals mould poetry, and the extent to which, conversely, the poets mould them. Yet more; it leads on to a still higher claim—perhaps the highest—which can be made for poetry, namely, that poetry is the ultimate expression of history, as of philosophy.

Geographically, Italy is one of the most striking instances of a country with definite natural boundaries. It is, in the classic phrase of Petrarch, *il bel paese ch' Apennin parte e 'l mar circonda e l' Alpe.*[1] It lies, with but one gap, within a ring-fence of sea and mountain-wall. That gap is the open gateway on the north-eastern frontier, through which from time immemorial the peninsula has again and again been invaded and repopulated,

[1] Sonnet xcvi.

and in whose fortunes lies the main key to Italian history. On its importance, both in Virgil's time and in Dante's, as long before Virgil and down to the present day, something more will have to be said. Otherwise, the Italian peninsula is to the geographer a single country, clean-cut and well-defined. Sicily and Sardinia are separate countries, connected with or disconnected from it politically by changes of events. The Alpine frontier on north and north-west has varied from time to time, but the precise line followed by it at one time or another has been chiefly a matter of the occupation of strategic points; otherwise the modifications in it have been neither extensive nor important.

But seldom, if ever, has this single geographical unity been fully either a single nation or a single state until the unification of the nineteenth century; and that unification, though now politically secured, is still nationally far from complete. Italy has throughout history been the seat of kingdoms, republics, principalities, confederacies, which were all local and partial, and generally in acute conflict, racial and cultural as well as political, among one another. And when it approached unity most nearly, it was not as a self-developed independent state, but as a portion or province of a larger empire.

At the dawn of systematically recorded history, behind which it is needless to go for the present purpose, Italy was occupied by four main groups among many others of minor importance. These were,

(1) The Celtic tribes of the north and north-west. They never coalesced into either a state or a nation.

(2) The Etruscan League, a powerful and well-organized confederacy, stretching slantwise across the peninsula from the north-eastern frontier down to the mouth of the Tiber, and at its greatest extension some way further. Its dominions covered the whole of the territory, and rather more, which was under the rule of the great Countess Matilda in the twelfth century.

(3) The Central-Italian populations. They were all seemingly of kindred blood, but were divided by language and tradition into the three groups of Oscans, Gabellians, and

Umbro-Latins. It was among them that municipal organization and conscious citizenship began. They had some sense of kinship, though not enough to keep them from incessant war among one another; and they had a tendency to combine into leagues formed of smaller groups. The most important among these was the Latin League, within or rather on the edge of which grew up the unique city-state of Rome. But Rome was a city, not a nation. For the Latins themselves, no less than for the expanding circles of tribes or peoples beyond them, Rome was the stone cut out without hands which smote them to pieces and became a great mountain and filled the whole earth.

(4) The Greek colonies in the south. The string of these towns with their territories was so nearly continuous all round the coast from Cumae to Bari that it received a common name, *Magna Graecia*, the greater Greece beyond the seas. The native populations along this strip of coast were more or less Hellenized; but Greek control nowhere reached far inland, and Greek influence not much further.

Among all these populations there was no trace and no sense of unity. The name of Italy, itself of uncertain origin, was for long used loosely and with a fluctuating sense. Records of the growth both of the name and of the thing it meant are almost wholly Roman. Beyond the Greek colonies on the southern coasts, the peninsula lay outside of the Greek world and of any special Greek interest. We do not know when the Romans began to use the word *Italia*, or what extent of country the name covered in its earliest use. At the time of the Pyrrhic wars it appears to have applied, though still very loosely, to the whole peninsula exclusive of Cisalpine Gaul and Liguria; it covered, that is to say, pretty nearly the "leg" of Italy south of the transverse upper section of the Apennine range. Its first definite extension to the full geographical sense, the country "which the sea and the Alps surround," is found in Polybius. At the time of the Second Punic War, "the Romans," he says, "had subdued all Italy except the land of the Gauls," and Hannibal, when he crossed the Alps, descended the valley of the Dora "into Italy." For a hundred and fifty years more, usage continued to fluctuate, often perplexingly, between the larger and the more restricted meaning.

But in whichever sense the term "Italy" were taken, Rome did not, either then or for long afterwards, identify herself with Italy, or seek to merge the Roman in an Italian commonwealth. The Roman primacy was that of a conqueror. Italy remained a complex aggregation of tribes, communities, and municipalities under Roman control, with a status ranging from that of full allies to that of mere subjects. It was dotted over at strategic points with garrisons of Roman colonies sharing the full citizenship. The defeat of Pyrrhus, in the words used by Mommsen,[1] "put an end to the last war which the Italians had waged for their independence"; but the independence sought was in no sense the independence of a nation.

As Roman control hardened and her Italian allies were treated more as subjects, a common desire to shake off this yoke led to a feeling towards joint Italian nationality. Concurrently, a movement arose at Rome for the incorporation of Italy in the Roman republic. Legislation in this sense was repeatedly brought forward. The question remained a burning one for a full generation. The assassination of Livius Drusus in 91 B.C. before he had brought in his proposed law extending Roman citizenship to all the allies was followed at once by that general Italian revolt known as the Social War. An Italian government, the first in history, was set up. Samnite and Latin were adopted as the joint official languages of the new state. Italian coinage was struck; and the town of Italica (afterwards known as Corfinium) was founded in the centre of the peninsula as the new capital. It was the first of many disastrous attempts made to create a unified Italy from which Rome was excluded.

After long and desperate fighting, the disciplined Roman armies conquered in the field; but as the result of the war, Roman citizenship was, two years later, extended over Italy including portions at least of southern Lombardy. The status of the north, however, remained anomalous and confused. In the eye of the law, all the territory beyond a line marked at its extremities by the little rivers of the Serchio and the

[1] Römische Geschichte, IV, vii.

Fiumicino was still a province. Its admission to citizenship took place gradually and irregularly, and was only formally completed in 42 B.C., the year of the battle of Philippi. A unified Italy then at last existed; and the Latin language, subject to local variations of dialect, soon became the common speech of the whole peninsula.

Virgil was born in 70 B.C., midway in the process of fusion. He combined in himself, in a singular and significant way, all the strains which have been noted as the main elements in the complex fabric of an earlier period. He was a native of the Cisalpina. Mantua had been an important Etruscan city, and there is reason to believe that Virgil himself was, on one side at least, of Etruscan blood. On more doubtful evidence, drawn partly from his name and partly from the temper of his genius, he has been claimed, and very widely accepted, as Celtic by parentage. He was either born, or became very early in life, a Roman citizen. In his education he absorbed Greek culture, and in later years lived at Tarentum and finally settled at Naples, both originally Greek towns of the South.

A dominant idea in his poetry, the keynote both of the Georgics and, still more definitely, of the Aeneid, is the reconciliation and coalescence of Rome and Italy. In the Georgics he is perhaps more an Italian than a Roman. The *Laudes Italiae*, the matchless panegyric of the Second Book, became a sort of sub-title for the whole poem. Yet it is interesting to note that the word *Romanus* occurs in the Georgics much oftener than *Italus*. In the Aeneid, their frequency is almost the same. Of set purpose, they are used so far as may be, interchangeably. The synthesis, as a doctrine, a faith, and a prophecy, has become complete. It is the running motive of the Aeneid throughout, emphasized over and over again in a hundred passages. The most striking in their setting are two at the beginning and end of the poem. In the prologue, Virgil gives his whole argument in the seven majestic lines which begin on the word *Italiam* and end on the word *Romae*. At the conclusion, he concentrates it into a single line in the scene of the reconciliation of the gods, at once a prayer, a decree, and a benediction, *Sit Romana potens Itala virtute propago.*[1] And midway between the two, he crystallizes it into two words, *Romula tellus*,[2] almost the last which came from the glorified spirit of Anchises. It was this, even more than his quality as an artist, which secured for Virgil his unique place among the poets of the world through age after age. He may be called, in a very real sense, the creator for all time of Italian Rome and Roman Italy.

The unified Italy of Augustus and Virgil had reached its definite natural boundaries except at the open gates of the north-eastern frontier. From the prologue to the third Georgic there may be inferred, in the difficult years between 36 and 31 B.C., a contemplated withdrawal and consolidation of that frontier upon, or but little in advance of, the short and easily defensible line of the Mincio. Something similar had to be contemplated by the Italian Chief Command in the autumn of 1917 after the disaster of Caporetto. But if this was so, the situation was changed some years later by the successful offensive campaigns of Tiberius and Drusus. The frontier, instead of being drawn back, was pushed well forward into the Tyrol and Istria; up beyond Trent on the left, down beyond Trieste on the right. The Region of Venetia, numbered X in the Augustan organization, included pretty nearly the whole of what was prior to the Great War known as Italia Irredenta. On the west and south, the Adige was the boundary between it and Region XI, Gallia Transpadana. Its northern limit was advanced from the foothills of the Venetian Alps to the watershed of the mountain chain, running roughly east and west, on the southern slopes of which are the sources of the Bacchiglione, Piave, and Tagliamento. From the further end of that line, in the mountains above the sources of the Isonzo, the frontier turned at a right angle and ran almost due south: following, at least approximately, the watershed between the basins of the Isonzo and the upper Save; crossing the plateau of the Carso near its south-eastern end; and apparently reaching the sea at the mouth of the Arsa on the further side of the Istrian peninsula, just outside the mouth of the Quernero channel. It thus followed almost exactly the line traced by the Treaty of London in 1915. In later years, the upper part of

[1] Aen. xii. 827.   [2] Aen. vi. 876.

this north-to-south line was again thrown forward in a deep salient, comprising the upper valley of the Save and its tributary streams, and extending at its apex a good way east of Laibach. Beyond this frontier were the provinces of Noricum to the north and Pannonia to the south of the Save. The covering legions were quartered far forward in these provinces along the line of the Drave. Italy was unified and complete, and except for trifling modifications, the Augustan limits remained good for more than three hundred years.

But that unified Italy, impressive and majestic as it was, could hardly be called either a state or a nationality. It was the central core of the Roman Empire, which itself was the state, and in which distinctions of nationality tended to become obliterated. *Fecisti patriam diversis gentibus unam*,[1] says the last classical panegyrist of the Imperial achievement. Italy continued to have an administrative and a fiscal system different from those of the provinces, but the distinction grew less and less. Its practical disappearance is registered, as an accepted fact which had to be regularized, by the historic Edict of Caracalla in A.D. 212. The Latin language and culture had before then spread over the entire West. Gaul, Spain, Africa ranked side by side with Italy, and gave rulers to the Empire. While Rome was still the *caput orbis*, the centre of the system and the seat of its central government, Italy was otherwise little more than one of the provinces.

Under Constantine's reorganization of the Empire, Italy becomes once more, as it was to be again in later ages, a mere geographical expression. Unity is lost. For other purposes than those of the geographer, the word Italy is used in three wholly different senses. The Prefecture of Italy included not only the Italian peninsula, but Rhaetia (i.e., Switzerland and Bavaria up to the line of the Danube), Sicily, Corsica, Sardinia, and the portion of Northern Africa now covered by Algeria, Tunisia, and Tripolitana. The Diocese of Italy was the peninsula; but it was little more than an administrative coupling-up of two Vicariates, corresponding in substance to the old Italy of the Republic and to Cisalpine Gaul: and it is the latter, not the former of these Vicariates, which bears the specific name of

[1] Rutilius Namatianus, De Reditu suo, l. 63.

Italy. North and South have fallen asunder again; and the capital is no longer Rome, but Milan. The visit of the Emperor Constantius to Rome in A.D. 357, so vividly described by Ammianus, is a transitory apparition, like that of some Saxon or Swabian Emperor in the Middle Ages. We are passing from the ancient to the medieval and modern world. The Virgilian unity of Italy, like the Virgilian ideal of the consubstantiation or identification of Italy with Rome, had definitely failed to accomplish itself.

To trace, even in brief summary, the course of Italian history between the fourth and the thirteenth century would be impossible within the limits of this sketch. But a few salient points may be noted as landmarks in the wide tract which lies between the Italy of Virgil and the Italy of Dante.

The deposition of Romulus Augustulus by Odovakar in A.D. 476 registers, as it were, the disappearance of the old Virgilian and Augustan world, while it emphasizes the complete severance of Italy and Rome. Odovakar took the title, now given for the first time in history, of King of Italy. But his kingdom was the Constantinian Vicariate, and the seat of government was Pavia. At the same, the Senate and People of Rome formally renounced their traditional world-sovereignty, accepted the position of a diocese of the Byzantine Empire, and thus left the way clear for the growth of the Temporal Power.

The Gothic kingdom founded by Theodoric seventeen years later was larger, and more of a reality. With better fortune, it might gradually have taken effective possession of the whole peninsula, and developed in it a nascent sense of common Italian nationality. But fate was adverse. When it was shattered by the military genius of Narses, the kingdom fell again into a bundle of fragments, under the nominal control of the Exarchs of Ravenna. A few years later came the Lombard invasion and the foundation of a Lombard kingdom, also with its capital at Pavia, which lasted for two centuries. At its greatest extent it covered the bulk of the peninsula, exclusive however of Genoa and Venice in the north, Rome and the Patrimony of Peter in the centre, and the coast towns of the south with their territories. But it was essentially, like its Gothic predecessor, a north-Italian kingdom; the duchies of Spoleto and Benevento being only in loose feudal adherence to it, and the divorce of Rome from Italy which has lasted until modern times having taken full effect.

The resettlement of Italy by Charlemagne is obscure. But under the provisions of the Peace of Verdun in A.D. 843, the kingdom of Italy stretched, nominally at least, from the Alps to Terracina. Its kings had little or no control over their feudatories; and later in that century the Eastern Empire re-established itself in the south, with Bari as the provincial capital. The last futile attempt towards the creation of an independent and unitary Italy was made by Berenger, Marquis of Ivrea, about the middle of the tenth century. But the hour of Piedmont had not yet come. Berenger ceded his kingdom to Otto the Great, who assumed the Iron Crown at Milan the year before he was crowned as Emperor. The kingdom of Italy as a substantive thing then ceased to exist for exactly nine hundred years.

During the three centuries from this point to the birth of Dante, the most important points to be noted as bearing on the Italian problem are perhaps these:

(1) The development of five prominent powers which were in some sense states. These were the Republics of Milan, Florence, and Venice, the Patrimony of Peter, and the Kingdom of Naples.

(2) The re-emergence of the municipal instinct which had been developed and fostered by the policy and genius of Rome. It was accompanied by the growth of civic life and institutions and by the expansion of commerce. With these there gradually arose the consciousness of an Italian race, though not of an Italian nation.

(3) A further separation between North and South brought about by the Norman conquests in lower Italy. These began early in the eleventh century; but the Norman dukes did not assume the title of king until A.D. 1130, and then called themselves Kings of Sicily. This became later the joint Kingdom of Sicily and Apulia.

(4) A series of transitory republics at Rome, which served to keep alive some memory of the great Roman past.

(5) The irreconcilable hostility between the Papacy and the Empire, from the time of Hildebrand (A.D. 1073–95) onwards.

Between these two last great forces, the fragments into which Italy had crumbled were used as gambling counters. Each of them passed from one side to the other according to the momentary preponderance of Guelfs or Ghibellines. Any latent sense of nationality was swallowed up in fierce local competition, hardly checked by shifting and short-lived alliances. Historians note that after the battle of Legnano in A.D. 1176 the name Italy is not once used in the terms of pacification. The idea of an independent Italy still lurked somewhere in the background. When Charles of Anjou was called in to crush Manfred, he received investiture in the indivisible *regno*—the Kingdom of Italy—on condition that it should not be held together with the Empire. But from that so-called indivisible kingdom, Rome with the Patrimony of Peter and the Duchy of Benevento was expressly reserved; and he was to hold the kingdom thus mutilated as a fief of the Church.

In the course of these three centuries, with the growth of inter-civic and foreign commerce, came increasing wealth. With wealth and the extension of relations to other countries and races, came culture. Culture could not be confined within municipal or provincial boundaries. The sense of something like common nationality grew up concurrently with the spread of a highly internationalized civilization. At the court of Frederick the Second, "Italian came into being as a language." Dante wrote in Tuscan; but the Tuscan in which he wrote was in fact Italian. He created Italian literature; and the immense power of words over human affairs is nowhere shown more remarkably than in the influence exercised on later history by that great achievement.

In the *De Vulgari Eloquentia*[1] there is an interesting passage illustrative of the interrelation between a common language and a common organized state. In the Italy of his own time, Dante says, there are fourteen distinct regional dialects, while the local sub-dialects run to not less than a thousand. The object of his inquiry is the discovery and definition of an

[1] V.E., x. 18.

established and regulated Italian language, the *vulgare illustre* as he calls it. One of the notes of such a language is that it should be *curiale*, the accepted language of a court. But here he anticipates an objection: is it not idle—*videtur nugatio*—to speak of a court-Italian *cum curia careamus*, when there is no such thing as an Italian Court? And his answer to this objection is very striking: *licet curia in Italia non sit, membra tamen eius non desunt; curiam habemus, licet corporaliter sit dispersa:* though there is no Italian Court, there are the elements of one. These are "corporeally severed," but in the body of detached fragments there is the material for, the potentiality of, an Italian Court as the functional organ of an Italian state or nation.

We may now turn to Dante's other writings, and attempt to examine in them both how he defines or describes Italy geographically, and also in what terms he speaks of it either as an organized community or as a nation; how it sorts itself in the ascending series of *vicinia, civitas, regnum, genus humanum,* or in the collateral organism of *nationes, regna et civitates.*[1]

Italia, Europae regio nobilissima, as he calls it elsewhere with national pride, extends *a Ianuensium finibus usque ad promontorium illud qua sinus Adriatici maris incipit et Siciliam.*[2] The area so defined is there named as that over which *sì affirmando loquuntur.* It is based, that is to say, on the ground of a common language rather than of a common race or citizenship. Thus likewise, in a corresponding passage in the *Inferno,* its inhabitants are described as *le genti* (not *la gente*) *del bel paese la dove il sì suona.*[3] From east to west it extends *tra due liti.*[4] *Lo dosso d'Italia*[5] is the backbone of the Apennines running right from end to end of it. The *Ianuensium fines* are practically the same as the Augustan boundary between Italy and Narbonese Gaul, which was fixed at the river Var. From that point its northern frontier is approximately defined in the lines

> Suso in Italia bella giace un laco
> Appiè dell' Alpe, che serra Lamagna
> Sopra Tiralli, ch' ha nome Benaco.[6]

[1] De Monarchia I. 3, 14.   [2] De Monarchia II. 3, V.E. I. 8.
[3] *Inf.* xxxiii. 79.   [4] *Par.* xxi. 106.   [5] *Purg.* xxx. 86.   [6] *Inf.* xx. 61-3.

G

It includes, that is, the whole of the Lago di Garda, and marches
with "Germany" in the sense in which that term includes
Teutonic-speaking Switzerland. Its north-eastern limit is
precisely assigned elsewhere as

> A Pola presso del Quarnaro
> Che Italia chiude e suoi termini bagna.[1]

The channel of Quarnero divides Istria from the island of
Cherso. West of its mouth, at the tip of the promontory of
the Istrian peninsula, is Pola. Thus Pola is definitely placed
in Italy. But if Dante's words are pressed closely, his frontier
does not reach up to the head of the Istrian Gulf beyond the
Quarnero channel, and *a fortiori* does not include Fiume.
North-west of this, and in the debateable land, Dante's Italy
includes the sources of the Brenta and Piave;[2] in other words,
it reaches up to the watershed of the Carnic Alps.

Virgil had, with a conscious and definite purpose, made the
words Roman and Italian, as nearly as might be, interchange-
able and equivalent. In Dante, Latin and Italian coalesce into
a single meaning, less as a matter of deliberate doctrine
than at the prompting of a mixed poetical and historical
instinct. Sordello calls Virgil *gloria de' Latin*.[3] The Sienese
Omberto says, *io fui Latino*.[4] When Virgil asks, in the *Inferno*:
Dinne s'alcun Latino è tra costoro che son quinc'entro, Grifolino
of Arezzo answers, for himself and Capocchio of Siena, *Latin
sem noi ambedue*.[5] So also to the question, *Conosci tu alcun
che sia Latino sotto la pece?* the reply given is

> Se voi volete vedere o udire
> Toschi o Lombardi, io ne farò venire.[6]

The identification is even more pointedly made in the reply to
the same question of souls in Purgatory.

> O frate mio, ciascuna è cittadina
> D' una vera città; ma tu vuoi dire,
> Che vivesse in Italia peregrina.[7]

[1] *Inf.* ix. 113–4   [2] *Par.* ix. 25–7   [3] *Purg.* vii. 16.   [4] *Purg.* xi. 58.
[5] *Inf.* xxix. 82–92.   [6] *Inf.* xxii. 65, 97.   [7] *Purg.* xiii. 94–6.

The supreme expression of the unity and solidarity of Italy by Dante is, of course, the magnificent outburst beginning *Ahi serva Italia* in canto VI of the *Purgatorio*, which was a storm-beacon through the centuries and became the watchword of the Risorgimento. Next to it in importance come the visions of Rudolf of Habsburg, *imperador che potea sanar le Piaghe ch'hanno Italia morta*, and of Henry of Luxemburg, who *a drizzare Italia verra in prima che ella sia disposta*.[1] Striking also is the bitter cry from the lips of St. Peter in the *Paradiso*:

> O difesa di Dio, perchè pur giaci?
> Del sangue nostro Caorsini e Guaschi
> S' apparecchian di bere: o buon principio,
> A che vil fine convien che tu caschi![2]

It is not only an expression of the Italian loathing for the French Popes, John XXII and Clement V, but a sombre prophecy of the Age of Invasions beginning with that of 1494 when once more, as once before, two hundred years earlier, *Carlo venne in Italia.*

The apostrophe to Italy in the *De Monarchia, O Ausoniam gloriosam si nunquam infirmator ille imperii tui* (the Emperor Constantine) *natus fuisset!*[3] identifies "Ausonia," classic Italy, with Rome to which belonged by divine ordinance the monarchy of the world. It is probably in this sense of a world-empire that Dante calls Italy *donna di provincie*:[4] though the eleven Augustan Regions also came to be called provinces (as with modifications they still are) as early as the fourth century. The title has in any case imposed itself on the imagination of the world; the Lady of Lands, the *donna e reina*, has ever since been known and passionately loved as such.

It would be beyond the scope of this inquiry to trace the faith and the doctrine of a unified Italy and a single Italian nation through the times after Dante had given them vital expression. During the successive periods which fill these six hundred years—the Age of the Despots, the Age of the Invasions, the Age of Spanish-Austrian ascendancy, the revolutionary Napoleonic changes, the reinstated Austrian

---

[1] *Purg.* vii. 94, 5, *Par.* xxx. 136–8. [2] *Par.* xxvii. 57–60.
[3] *Mon.* II. xiii. [4] *Purg.* vi. 78.

predominance, the complex movements which resulted in the
creation of the Kingdom of Italy in 1861 and its extension,
which has only now been completed, to its full natural
boundaries—Dante's vision has been a spiritual influence, a
constructive force, which has waxed or waned, but has never
ceased to operate.

Still less can the attempt be made here to follow out the
equally important history of the politico-ecclesiastical relations
between Italy and Rome, or to trace more fully the causes and
results of that inherent duality which goes back, as we have
seen, to the beginnings of Roman and Italian history. The
resolution of that duality in a higher synthesis was the prophetic message of Virgil, and, in a different way, of Dante
also. It still remains an unrealized ideal. The *Fortuna Urbis* of
the Roman Empire never became a *Fortuna Italiae*. Rome
the city has for just fifty years been the Italian capital; but the
spiritual Rome, like her imperial predecessor, has reached out
beyond and become separated from Italy in the gigantic claim
to include the world.

If we try to define Virgil's position on the graded scale of
patriotism, we may say that he was first and foremost an
Italian; that he was a Roman in so far as he identified the
mission and the glory of Rome with the glory and the mission
of Italy; and that he was a Cisalpine, and more particularly a
Mantuan, mainly by blood, birth, and early associations. Of
Mantua he speaks over and over again with a thrill of pride
and affection; not only in the *superet modo Mantua nobis* of the
Eclogues,[1] and the *Et qualem infelix amisit Mantua campum* of
the Georgics,[2] but most conspicuously in two great passages,
the proem to the third Georgic beginning with

> Primus Idumaeas referam tibi, Mantua, palmas,

and the record in the tenth Aeneid,

> Tusci filius amnis
> Qui muros matrisque dedit tibi, Mantua, nomen,
> Mantua dives avis, sed non genus omnibus unum.
> Gens illi triplex, populi sub gente quaterni,
> Ipse caput populis, Tusco de sanguine vires.

[1] Ecl. ix. 27.   [2] Georg. ii. 198.

where the personal note of local patriotism in *ipse caput populis* is clear and unmistakable. But the *carità del natio loco*, though strong, was not nearly so powerful in him as that of Florence in Dante. It does not appear that he ever lived in northern Italy after the period which gave birth to the Eclogues. His life was passed, his poetry written, mainly in the centre and the south. Even in the second Georgic the reference to his birthplace quoted above is coupled with one to the extreme south, *saltus et saturi longinqua Tarenti*, as a rival affection. The years of the composition of the Aeneid were mainly spent in Campania.

For Dante, to be out of Florence was to be in exile. Florence was not only his city, but his *patria terra*, a microcosm of the Italy of his ideals or dreams. He speaks of it as *nostra terra prava*,[1] just as he makes Cunizza in the Sphere of Venus speak of the *terra prava Italica*.[2] Further, the Italy that he actually knew and cared about was northern Italy. The South, the *corno d'Ausonia* as he calls it, is hardly taken into account by him. It was, in fact, a separate kingdom. It does not appear that he was ever in it, or indeed that he was ever even as far south as Rome except on the embassy of 1300. When he writes that after his banishment, *per le parte quasi tutte alle quali questa lingua si stende, peregrino quasi mendicando sono andato*,[3] the words must be taken with this qualification; and even so, stress must be laid on the original as well the acquired sense of the word *peregrinus*. In these wanderings he felt himself an exile in the full sense; not only a pilgrim, but a foreigner.

The Homeric poems gave some sense of unity, and even of common nationality, to the Hellenic world. Virgil and Dante, more directly and more powerfully, created a sense of the nationality and unity of Italy. The effect of poetry on history is incalculably great: not immediately, it may be, but in its cumulative and often long-deferred action. As poetry is the final distillation of both history and philosophy, the ideal expression towards which they both tend, so it re-descends from its own empyrean and acts as a germinal force, the "shaeping spirit" of Coleridge, the "élan vital" of modern thought, to create new philosophy and make new history.

[1] *Inf.* xvi. 9. [2] *Par.* ix. 25. [3] Convivio, i. 3.

The Italy of Virgil and Dante is not yet fully substantialized. This means that their work is not yet fully done. That it will be completed is the faith and the assured hope of England as well as of Italy.

DANTE'S PARADISO

[An Introduction to C. L. Shadwell's verse translation published 1915]

DURING the last generation, the study of Dante in England has immensely increased, not among scholars or theologians only, but in a wider circle. He has fully secured his place, even in popular estimation, among the great classics who are the common inheritance of all nations and languages. The Italian poets as a whole do not bulk so largely in our reading as they did a hundred years ago. Neither Petrarch, nor Ariosto, nor Tasso is now accounted a part of the ordinary reading of educated English men and women. Guarini, once a common school-book among us, is probably only read now by professed students of literature. Alfieri and Metastasio are spent fames. Leopardi, a poet in whom not only the Italian Risorgimento, but the new European Renaissance of the earlier nineteenth century, found an interpreter of unsurpassed potency and beauty, has never reached a wide audience among English-speaking readers. It is at once a symbol and a consequence of their comparative neglect of the Italian poets, that the Italian language itself has ceased, in common estimation, to be, like French or German, a necessary part of education.

But in this disorientation, this shifting of the axis of letters, the greatest of Italian poets has more and more come by his own. When Italian classics occupied a place in English reading only second to the classics of France, Dante was not one of them; or if he was, it was only by courtesy and with a sort of amused indulgence. His position as the fountain-head of Italian poetry, like that of Chaucer as the fountain-head of our own, had to be admitted. But it was admitted perfunctorily. The *Commedia* was thought of, loosely and ignorantly, as a poem remarkable indeed for its time and containing many beauties, but on the whole grotesque, insipid, and even barbarous. It has taken many revolutions of the sun to reinstate it, side by side with the Iliad and the Aeneid, as one of the greatest achievements of human art and genius, as a masterpiece of construction, as the voice of a whole civilization, as one of the lights in the darkness of the world. Just one hundred years have passed since Cary completed the translation which first brought Dante really within the compass of English readers, and spoke in his preface of "the music of nobler thoughts" amid which, for the years during which he had been engaged upon it, other recollections had been lulled and a new amplitude given to life. Since then, and more particularly in the course of the last half-century, appreciation of Dante's poetical greatness has increased with prolonged study. That study, or body of studies, pursued individually or in concert by countless numbers of students, has not indeed been confined to, or even chiefly centred upon, Dante's work in its specific quality of poetry. As with the Homeric poems, the *Commedia* has been taken as a text for the study of the whole world in which it was produced, of which it gives the pattern and records the operative forces. It has been a primary document for the history of life and thought in the Middle Ages; for their politics, their science, their theology, their metaphysic. Nor was it possible that these complex and exacting investigations should not, in some measure, divert attention from the central poetic quality of what is, first and last, a poem. But that poetic quality reasserts itself through its own vital energy. Poetry, as the pattern and interpretation of life, is the ultimate convergence of all thought and of all knowledge: as the expression of mankind begins with poetry, so it ends on it; and the great poet who appears at intervals of many generations sums up or interprets—one might almost say, incarnates—the whole material, social, intellectual and spiritual movement of the race. Poetry is not philosophy; it is not history: but it is, in a very profound sense, the ideal which both history and philosophy tend—*wish* is the Aristotelian word—to reach. At any moment, the poetical value of any great poem, while on the one hand it has the absolute quality of art, is likewise on the other hand the integration of all the knowledge and thought which went to make it, or which have since accrued round it.

As art pure and simple, poetry is, like all other art, untranslatable; in the process of translation, the work of art ceases to be itself. Yet the instinct to translate poetry is natural, and the translation executed need be neither meaningless nor useless. Only, it might be well, both in executing and in reading such work, to replace or at least to supplement the term "translation" by the term "transvaluation." For a translation does not purport to replace its original; hardly even, in any real sense, to be equivalent to it. It gives so much of the effect of the original on the translator's intellectual and aesthetic perception as he is able to re-condense within the limits of certain forms through the operation of an art of his own—an art secondary indeed and subsidiary, but yet, like all art, creative. In offering a translation of Dante to his readers, what the translator in effect says to them is, Here I place before you so much of what Dante means to me as can be gathered and fixed in a single transvaluation executed in accordance with a single artistic convention: whatever more Dante means to me (and that is much, it may be even infinitely much) he means to me at least this.

The extended knowledge of Dante among English readers, the increased domination which his genius exercises over them as that knowledge ripens into appreciative admiration, are reflected in the large numbers of translations of the *Commedia*, as well as of Dante's other works, and of the *Vita Nuova* more particularly, which have appeared and continue to appear in the present generation. Each of these represents so much of the effective meaning of the original to the translator as his own imagination and craftsmanship have enabled him to project upon the metrical pattern chosen by him as the fittest for his purpose. They are not meant to compete with one another, and need not be put into competition. As often happens, the earliest adventurer had the first success. However little idea of competition there may be, succeeding translators are perhaps to some degree hampered, the lines on which they work restricted, by the mere existence of a predecessor. After a century, Cary's dignified and sober rendering (the defects and limitations of which it would be irrelevant to discuss here) retains value and may be read with undiminished pleasure and profit; the more so, doubtless, because he had the good sense to reject the fatal allurements of a line-for-line rendering on which so many attempts, with Dante as with other poets, have made shipwreck. But the Miltonic blank verse which he chose as his vehicle is essentially unsuited to the purpose in two ways; not only because it is a metrical form which is beyond the compass of most artists, but because it ignores the formal quality of the *Commedia* as poetry; and in poetry, it cannot be too often repeated, the form is not separable from the substance, for the form is the substance.

The Provost of Oriel's rendering of the *Purgatorio* (1892 and 1899), to which that of the *Paradiso* has now been added, won recognition among students of Dante and among lovers of poetry, as an attempt to solve the problem of transvaluation on new lines and in a new medium. He saw that this problem was one not merely of vocabulary and diction, but above and beyond these, of metrical form. He saw that the metrical unit, the key of the pattern, in the *Commedia* is not the line, but the terzina or group of three lines. In the original, these units are interlocked throughout by the rhyming system, and fastened off at the end of each canto by a final line which converts the last terzina into a quatrain. But it remains true that the poem throughout is cast in the form of three-line stanzas; and this form is emphasized by Dante's management of the period. There is a marked pause at the end of the stanza-unit so habitually that its absence is a rare and marked exception; and the more elaborate poetical ornament, the "Dantesque similes" and their equivalents, are normally so arranged as exactly to fill one or more stanzas.

Of the English quatrain best known from its use in Marvell's famous Horatian Ode, and adopted by the Provost of Oriel as a near equivalent in its total effect to Dante's terzina, the translator has himself discoursed in the preface to his rendering of the *Purgatorio*. It would be superfluous to go over the ground again. The stanza presents (like any other actual or conceivable form of verse) its own difficulties and drawbacks. To problems of this kind there is, and can be, no absolute solution. Of even the best and most successful efforts in poetical translation it has to be said that

> forma non s' accorda
> Molte fiate alla intenzione dell' arte,
> Perch' a risponder la materia è sorda;[1]

And the reader may now and then have to murmur to himself, *Ma non con questa moderna favella!* But the merits of this particular metrical form are great. It has been shown to bear surprisingly well the test of continuous use on a large scale. With the skilful management that has been applied to it, it gives a striking approximation to the colour and movement of the original. The objection, if it be a real one, that as a lyric form of verse it is unsuited to a long poem akin in nature to the epic, might equally well have been made against the metre of the original, which was Dante's own invention. In such matters, *a priori* considerations count for little; effective success is the only real criterion. This metre in its continuous use is structurally akin to Dante's; it marks the same unit, and carries on where necessary from one unit to another without awkwardness or discontinuity; and by the brevity and succinctness of its rhythms it keeps before the reader, as it imposes on the writer, that quality of terse precision in which Dante is supreme if not unique among poets. The translator, it might be said, has invoked the spirit of Dante somewhat as Dante himself invokes the "Pegasean Goddess,"

> Illustrami di te, sì ch' io rilevi
> Le lor figure com' io l' ho concetto:
> Paia tua possa in questi versi brevi:[2]

And the invocation has not been left unanswered.

In the *Paradiso*, the genius of Dante has reached its consummation. He moves in it with a larger sweep of imagination, with a fuller certainty of hand. His own words give the best account of this:

> Se fosse a punto la cera dedutta,
> E fosse il cielo in sua virtù suprema,
> La luce del suggel parrebbe tutta;
> Ma la natura la dà sempre scema,

---

[1] *Par.* i. 127-9.   [2] *Par.* xviii. 85-7.

Similemente operando all' artista
Ch' ha l' abito dell' arte, e man che trema.
Però se il caldo amor, la chiara vista
Della prima virtù dispone e segna,
Tutta la perfezion quivi s' acquista.[1]

Yet it is not through the *Paradiso*, but through the other two
cantiche of the *Commedia*, and most of all through the *Inferno*,
that Dante acquired, and retains, his wide popular fame. It is
"Dante of the dread Inferno" who has most impressed himself
on the general imagination; just as, during his own life, he was
pointed at with awe, and spoken of in whispers, not as the
man who had been rapt into heaven and seen the Rose of the
Blessed, but as the man who had passed through Hell and bore
on his dark face the marks of its burning. For this partial and
even misleading view, there are more reasons than one. The
simplest is the mere fact that the *Inferno* comes first and is
consequently read first. Many readers, flagging in their interest,
or repelled by the difficulties of the poem and feeling that they
have "supped full with horrors," never proceed farther. But
the *Inferno* also makes a more potent appeal to the ordinary
mind from its highly dramatic and—if one may use the word—
sensational quality. It displays, in a way that the other two
cantiche do not, the more obvious side of romanticism as
embodied in medieval art. It is not only a poem but a thrilling
narrative of adventure; it stirs the cruder as well as the nobler
instincts. It has the fascination of horror; it excites the imagination through the nerves, through the almost physical attraction
exercised by all portraitures, from the Odyssey onwards, of a
mysterious subterranean world. Further, and as a consequence
of this quality, it lends itself more readily to pictorial representation. Painters and designers have for the last five centuries
had continual recourse to the *Commedia* for subjects; it is from
the *Inferno* that the great majority of them have been taken.
Finally, it is the *Inferno* which contains, with insignificant
exceptions, not only the heathen, that is to say, all the great
figures of the classical world whether in mythology or in
history, but also the men and women of post-Christian history

[1] *Par.* xiii. 73–81.

and romance who died in sin; and in it accordingly come the
most famous romantic or tragic episodes, those "show-pieces"
which stand out from their surroundings and are almost
universally known, like those of Francesca of Rimini, of
Count Ugolino, of the last voyage of Ulysses.

In passing from the *Inferno* to the *Purgatorio*, the reader is
transferred from that crowded and clamorous realm to a
world imagined and portrayed with the same precision, but,
in its unearthly stillness and beauty, less immediate and less
overpowering in its effect on those who are first introduced
to it. As Dante and his guide ascend that strange mountain
beneath those unfamiliar skies, we follow them, with eager
suspense, as through the breathless atmosphere of a dream.
All the souls in Purgatory are waiting; and the sense of waiting
overcomes us likewise as the poet leads us up and up among
them. The key-note of the whole cantica is deliberately struck
in the two highly elaborated descriptions of dawn at the
opening of the first and second canti, beginning *Dolce color
d' oriental saffiro*[1] and *Si che le bianche e le vermiglie guance*.[2]
It is repeated, with extraordinary effect, in the twenty-seventh,
where Dante has passed through the fire and is about to enter
the Earthly Paradise: *Nell' ora, credo, che dell' oriente prima
ragg io' nel monte Citerea*[3] and *E già, per gli splendori antelucani*.[4]
Even in the Earthly Paradise itself there is the same sense of
troubled expectancy. In that "divine woodland," among the
long shadows of sunrise, the morning blossoms, and the
morning songs of birds, strange, perplexing pageants pass.
A harlot is seen seated in the triumphal chariot; the holy
virgins, weeping, intone the Psalm *Deus, venerunt gentes*; and
Beatrice herself, *sospirosa e pia*, changes her beauty and
becomes, for a little, like Mary at the foot of the Cross. Only
in the very last lines of the cantica does Dante drink of Eunoë
and become ready for the ascent:

> Io ritornai dalla santissim' onda
> Rifatto sì, come piante novelle
> Rinnovellate di novella fronda,
> Puro e disposto a salire alle stelle.[5]

[1] *Purg.* i. 13.   [2] *Purg.* ii. 7.
[3] *Purg.* xxvii. 94, 5.   [4] *Purg.* xxvii. 109.   [5] *Purg.* xxxiii. 142-5.

---

94   STUDIES IN HUMANISM

That triple emphasis gives the key-note for the *Paradiso*; and at the opening of the *Paradiso* itself, Dante tells us that he is "transhumanized"; a change has passed over him "which cannot be signified by words."[1] A like change comes over the poem. It moves henceforth in a more supernatural world. This of itself is sufficient explanation why the *Paradiso* should not be "popular" to the same degree as the *Inferno*, or even as the *Purgatorio*. It is all at a higher tension, and makes more exacting demands both on the intellect and on the imagination. But for the charge of monotony which has been made against it, and for the sense of monotony indistinctly felt by many readers who have not formulated their impressions, there are particular reasons which have to do partly indeed with the nature of the subject, but partly also with Dante's handling of it, that is to say, with the quality of his art as a poet.

One of the dangers which beset all artists is the overdoing of a successful device. The device of repetition is one of the most potent instruments in the conduct of a large poem; and it is also one which has to be most sedulously limited by instinctive tact. In the *Paradiso*, as two thousand years earlier in the Odyssey, though both poems are miracles of construction, this particular device is pushed up to, perhaps even a little beyond, its limit. Much of the impression of monotony which beginners receive from the *Paradiso* is simply due to the reiteration by Dante of his incapacity to describe the experience which he is recording. This is done by him—with great skill and immense effect—twice in the first and no less than four times in the last canto: but between them, it is repeated over and over (see for instance canti x, xiv, xviii, xxiv, xxx) at comparatively short intervals. In this as in other matters, an artist is apt to be taken at his own valuation.

Similarly, his insistence on the increasing beauty of Beatrice, designed to be felt as a key-note throughout, is repeated so often that it comes perilously near overshooting its mark. The scale begins so high that its upper notes are all but inaudible. Between the goddess beloved of the First Lover in the fourth canto,

O amanza del primo amante, O diva![2]

[1] *Par.* i. 70-1.   [2] *Par.* iv. 118.

and her who has the joy of God in her face, in the twenty-seventh,

> Che Dio parea nel suo volto gioire,[1]

we have been told again and again how she has been perpetually becoming more beautiful,

> La donna mia, ch' io vidi far più bella;
>
> La sua sembianza
> Vinceva gl' altri e l' ultimo solere;
>
> La bellezza mia più s' accende,[2]

Yet at the end we seem to be just where we were at the beginning. Nor in truth is it the end; for from this point the poet still strains to soar upwards:

> Se quanto infino a qui di lei si dice
> Fosse conchiuso tutto in una loda,
> Poco sarebbe a fornir questa vice:
> La bellezza ch' io vidi si trasmoda
> Non pur di là da noi, ma certo io credo
> Che solo il suo fattor tutta la goda.[3]

In the lines which immediately follow, he elaborates this thought: they are also the lines in which he speaks most explicitly of the range and limits of his own art:

> Dal primo giorno ch' io vidi il suo viso
> In questa vita infino a questa vista
> Non m' è il seguire al mio cantar preciso,
> Ma or convien che mio seguir desista
> Più dietro a sua bellezza poetando,
> Come all' ultimo suo ciascun artista.[4]

The ideal of art is, like all ideals, unattainable; it always remains ahead of any actual achievement. But this truth is one rather to be present to the mind of the artist than to be expressly stated, with all the emphasis of reiteration, in the work of art itself. It is of the essence of Paradise, as Piccarda

---

[1] *Par.* xxvii. 105.   [2] *Par.* viii. 15; xviii. 56–7; xxi. 7, 8.
[3] *Par.* xxx. 16–21.   [4] *Par.* xxx. 28–33.

explains to Dante, that through its ascending spheres there is no unsatisfied desire. *Ogni dove in cielo è Paradiso*,[1] everywhere in heaven is Paradise: *in la sua volontade è nostra pace*,[2] and his will is our peace. But it is likewise of the essence of art that it cannot transcend its own boundaries, and can only project upon the human material in which it works an imperfect image of the eternal qualities which it apprehends.

Thus to the increasing subtilization of beauty, in words no less than in lines and colours, there is a limit put not merely by the *man che trema*,[3] the faltering touch of the artist, but also by the *cera di cose generate*,[4] the finite material in which he has to work. In Botticelli's designs for the *Commedia*, the whole thirty drawings for the *Paradiso* consist of the repetition of what is in effect a single subject, the two figures of Beatrice and Dante, with "white-upturnèd wondering eyes," ascending and ascending, from where they leave the tree-tops of the Earthly Paradise, through the nine heavens, to where they appear against a background of the Paradisal Rose unfolding itself and distinguishable at last as the clear-ranged unnumbered figures of the blessed, or as a celestial flowerage in which each flower is also a winged soul. This is not idle repetition. In each fresh delineation, the artist has set himself anew to reach by some more intimate handling, some added subtlety of line and modelling, nearer an ideal and unattainable perfection. Neither in these designs, nor in the poem itself, will the student who is himself an artist feel any of the monotony which superficial acquaintance or careless reading may suggest.

But there is yet a further source for comparative failure to appreciate the excellence of the *Paradiso*, and one which may not be at once obvious. It is simply this, that it is not read fast enough.

This may seem a paradox, or even an absurdity. It is of course not only true, but undisputed, that the *Paradiso*, like all Dante's work, demands, as it repays, the most careful and minute study. Without such study it is, and must needs be, largely unintelligible. To read it through rapidly without preparation and without detailed knowledge is, if not possible, at least quite ineffective. But when some groundwork has

---

[1] *Par.* iii. 88, 9.   [2] *Par.* iii. 85.   [3] *Par.* xiii. 78.   [4] *Par.* xiii. 65–7.

been laid, it must be read swiftly, and as a whole. Only thus can one appreciate its vast movement and the magnificence of its structure. And then it will appear not only much greater, but also much more varied: its large modelling will come out, its subtle planes will tell, its organic movement will be felt. Again and again we must return from the endlessness of minute scholarly study to the broad view of the poem as a single complete work of art. The ideal to be aimed at—never, perhaps, to be fully realized—is that of knowing the whole poem by heart, of being able to understand each line and phrase taken in isolation and to place them in relationship to one another, and at the same time of embracing it comprehensively not as a succession of parts, but as a whole.

Once this totality has been apprehended, the study of the *Paradiso* will become increasingly fruitful and endlessly stimulating. The words of Beatrice to Dante when they have reached the Eighth Heaven will begin to take their meaning in our own experience,

> Rimira in giù, e vedi quanto mondo
> Sotto li piedi già esser ti fei.[1]

We shall begin to see, likewise, how in this *ultimo lavoro* the art of the poet becomes finer as the demands he makes on it become more exacting. "The sensibility, the fineness of touch," Pater says, "is at its height in the placid and temperate regions of the *Purgatorio*." This is no doubt true; but put without reservation it may tend to mislead. Sensibility, with its implication of the *man che trema*, is one of those qualities which in its final ascent art divests itself of or transcends. That ascent is made at immense sacrifices. The ardour of poetry burns away more and more of poetical ornament, of the flowerage of an earlier and less mature beauty. In Dante, as in Milton, we can trace this arduous process towards an ultimate, perhaps an actually elusory perfection. With both, we seem to reach a point at which substance and form merge, and become something beyond themselves. Concentration on the essential is sometimes carried so far that the poetry, at least to an unpurged sight, seems to have almost burned itself away,

[1] *Par.* xxii. 128, 9.

H

to have been vaporized into an imponderable essence. Instances are capricious and imperfect, but one may be given.

Among the expanded decorative similes which Dante reintroduced into European poetry, and which are a distinctive note of his poetical style, one of the most elaborately beautiful is that in canto xxx of the *Purgatorio*:

> Sì come neve tra le vive travi
> Per lo dosso d' Italia si congela,
> Soffiata e stretta dagli venti schiavi,
> Poi liquefatta in sè stessa trapela
> Pur che la terra che perde ombra spiri,
> Sì che par fuoco fonder la candela.[1]

It is one of those pieces of loaded and enriched ornament which are so effective, "like stones of worth that thinly placèd are," in the hands of an artist who is in his habitual usage a master of austere and reserved simplicity; and it is specially notable for the artifice by which the transition back from it to the more unadorned diction of the narrative is managed in the last line through what is in itself a further superflux of enrichment, the comparison of the compared image itself to something else. In the last canto of the *Paradiso* the image is repeated, but now it has discarded its draperies and become a precise unornamented figure drawn at a single stroke, *Così la neve al sol si disigilla.*[2] Just so in Milton likewise, the rich ornament and long-drawn harmonies of a famous passage in the Ludlow masque,

> At last a soft and solemn-breathing sound
> Rose like a stem of rich distilled perfumes
> And stole upon the air, that even Silence
> Was took ere she was ware, and wished she might
> Deny her nature, and be never more,
> Still to be so displaced,

give place, in the *Paradise Lost*, to the single terse and almost metallic phrase, *Silence was pleased.*

Study of the similes in the *Paradiso*, as the most patent and typical form which poetical ornament may take, will bring out this movement of ascent through concentration: the more so, because the Dantesque simile is so characteristic of Dante's

---

[1] *Purg.* xxx. 85–90.   [2] *Par.* xxxiii. 64.

individual style. Of these similes there may be in all about two hundred; precise figures are needless, and are in fact impossible where, as is often the case, the simile is inverted, or might rather be described either as an identification or as an explanatory analogy. If we confine ourselves to the fifty-two or fifty-three developed and formally detachable similes filling either one or two terzine—in a few cases of unusual elaboration, even three—it is interesting to observe that the great majority of them deal with a strictly, and doubtless deliberately, limited subject-matter: with celestial phenomena and effects of light (these are the most numerous, about one-third of the whole); with the life of birds, those "angels of the air"; and with the movements and tones of dancers and musicians. There are only three landscape-pictures, and only two similes drawn from classical mythology. A few are taken from the operations of science, the astronomer or geometer at work; and two from the mechanism of a clock, which must have impressed Dante's imagination strongly. One from the life of bees, and one from the psychology of dreams, are drawn directly from Virgil. The image of mother and infant occurs three times. The beautiful simile of the pilgrim at the goal of his pilgrimage has the special interest that Dante repeats and elaborates it only a few lines lower, in what is perhaps the most fervid and thrilling of all the passages in the *Commedia* which can be regarded as detachable ornament.[1] When we add to these the images—a single one in each case—of the bachelor undergoing his proofs, of a fish in a pond, of the animal wriggling under a cover, of the fading of a blush, of the lady shrinking at a story of dishonour, and of a galley stopping at the master's whistle, we have exhausted the list. The massed effect of the whole is to emphasize the ethereal atmosphere in which the whole action passes, and attune the imagination to it. Purely decorative similes, like that for instance in the *Purgatorio* just before Dante passes through the fire which cleanses him from the stains of mortality,

> Come al nome di Tisbe apersi il ciglio
> Piramo in sulla morte e riguardolla,
> Allor che il gelso diventò vermiglio,[2]

[1] *Par.* xxxi. 43–5; 103–8.   [2] *Purg.* xxvii. 37–9.

hardly, if at all, occur in the *Paradiso*. The poetry has got beyond them.

It has been found remarkable, it has even been thought a curious defect of judgment or of taste, that at the very consummation of the Beatific Vision the one image used by St. Bernard is almost prosaic in its bald simplicity:

> Qui farem punto, come buon sartore
> Che, com' egli ha del panno, fa la gonna.[1]

Elsewhere, it is rather Dante's poetical habit to elevate common images by some height and reinforcement of diction;

> Nè giugneriesi numerando al venti
> Sì tosto, come—[2]

that is his august way of saying "quicker than one can count twenty." But the bareness in St. Bernard's words is calculated. It is a specific instance of what becomes more and more the burden of the whole poem as it approaches its conclusion, *All' alta fantasia qui mancò possa.*[3] In the last resort he becomes careless of any verbal or rhetorical artifices. The simplest language comes nearest to expressing what is beyond expression.

He frees himself too in the *Paradiso* of a quality which he shared with his age, but which is one of the defects in the literature of that age that prevent it from being fully classical. This is the irrepressible tendency of the medieval writers to allegorize. It made their art often approach mystification. It is the fatal attraction they had to it which makes so much of their poetry, to minds which have outworn or discarded that method, unattractive, tiresome, and sometimes almost unintelligible. To the modern mind, those intricate medieval allegories seem to be little better than *ambage in che la gente folle già s' inviscava.*[4] In the *Paradiso* however while there is much to tax our apprehension to the highest, there is nothing that is there merely, as it would seem, to perplex us in puzzles, like the spotted panther and the hound of the *Inferno* or the enigmatic gryphon of the *Purgatorio*.

But the transition, in atmosphere and in consequent handling, from the *Purgatorio* to the *Paradiso* is gradual, like the melting of dawn into full day; there is no such sharp change as that

---

[1] *Par.* xxxii. 140–1. [2] *Par.* xxix. 49. [3] *Par.* xxxiii. 142. [4] *Par.* xvii. 31.

which came when Dante issued from Hell. The "placid and temperate regions of the *Purgatorio*" have been suggestively described as "a realm of grey but clear light." Their light is subdued perhaps, but hardly grey; it is full of the *splendori antelucani*,[1] the lustrous flushings of a divine dawn:

> The grave East deepens
> Glowing, and with crimson a long cloud swells.

And in the *Paradiso*, the access of light, though so great as to be dazzling (and this is a further reason for the alleged "monotony" of its effect), is gradual, and leaves room both for successive heightenings and for delicacies of tone and colour that only tell in their full effect when the eye has become used to the overpowering light in which they float.

> That glorious Form, that Light unsufferable,
> And that far-beaming blaze of Majesty

are approached by stages; even in Paradise, though *ogni dove è Paradiso*, yet *la gloria risplende in una parte più, e meno altrove*.[2] Colour tells in the Paradisal radiance hardly less than in the luminous and pearly atmosphere of Purgatory. Pearl itself, and alabaster, are employed repeatedly as images. In the Ninth Heaven there are the colours of morning and evening clouds. Ruby, topaz, sapphire give frequent notes of pure colour at its highest: but alongside of these are the more familiar hues of the flowering meadows of earth,

> Come raggio di sol, che puro mei
> Per fratta nube, già prato di fiori
> Vider, coperti d' ombra, gli occhi miei.[3]

Thus too, while in the Sphere of the Sun Dante says of what he saw that it reached him not as colour but as light, *non per color ma per lume parvente*,[4] yet even after he has entered the Empyrean, the *Ciel ch' è pura luce*,[5] his purged sight distinguishes in it ruby and topaz, white and gold, and

> per la vista che s' avvalorava
> Nella profonda e chiara sussistenza
> Dell' alto lume parvemi tre giri
> Di tre colori e d' una continenza.[6]

---

[1] *Purg.* xxvii. 108.   [2] *Par.* iii. 88, 9; i. 1–3.   [3] *Par.* xxiii. 79–81.
[4] *Par.* x. 42.   [5] *Par.* xxx. 37.   [6] *Par.* xxxiii. 112, 115–117.

So likewise, and more largely, the reader who has mastered the structure of the *Paradiso* and learned to breathe its air will appreciate more and more not only its large magnificence, but its delicacy of modelling, its tone-values, its breadth and fineness of touch. Dante has disengaged himself from the grosser, the more local and temporary material in which he had at first to work, and which must needs be, in some sense, the soil in which poetry has its roots. The parochial detail, so one might almost call it, which has so large a place in the other cantiche, and which for readers in other countries and later ages comes to have less and less poetical relevance, or may even become absolutely distasteful, has in the *Paradiso* mainly melted away. What remains of it is, with great skill, collected and concentrated in the long discourse of Cacciaguida which occupies three whole cantos at the central point of the cantica, where it is also sublimated and touched to fine, more far-ranging issues by being brought into one structure with the description of the Golden Age of Florence—that imaginary Golden Age to which mankind in its progress always looks longingly back— and with the majestic prophecy of the poet's own life and fortunes, and of some new Golden Age to come, *così incredibili a quei che fien presente.*[1] Elsewhere the specifically Florentine allusions are so few, that the mention of the Lapi and Bindi[2] towards the end of the poem would come almost as a discord if we did not realize that it is one of those calculated touches through which Dante makes his transhumanized argosy keep anchorage, as it were, to the concrete world of earth. Their rarity makes them tell with enhanced effect. The most striking instance is in the passage where Dante has been comparing himself, when come into the full view of the white Rose of Paradise, to the barbarians of the furthest North struck dumb at the sight of Rome.

> Io, che al divino dall' umano,
>   All' eterno dal tempo, era venuto,
>   E di Fiorenza in popol giusto e sano,
>   Di che stupor dovea esser compiuto![3]

The single word "Florence" gives, with a force which would

be only weakened by amplification, the whole distilled essence
of those great arraignments which he has made so often against
his city and his contemporaries. The "vile semblance" of this
globe of earth as seen through the Seven Spheres has become
matter for a smile and a single glance, rather than for serious
thought or eloquent speech:

> Col viso ritornai per tutte e quante
> Le sette spere, e vidi questo globo
> Tal, ch' io sorrisi del suo vil sembiante.[1]

Yet, even among these high verities, in the most exalted sphere
of his vision, there is, once or twice, a very human touch of
bewilderment, a Virgilian tremor in the voice: it is borne
faintly across the poet's mind, and overcomes him like a
summer cloud, that all this may be but a dream. He puts the
doubt, if it be a doubt—it is something more remote and
impalpable—in the mouth of St. Bernard: *Ma perche il tempo
fugge che t'assonna.*[2] Was it all a dream? *Credoc h' io vidi,*[3]
"I think I saw," is all that he finally trusts himself to
say. The *maggior letargo che venticinque secoli,*[4] even if it occupied
but a moment, *un punto solo,* has nevertheless snapped something, has broken what may have been in some sense an
enchantment. It could only be one step more, to reach the
thought of waking, with its implication of something like
disillusion. But this step he does not take. He leaves the matter
at that faint hint, that barely perceptible accent or undertone
of questioning.

There are times, like the present, when we feel in an increased
measure the value, and the necessity, of looking beyond the
shows of the world and moving (if it be but in a dream or
a vision) among the eternal things. Custom, the social fabric,
civilization itself, are hung precariously over an abyss of
blackness, like a thin crust that trembles and may give way.
In something greater, beneath and above them, around them
and in them, is the only solid base of life, the reality of which
life is but a moving shadow. Dante is one of the great masters
to whom at such a time we can turn, not to seek distraction or

[1] *Par.* xxii. 133-5.   [2] *Par.* xxxii. 139.   [3] *Par.* xxxiii. 92.
[4] *Par.* xxxiii. 94.

to drug our senses in dreams, but to be enabled to see the things about us in their true proportion, to realize how slight and transitory they are. Science tells us that the densest and most solid matter is a mere film, a thin network of vapour. This is the point to which, in the spiritual sphere, Dante leads us in the *Paradiso*. The *nuova belva* that had made its awful epiphany on the very threshold of heaven, and dragged away the car of Christ, disappears, the lamentation of the *Deus, venerunt gentes* ends, and Beatrice stands erect, "coloured like fire."[1] Before we enter Paradise with Dante, not only has the defilement of sin been cleansed away in the Purgatorial fire, but the memory and consciousness of it in the water of Lethe. The miseries and agonies of earth have sunk out of sight. Even the cry of the souls under the altar for judgment, *Usque quo, Domine, non iudicas et non vindicas sanguinem nostrum?* is no longer audible. That cry may go up even from the highest circles of the Purgatorial Mountain, which is, in Dante's cosmography, still upon this earth, as Hell is beneath and within it. But Heaven is beyond this earth; and in the vision of Heaven which poetry gives us, all else, grief and passion, hope and remembrance, is swallowed up in contemplation of the heavenly order with which the vision makes us one.

That order is peace. Looking down through the seven spheres, Dante sees *l'aiuola che ci fa tanto feroci*[2] like a speck in the distance. But that very phrase is an echo of the noble words at the end of the *De Monarchia* in which his eyes are fixed on the vision of an earthly world planned on the heavenly model: *Quum dispositio mundi huius dispositionem inhaerentem coelorum circulationi sequatur, hoc est ad quod maxime debet intendere curator orbis, ut in areola ista mortalium libere cum pace vivatur.* Only souls in Paradise can say unreservedly, and as the realization of a peace perfected, *in la sua volontade è nostra pace.* But that profound sentence is double-faceted; and in the other and no less vital sense of t   h as it is in heaven.

[1] *Purg.* xxx.

ERASMUS ON WAR

[*Introduction to a Reprint of the Tudor translation*, 1907]

THE treatise of Erasmus on War, with the text *Dulce Bellum Inexpertis* for its title, was among the most famous writings of the most illustrious writer of his age. Few now read Erasmus; he has become for the world in general a somewhat vague name. Only by some effort of the historical imagination is it possible for those who are not professional scholars or historians to realize the enormous force which he was at a critical period of European civilization. The free institutions and the material progress of the modern world have alike their roots in humanism: humanism as a movement of the human mind culminated in the age, and even in a sense in the person, of Erasmus. Its brilliant flower was earlier; its fruits developed and matured later: but it was in his time, and in him, that the fruit set. The earlier sixteenth century is not so romantic as its predecessors, nor so rich in solid achievement as others that have followed it. As in some orchard when spring is over, the blossom lies withered on the grass, and there is long to wait before the fruit can ripen on the boughs. Yet here, in the dull hot midsummer days, is the central and critical period of the year's growth.

The life of Erasmus is accessible in many popular forms as well as in more learned and scholarly works. It need not be recapitulated here. But in order to appreciate this treatise on War at all fully, it is necessary to realize the time and circumstances in which it appeared, and to recall some of the main features of the author's life and work up to the date of its composition.

That date can be fixed with certainty, from a combination of external and internal evidence, between the years 1513 and 1515; in all probability, it was the winter of 1514-5. It was printed in the latter year, in the *Editio princeps* of Erasmus' enlarged and rewritten *Adagia* then issued from Froben's great

printing works at Basel. The stormy decennate of Pope
Julius II had ended that February. To his successor Giovanni
de' Medici, who succeeded to the Papal throne under the name
of Leo X, the treatise is particularly addressed.

The years which ensued were a time singularly momentous
in the history of religion, of letters, and of the whole life of
the civilized world. The eulogy of Leo with which Erasmus
ends indicates the hopes then entertained of a new Augustan
Age of peace and reconciliation. The Reformation was still
capable of being regarded as an internal and constructive force,
within the framework of society built up by the Middle Ages.
The final divorce between humanism and the Church had not
yet been made. The long and disastrous epoch of the wars of
religion was still only a dark cloud on the horizon. The
Renaissance was really dead, but few yet realized the fact.
The new head of the Church was a lover of peace, a friend of
scholars, a munificent patron of the arts. This treatise shows
that Erasmus to a large extent shared or strove to share in an
illusion widely spread among the educated classes of Europe.
With a keener instinct for what the souls of men required,
Luther, when he visited Rome two years earlier, had turned
away indignantly from the temple where a corpse lay swathed
in gold and half-hid in the steam of incense. With a keener
insight into realities, Machiavelli was, just at this time, composing *The Prince*.

The subject of his impassioned pleading for peace among
beings human, civilized, and Christian, had in one form or
another been long in Erasmus' mind. In his most celebrated
single work, *The Praise of Folly*, he had bitterly attacked the
attitude towards war habitual, and evilly consecrated by usage,
among spiritual and temporal monarchs. The same argument
had formed the substance of a document addressed by him to
Pope Julius in 1507 under the title of *Anti-Polemus*. Much of
the substance, much even of the phraseology of that earlier
work is doubtless now repeated. Beyond the express reference
to the new Pope, the other notes of time in the treatise we are
now considering are few and faint. Allusions to Louis XII
of France (1498–1515), to Ferdinand the Catholic (1479–1516),
to Philip of Aragon (1504–16) and Sigismund of Poland

(1506–48), are all consistent with the composition of the treatise some years earlier. At the end of it he promises to treat of the matter more largely when he publishes his *Anti-Polemus*. But this intention was never carried into effect. Perhaps Erasmus had become convinced of its futility; for the events of the years which followed soon showed that the new Augustan Age was but a false dawn over which night settled more stormily and darkly than before.

For ten or a dozen years Erasmus had stood at the head of European scholarship. His name was as famous in France and England as in the Low Countries and Germany. The age indeed was one of those in which the much-abused term of the republic of letters has had a real and vital meaning. The nationalities of modern Europe had already formed themselves; the idea of the Empire had become obsolete, and if the Imperial title was still coveted by princes, that was under no illusion as to the amount of effective supremacy which it carried with it, or as to any life yet remaining in the medieval doctrine of the unity of Christendom. The discovery of the New World towards the end of the previous century precipitated a revolution in European politics towards which events had long been moving, and finally broke up the political framework of the Middle Ages. But the other great event of the same period, the invention and diffusion of the art of printing, had created a new European commonwealth of the mind. The history of the century which followed it is a history of which the landmarks are found less in battles and treaties than in books.

The earlier life of the man who occupies the central place in the literary and spiritual movement of his time differs in no important way from the youth of many contemporary scholars and authors. Even the illegitimacy of his birth was an accident shared with so many others that it does not mark him out in any way from his fellows. His early education at Utrecht, at Deventer, at Herzogenbosch; his enforced and unhappy novitiate in a house of Augustinian Canons near Gouda; his secretaryship to the Bishop of Cambray, the grudging patron who allowed rather than assisted him to complete his training at the University of Paris—all this was at the time mere matter of common form. It is with his arrival in England at the age of thirty-one that his effective life really begins.

For the next twenty years that life was one of restless movement and incessant production. In England, France, the Low Countries, the Rhine valley and Italy, he flitted about gathering up the whole intellectual movement of the age, and pouring forth the results in that admirable Latin which was not only the common language of scholars in all countries, but the single language in which he himself thought instinctively and wrote freely. Between the *Adagia* of 1500 and the *Colloquia* of 1516 comes a mass of writings equivalent to the total product of many fertile and illustrious pens. He worked in the cause of humanism with a sacred fury, striving with all his might to connect it with what was living in the old and what was developing in the modern world.

In his travels no less than in his studies, war perpetually met him as at once the cause and the effect of barbarism, as the symbol of everything to which humanism in its broader as well as its narrower aspect was utterly opposed and repugnant. He was a student at Paris in the ominous year of the French invasion of Italy; a year in which the death of Pico della Mirandola and Politian came like a symbol of the death of the Italian Renaissance itself. From that expedition Charles VIII, in the well-known phrase, brought the Renaissance to France, but brought her as a captive chained to the wheels of his cannon. The epoch of the Italian wars began. Sandro Botticelli, in 1500, painted that marvellous "Nativity" which is one of the chief treasures of the National Gallery of London. The painter's own words may still be read in Greek upon the panel: "This picture was painted by me Alexander amid the confusions of Italy, at the time prophesied in the Second Woe of the Apocalypse, when Satan shall be loosed upon the earth." In November, 1506, Erasmus was at Bologna and saw the triumphal entry of Pope Julius into the city at the head of a great mercenary army. Two years later, the League of Cambray, a combination of folly, treachery and shame which horrified even hardened politicians, plunged half Europe into a war in which no one was a gainer and which finally ruined Italy: *bellum quo nullum*, says the historian, *vel atrocius vel diuturnius in Italia post exactos Gothos maiores nostri meminerunt.* In England Erasmus had found, on his first visit in 1498, a country exhausted by the Wars of the Roses, from which she had emerged with half her ruling class killed in the field or on the scaffold, and the whole fabric of society to reconstruct. The Empire was in a state of confusion no less deplorable and much more extensive. The Diet of 1495 had indeed, by an expiring effort towards the suppression of complete anarchy, decreed the abolition of private war. But in a society where every owner of a castle, every lord of a few square miles of territory, could conduct public war on his own account, the prohibition was little more than an empty phrase. Humanism had found a place by the end of the fifteenth century, but too late to have much effect on the growing fury of religious controversy. The same year in which this treatise against war appeared gave to the world another work of still wider circulation and of more profound consequences. The famous *Epistolae Obscurorum Virorum*, first published in 1515, and circulated rapidly among all the educated readers of Europe, made an open breach between the humanists and the Church. That breach was never closed; nor on the other hand could the efforts of well-meaning reformers like Melancthon bring humanism into any organic relation with the Reformed movement. When mutual exhaustion brought the long European struggle to a close, civilization had to start afresh; it took a century more to recover the lost ground. The very idea of humanism had long before then disappeared.

War, pestilence, the theologians: these were the three great enemies with which Erasmus says he had throughout life to contend. It was during the years he spent in England that he was perhaps least harassed by them. His three visits to this country—a fourth, in 1517, appears to have been brief and not marked by any very notable incident—were of the utmost importance in his life. During the first, in his residence between 1497 and 1499 at London and Oxford, the English Renaissance, if the name be fully applicable to so partial and inconclusive a movement, was in the promise and ardour of its brief spring. It was then that Erasmus made the acquaintance of four great English humanists, Colet, Grocyn, Latimer and Linacre. These men were the makers of modern England to a degree seldom quite realized. They carried the future in their hands. Peace had descended upon a weary country, and the younger generation was full of new hopes. The *Enchiridion Militis Christiani*, written soon after Erasmus returned to France, breathes the spirit of one who had not lost hope in the reconciliation of the Church and the world, of the old and the new. When Erasmus made his second visit in 1506, that fair promise had grown and spread. Colet had then become Dean of St. Paul's; and through him, as it would appear, Erasmus now made the acquaintance of a man even greater, with whom he soon formed as close an intimacy, Thomas More.

His Italian journey followed; he was in Italy for nearly three years, at Turin, Bologna, Venice, Padua, Siena, Rome. It was in the first of these years that Albert Dürer was also in Venice, where he met Bellini and was recognized by the Italian master-painters as the head of a transalpine art in no way inferior to their own. The year after Erasmus left Italy, Botticelli, the last survivor in art of the ancient world, died at Florence.

Meanwhile, Henry VIII, a prince young, handsome, generous, pious, had succeeded to the throne of England. A golden age was thought to have dawned. Lord Mountjoy, who had been a pupil of Erasmus at Paris and with whom he had first come to England, lost no time in urging Henry to send for the most brilliant and famous of European scholars and attach him to his court. The King, who had already met and admired him, needed no pressing. In the letter which Henry himself wrote to Erasmus entreating him to take up his residence in England, the language employed is that of sincere admiration; nor was there any conscious insincerity in the main motive which he urged. "It is my earnest wish," wrote the King, "to restore Christ's religion to its primitive purity." The history of the English Reformation supplies a strange commentary on these words.

But the first few years of the new reign (1509–13) which coincide with the third and longest sojourn of Erasmus in England, were a time in which high hopes might seem not unreasonable. While Italy was ravaged by war, and the rest of

Europe was in uneasy ferment, England was peaceful and prosperous. The lust of the eyes and the pride of life were indeed the motive forces of the court; but alongside of these was a real desire for reform, and a real if very imperfect attempt to cultivate the nobler arts of peace, to establish learning and to purify religion. Colet's foundation of St. Paul's School in 1510 is one of the landmarks of English history. Erasmus joined the founder and the first High Master, Colet and Lily, in composing the school books to be used in it. He had already written, in More's house at Chelsea, where pure religion reigned alongside of high culture, the *Encomium Moriae*, in which his immense gifts of eloquence and wit were lavished on the cause of humanism and the larger cause of humanity.

That war was at once a sin, a scandal and a folly, was one of the central doctrines of the group of eminent Englishmen with whom Erasmus was now associated. It was a doctrine held by them, however, with some ambiguity and in varying degrees. In the *Utopia* of 1516, More condemns wars of aggression while taking the common view as to wars of defence. In 1513, when Henry, swept away into the seductive scheme for the partition of France by a European confederacy, was preparing for the first of his useless and inglorious Continental campaigns, Colet spoke out more freely. He preached before the King and the Court against war itself as barbarous and unchristian, and did not spare condemnation of either kings or popes who acted otherwise. Henry was disturbed. He sent for Colet, and pressed him hard on the point whether he meant that all wars were unjustifiable. Colet was in advance of his age, but not to that extent; he gave some kind of answer which satisfied the King. The preparations for war went forward. The Battle of Spurs plunged the Court and the whole nation into the intoxication of victory, while at Floddenedge in the same autumn, the ancestral allies of France sustained the most crushing defeat recorded in Scottish history. When both sides in a war have invoked God's favour, the successful side is apt enough to believe that its prayers have been heard and its action accepted by God.

Erasmus was now Reader in Greek and Professor of Divinity

at Cambridge; but Cambridge was far away from the centre of European thought and of literary activities. He left England before the end of the year for Basel, where the greater part of his life thenceforth was passed. Froben had made Basel the chief literary centre of production for the whole of Europe. Through his printing-presses, Erasmus could reach a wider audience than was attainable at any court however favourable to pure religion and the new learning. It was at this juncture that he made an eloquent and far-reaching appeal, on a matter which lay very near his heart, to the conscience of Christendom.

The *Adagia*, that vast work which was, to his own contemporaries at least, Erasmus' foremost title to fame, has long ago passed into the rank of those monuments of literature "dont la réputation s'affermira toujours parce qu'on ne les lit guère." So far as Erasmus is more than a name for most modern readers, it is on slighter and more popular works that any direct knowledge of him is grounded: on the *Colloquies* which only ceased to be a school book within living memory, on the *Praise of Folly*, and on selections from the enormous mass of his letters. The *Adagia* has been described by a distinguished Oxford scholar of the nineteenth century as "a manual of the wit and wisdom of the ancient world for the use of the modern, enlivened by commentary in Erasmus' finest vein." In its first form, the *Adagiorum Collectanea*, it was published at Paris in 1500, just after Erasmus had left England; in an epistle dedicatory to Mountjoy, he ascribes the inspiration of the work to him and to Richard Charnock, the Prior of St. Mary's College in Oxford.

The volume consists of a series of between eight and nine hundred short essays or comments, each suggested by some terse or proverbial phrase from a Latin author. It gave full scope for the display, not only of the immense treasures of his learning, but of those other qualities the combination of which raised him far above all his contemporaries; his keen wit, his copiousness and facility, his complete control of Latin as a living language. It had an enthusiastic reception, and established him as the unquestioned head of European men of letters. Edition after edition poured from the press. It was ten times re-issued at Paris within a generation. Eleven editions were published at Strasburg between 1509 and 1521. Within the same period it was reprinted at Erfurt, Cologne, the Hague, Mayence, Leyden and elsewhere. The Rhine valley was the great nursery of letters north of the Alps, and along the Rhine from source to sea the book spread and was multiplied.

This success induced Erasmus to expand and supplement the collection. The *Adagiorum Chiliades*, the title of the book in its new form, was completed by him during his residence in Italy, and was published at Venice by Aldus in September, 1508. The enlarged collection, which is in effect a new work, consists of no less than three thousand two hundred and sixty heads. In his preface, Erasmus, with that affectation from which few authors are wholly free, speaks of the earlier work as a little collection carelessly made. "Some people got hold of it," he adds—and here the affectation becomes absolute untruth— "and had it printed very incorrectly." In the new work, however, much of the old disappears, much more is partially or completely recast, and such of the old matter as is retained is dispersed at random among the new. In the *Collectanea*, the Comments had all been brief: here, many are expanded into substantial treatises covering four or five pages of closely printed folio.

The Aldine edition had been reprinted at Basel by Froben in 1513 not long before Erasmus himself took up his permanent residence there. Under his immediate supervision there presently appeared what is to all intents and purposes the definitive edition of 1515. It is a book of nearly seven hundred folio pages, and contains, besides the introductory matter, three thousand four hundred and eleven headings. In the preface, Erasmus gives some details with regard to its composition. Of the earlier work he now says, no doubt with truth, that it was undertaken by him hastily and with too little attention to method: when preparing the Venice edition, he had better realized the magnitude of the enterprise, and was better fitted for it by reading and learning; more especially, by the numerous Greek manuscripts and newly printed Greek first editions to which he had access in Venice as well as elsewhere in Italy. In England also, owing largely to the kindness of Archbishop

I

Warham, more leisure and an ampler library had been available.

Among several important additions made in the *Adagia* of 1515, the "Essay on War" is at once the longest and the most remarkable. The text which forms its title had indeed been in the earlier collection, with a few lines of commentary; but the treatise, in itself a substantial work, now appeared for the first time. It occupied a conspicuous place as the first heading in the fourth Chiliad of the complete work. It was at once singled out as of special note and profound import. Froben was soon called upon for a separate edition, which he produced in April, 1517, as a quarto of twenty pages. This little book, the *Bellum Erasmi* as it was popularly called, found an unprecedented public. Half the scholarly presses of Europe were soon employed in reprinting it. Within ten years it had been re-issued at Louvain, Leipsic, Antwerp, Venice, and twice over at Strasburg, Mayence, Paris, and Cologne. German translations of it were published at Basel and at Strasburg in 1519 and 1520. Through these and other sources it soon made its way to England; and a translation into English was issued by Berthelet, the King's printer, in the winter of 1533-4.

There is no direct evidence whether this translation be by Richard Taverner, the translator and editor a few years later of selections from the *Adagia*, or by some other hand; nor except for purposes of curiosity is the question of any importance. For the version wholly lacks distinction; it is a work of adequate scholarship but of no independent literary merit. English prose was then hardly formed. The Revival of Letters had reached the country, but for political and social reasons which may be found in any handbook of English history, it had found the soil fertile indeed, but not yet broken up. Since Chaucer, English poetry had practically stood still; and except where poetry has cleared the way, prose does not in ordinary circumstances advance. A few adventurers in setting forth had appeared. More's *Utopia* is an English classic in virtue of its style as well as of its matter. Berners' *Froissart*, published in 1523, was the first and one of the finest of that series of translations which from this time onwards for about a century were produced in an almost continuous stream, and through which the secret of prose was slowly wrung from older and more accomplished languages. Latimer, about the same time, showed his countrymen how a vernacular prose, flexible, well-knit and nervous, might be written without its lines being traced on any ancient or foreign model. Coverdale, the greatest master of English prose whom the century produced, whose name has just missed the immortality that is secure for his work, must by this time have substantially completed that noble version of the Bible which appeared in 1535, and to which the Authorized Version of the seventeenth century owes all that one work of genius can owe to another. It is not with those great men that the translator of this treatise can be compared. But he wrought, after his measure, on the same structure as they.

It is then to the original Latin, not to this awkward and stammering version, that students must turn now, as still more certainly they turned then, for the mind of Erasmus; for with him, even more than with most authors, the style is the man, and his Latin is the substance, not merely the dress, of his thought. When he wrote it, he was about forty-eight years old, and still in the fullness of his powers. If he was often crippled by poor health, that was no more than he had habitually been from boyhood. In this treatise we come very near the real man, with his strange mixture of liberalism and orthodoxy, of clear-sighted courage and a delicacy which bordered on timidity.

His text is that (in the translator's words) "nothing is either more wicked or more wretched, nothing doth more become a man (I will not say a Christian man) than war." War was shocking to Erasmus on every side alike of his complex and sensitive nature. It was impious; it was inhuman; it was ugly; it was, in every sense of the word, barbarous, to one who, before all things and in the full sense of the term, was civilized and a lover of civilization. All these aspects of the case, seen by others singly and partially, were to him facets of one truth, rays from one light. His argument circles and flickers among them, hardly pausing to enforce one before sliding insensibly to another. In the splendid vindication of the nature of man with which the treatise opens, the tone is rather that of Cicero than of the Gospels. The majesty of man resides above all in his capacity "to behold the very pure strength and nature of things." In essence he is no fallen and corrupt creature, but a piece of workmanship such as Shakespeare describes him through the mouth of Hamlet. He was shaped to this heroic mould "by Nature, or rather god," so the Tudor translation reads, and its use of capital letters, though probably only a freak of the printer, brings out with singular suggestiveness the latent pantheism which underlies the thought of all the humanists.

To this wonderful creature, strife and warfare are naturally repugnant. Not only is his frame "weak and tender," but he is "born to love and amity." His chief end, the object to which all his highest and most distinctively human powers are directed, is co-operant labour in pursuit of knowledge. War comes out of ignorance, and into ignorance it leads: of war comes contempt of virtue and of godly living. In the age of Machiavelli the word virtue had a double and sinister meaning, but here it is taken in its nobler sense. Yet, the argument continues, war gives but little room for virtue even in the Florentine statesman's use of the term. It is waged mainly for "vain titles or childish wrath." It does not foster, in those responsible for it or in their instruments, any one of the nobler excellences. The argument in this part of the treatise is, both in its substance and in its ornament, wholly apart from the precepts of religion. The Furies of War are described as rising out of a very pagan hell. The apostrophe of Nature to mankind immediately suggests the spirit and recalls the language of Lucretius. Erasmus had clearly been reading the De Rerum Natura, and borrows some of his finest touches from the Roman poet's description of the growth of civilization in the fifth book which is one of the noblest contributions of antiquity towards a real conception of the nature of the world and of man. The progressive degeneration of morality, because, as its scope becomes higher, practice falls farther and farther short of it, is insisted upon by both thinkers in much the same spirit and with much the same illustrations. The rise of empires, "of which there was never none yet in any nation but it was gotten with the great shedding of man's blood," is seen by both in the same light. But Erasmus passes on to the expressly religious aspect of the whole matter in the great double climax with which he crowns his argument, the wickedness of a Christian fighting against a fellow-man, the horror of a Christian fighting against another Christian. "Yea, and with a thing so devilish," he breaks out in a mingling of intense scorn and profound pity, "we mingle Christ."

From this passionate appeal he passes to the praise of peace. Why should men add the horrors of war to all the other miseries and dangers of life? Why should one man's gain be sought only through another's loss? All victories in war are Cadmean; not only from their cost in blood and treasure, but because we are in very truth the members of one body, redeemed with Christ's blood. Such was the clear, unmistakable teaching of our Lord Himself, such of His apostles. But the law of Christ has been "plied to worldly opinion." Worldly men, philosophers following the sophistries of Aristotle, worst of all, divines and theologians, have corrupted the Gospel to the heathenish doctrine that every man must first provide for himself. The very words of Scripture are wrested to this abuse; self-defence is held, not merely to excuse, but to sanction, any violence. "Peter fought," they say, "in the garden." Yes, and that same night he denied his Master! "Punishment of wrong is a divine ordinance." In war, the punishment falls on the innocent. "The law of nature bids us repel violence by violence." What is the law of Christ? "May not a prince go to war justly for his right?" Did any war ever lack a title? "But what of wars against the Turk?" Such wars are of Turk against Turk: let us overcome evil with good; let us spread the Gospel by doing what the Gospel commands: did Christ say, Hate them that hate you?

Then, with the tact of an accomplished orator, he lets the tension relax, and drops to a lower tone. Even apart from all that has been urged, even if war were ever justifiable, think of the price that has to be paid for it. On this ground alone an unjust peace is far preferable to a just war. (These had been the very words of Colet to Henry VIII.) Men go to war under fine pretexts, but really to get riches, to satisfy hatred, or to win the poor glory of destroying. The hatred is but exasperated; the glory is won by and for the dregs of mankind; the riches are in the most prosperous event swallowed up ten times over. Yet if it be impossible but war should be, if there may sometimes be "a colour of equity" in it, and if the tyrant's plea, necessity, be ever well-founded, then at least, so Erasmus concludes, let it be conducted mercifully. Let us live in fervent desire of the peace that we may not fully attain. Let princes restrain their subjects. Let churchmen above all be peacemakers.

So the treatise passes to its conclusion with that eulogy of the Medicean Pope already mentioned, which perhaps was not wholly undeserved. To the modern world the name of Leo X has come down marked with a note of censure or even of ignominy. It is fair to remember that it did not bear quite the same aspect to contemporaries, nor to the ages which immediately followed. Under Rodrigo Borgia it might well seem to others, as well as to the Florentine mystic, that Antichrist was enthroned, and Satan let loose upon the earth. The eight years of Leo's pontificate (1513–21) were at least a period of outward splendour and of a refinement previously unknown. The corruption half veiled by that refinement and splendour was deep and mortal, but the collapse did not come until later. By comparison with the disastrous Papacy of Clement VII, his bastard cousin, that of Giovanni de' Medici seemed a last gleam of light before blackness descended on the world. Even the licence of a dissolute age was contrasted, to its favour, with the gloom which settled down over Europe with the great Catholic reaction. The age of Leo X has descended to history as the age of Bembo, Sanazzaro, Lascaris, of the Stanze of the Vatican, of Raphael's Sistine Madonna and Titian's Assumption; of the conquest of Mexico and the circumnavigation of Magellan; of Magdalen Tower and King's College Chapel. It was an interval of comparative peace before a long epoch of wars more cruel and more devastating than any within men's memory. The general European conflagration did not break out until ten years after Erasmus' death, though it had then been long foreseen as inevitable. But he lived to see the conquest of Rhodes by Soliman, the sack of Rome, the breach between England and the Papacy, the ill-omened marriage of Catherine de' Medici to the heir of the French crown. Humanism had done all that it could, and had failed. In the sanguinary era of one hundred years between the outbreak of civil war in the Empire and the Peace of Westphalia, the Renaissance followed the Middle Ages to the grave, and the modern world was born.

The mere fact of this treatise having been translated into English and published by the King's printer, in an age when the literary product of England was as yet scanty, shows that it had some prestige and some influence in this country. But only a few copies of the translation are known to exist; and it was never reprinted until now. Not until nearly three centuries later, and then amid the throes of a European revolution equally vast, was the work of Erasmus again presented in an English dress. Vicesimus Knox, a Whig essayist, compiler, and publicist of some repute in his time, was the author of a book which was published anonymously in 1794, and found a considerable number of readers in a year filled with great events in English history and English literature. It was entitled *Anti-Polemus: or the Plea of Reason: Religion: and Humanity against War: a Fragment translated from Erasmus and addressed to Aggressors.* That was the year when the first breach took place in the Whig party, and when Pitt initiated his brief and ill-fated policy of conciliation in Ireland. It was also the year of two works which had an immense influence, Paley's *Evidences* and Paine's *Age of Reason.* Among these great movements and shattering events, Knox's book had little chance of appealing to a wide audience. *Sed quid ad nos?* the bitter motto on the title-page, probably expresses the feelings with which it was generally regarded. A version of the treatise of Erasmus, made from the Latin text of the *Adagia* with some omissions, is the main substance of the volume; and Knox added a few extracts on the same subject from other writings of Erasmus. It does not appear to have been reprinted in England except in a collected edition of Knox's works which may be found on the dustiest shelves of old-fashioned libraries, until, after the close of the Napoleonic Wars, it was again published as a tract by the Society for the Promotion of Permanent and Universal Peace. Some half-dozen impressions of this tract appeared at intervals up to the middle of the century; its publication passed into the hands of the Society of Friends, and the last issue of which any record can be found was made just before the outbreak of the Crimean War. At the present day, the noble pleading of Erasmus has more than a merely literary or antiquarian interest. For the appeal of humanism still is, as it was then, to the dignity of human nature itself.

ARIOSTO

[1924]

IT is both singular and unfortunate that during the last hundred years the growth in this country of sympathy with the Italian nation has, with one notable exception, been accompanied by growing loss of familiarity with Italian literature and in particular with that body of noble Italian poetry which extends from the predecessors of Dante down to the present day. The neglect into which Italian studies have fallen means not only that we have allowed ourselves to become, to that extent, intellectually and artistically impoverished, but that we have cut ourselves away from one of the great formative influences of our own poetry. "The descent of poetry," in Gray's memorable phrase, "was from Greece to Italy, and from Italy to England."

At all the turning points of our poetry for the four centuries which lie between Chaucer and Wordsworth, the Italian influence has been marked, the Italian inspiration has been vital. They reached this country, in literature as in the other arts, very largely through France, but their transmission was also direct. Boccaccio was the poetical inspirer of Chaucer even more than his French models. Petrarch and his school were the originators of the renewed poetical expansion of England in the splendid, but brief and early clouded, period of our English Renaissance. Tasso and Guarini had a most powerful effect on the English poetry of the seventeenth and even of the earlier eighteenth century. Still later, the names of Chiabrera, Metastasio and Alfieri are those of poets once well known and widely read in England, and notable, if in a less degree, in the direction they gave to the evolution of our poetry.

The one exception to the general decay or disuse of Italian studies in this country since then is, of course, Dante. The growth, in quantity and quality, of knowledge and appreciation of the sovereign Italian poet does not require to be dwelt upon. It is a movement which has been running for sixty or seventy years, and which runs as strongly as ever. But its existence, however welcome in itself, only throws into stronger relief the comparative desuetude into which the study of Dante's successors has fallen. It is a curious question how far concentration on Dante may have actually tended to withdraw attention or interest from the line of poets who seem to stand half obscured in his gigantic shadow.

A century ago, Dante was just emerging from his long eclipse. But Italian poetry as a whole still then remained, what it long had been, an integral part of national culture. In educated men and women, knowledge of Italian was assumed. Of women's education in particular it was a normal and accepted part. In any old country house with an intact library one may still find the row of volumes lettered *Poesie Raccolte* or *Poesie Scelte*, and at all events a Petrarch, an Ariosto and a Tasso, whether in the more sumptuous form of the quartos with their elaborate engravings dear to the eighteenth century, or in the neat duodecimos suitable to lie on a lady's worktable. Peacock's Morgana, who is found by Algernon Falconer reading the *Orlando Innamorato* and who quotes freely from it, is drawn from the life. Scott told Cheney at Rome in 1832 that he had long made it a practice to read through both the *Orlando Innamorato* and the *Orlando Furioso* once every year; and when he was called the Northern Ariosto, the phrase was neither pedantic nor meaningless to the ordinary educated reader. In quite recent times, the study of Italian has been reinstated in our Universities, and one is glad to think that it is growing, if slowly, yet steadily. But from our education short of the Universities it long ago disappeared. A few years ago I found on inquiry that so far as official statistics covered the ground, it was taught in no boys' school and in only two girls' schools in England. The loss to our national culture, the loss to intelligent study of our own national poetry, is very great. For this reason, no less than for the more obvious reason that Englishmen and Englishwomen should be acquainted with the literature of a great and friendly nation, it may be hoped that effective influence will be exercised towards the fuller recognition and more adequate study of Italian, and of the great Italian classics.

Of those classics Ariosto is one of the greatest; and he is the one whose effect on the evolution and civilization of English poetry has been most direct and most potent. To the *Orlando Furioso*, the *Faerie Queene* owes, it may be said poetically and artistically everything; owes its existence. And Spenser is in poetry the central and culminating figure of the Elizabethan age. Milton was, and acknowledged himself to be, Spenser's pupil and successor. In that sense he also derives from Ariosto, at a double remove. But his own saturation in youth with the Italian romantic epic, from the *Morgante* and the *Mambriano* to the *Gerusalemme Liberata*, was what made it possible for Puritanism to break, for once, into amazing flower, for English poetry to rise beyond insularity and provincialism, and for a new name and a new language to take their place among the world classics.

Milton himself has recorded, in words of exalted beauty, the time when "my younger feet wandered . . . among those lofty fables and romances which recount in solemn cantos the deeds of knighthood." Perhaps it is the more naïve earlier romances that were primarily in his mind when he spoke of solemn cantos; but Ariosto, for all his gaiety and brightness, can be solemn, too, when he chooses; can rise to the loftiness of tragic events, of grief and endurance, of unselfish love and invincible honour. In the famous passage in the *Paradise Regained*,

> When Agrican with all his Northern powers
> Besieged Albracca, as romances tell,
> The city of Gallaphrone, from thence to win
> The fairest of her sex, Angelica
> His daughter, sought by many prowest knights
> Both Paynim, and the Peers of Charlemain—

it is to Boiardo that Milton is referring; and in the equally splendid passage in the *Paradise Lost*,

All who since, baptized or infidel,
Jousted in Aspramont or Montalban,
Damasco or Marocco or Trebisond,
Or whom Biserta sent from Afric shore
When Charlemain with all his peerage fell
By Fontarabbia—

the scope he includes is that of the *Mambriano* as well as of
the two Orlandi. But the jousting at Damascus is one of the
great episodes in Ariosto, and Milton's opening phrase repeats
and is meant to recall Ariosto's *Macomettani e gente di battesmo*.

In many Miltonic similes, in many touches of description or
imagination, the saturation of Milton's mind with the language,
the melody, the enriched ornament of Ariosto is evident,
though he adds his own inimitable and unswerving dignity—
now and then, it must be confessed, with unhappy result; for
Ariosto never for a moment loses his sense of humour and his
lightness of touch, and Milton's attempts at humour, as also
indeed Spenser's, are seldom happy.

I do not propose to enter even in summary on the circumstances and surroundings of Ariosto's life. It would be superfluous here; to those who wish to pursue the subject, Professor
Edmund Gardner's full, elaborate and fascinating study
entitled *The King of Court Poets*, is accessible. But to place
him, not merely in relation to the course of Italian poetry but
to the whole movement of European history and art, a few
notes may be given. His life, 1474–1533, almost exactly covers
the last and culminating phase of the Italian Renaissance, in
that amazing and unequalled splendour which was to be
succeeded by swift decay. When, at the age of twelve, he
removed with his family from his native Reggio to Ferrara,
the ducal court there was the most splendid in Italy, or in the
world; and the years between then and the beginning of
sorrows, the coming of Charles VIII into Italy in 1494, were
the golden age of humanism.

It was the horror of the French invasion which made
Boiardo break off his *Orlando Innamorato*, though he lived
for ten years more. In effect, he passed over the task of
completing the creation of the romantic epic to the boy of
twenty who was to accomplish it. Ariosto then or soon

afterwards became attached to the Ducal household. He wrote a Latin epithalamium for the marriage, in 1502, of Alfonso d'Este and Lucrezia Borgia, that pathetic and enigmatic figure who died, and perhaps lived, something like a saint, and descended to the fevered imagination of the next age as a devil incarnate: "beautiful, good, sweet and courteous," says the *Loyal Serviteur* who wrote the life of the Chevalier Bayard; and the laudation of her in the *Orlando* (xiii, 69–71) sounds as sincere as it is magnificent.

At all events, it must not be forgotten that Ariosto reserves his highest praise for one on whom flattery would have been wasted, and on whose virtue no shadow was ever thrown, the widowed Marchioness of Pescara, the Puritan saint Vittoria Colonna. It was to the service of Cardinal Ippolito, Alfonso's younger brother, that Ariosto was specially attached. Of him historians have no good to say except that he seems always to have stuck loyally by Alfonso, both in the domestic horrors which followed his succession and in the tortuous, inconclusive politics of his reign. The loaded and extravagant panegyrics on both with which the *Orlando Furioso* is filled were common form in the Age of the Despots. Some readers find in their very extravagance a hint of sarcasm; we may be content to admire, as art, their adroit insertion, their inexhaustible fertility of variation, and the melodious splendour of their language.

Ariosto's youth was passed in the full day of the Renaissance; his great work was executed in its even more gorgeous sunset. He outlived Leonardo and Raffaele; he was almost the exact contemporary of Michael Angelo and Titian. Machiavelli's *Prince* and Rabelais' *Gargantua* (both published within a few months of the *Orlando Furioso* in its final form) give in some sense the two extremes of the vast revolution which that age brought into human thought and the art of letters. In England, Malory's *Morte d'Arthur* appeared in Ariosto's boyhood, More's *Utopia* in the year of the first publication of the *Orlando*. In the year of Ariosto's death come the earliest plays of Heywood, and we are on the brink of the Elizabethan age. But, indeed, the Renaissance in its wide European significance may be said to have come to an end

just then. That stormy sunset was the age of Bayard and of
Cesare Borgia, of the typical decadent Giuliano de' Medici
and the pasteboard Paladin Francis I, of Castiglione's *Courtier*
and Machiavelli's *Prince*. The sack of Rome in 1527 was in
itself a mere incident, as was its sack by Alaric eleven centuries
before; but both were dramatic and startling symbols of the
end of one world and the beginning of another. Three years
later, Charles V was crowned Emperor at Bologna. The
magnificent stanzas then incorporated by Ariosto in canto
xv (24–39) of the *Orlando* are the last swan-song over the
phantom of prestige and majesty that still lingered on the
relics of the medieval Empire: in their concluding lines,

> E vuol che sotto a questo Imperatore
> Solo un ovile sia, solo un pastore—

we seem to hear, and to hear for the last time, the voice of
Dante speaking across the ashes of two hundred years.

Duke Alfonso died the year after Ariosto; in the same year
the Society of Jesus was created, and the Counter-Reformation
began. Humanism went to the grave with Erasmus two years
later; and already there loomed on the near horizon the
century-long wars of Religion. The story is well known, but
bears repetition, of Alfonso's last commission to Titian; the
mythological subject which, left unfinished at Alfonso's death,
was many years later recomposed by the artist into a painting
executed for Philip II after Lepanto, under the title "Religion
defended by Spain." In a smaller way it is worth remembering
too that Alfonso's grandson, born in the year of Ariosto's
death, was the last sovereign prince of Ferrara, which then
became incorporated in the Papal States.

Ariosto's literary production was not only very large but
very various. That age of giants was one of high intellectual
and imaginative tension and of extraordinary fecundity, in
poetry as in the other arts. He abandoned the study of law
to devote himself to poetry at the age of twenty; but soon after,
on the death of his unlucky father, he found himself obliged to
look after and sustain nine younger brothers and sisters; his
position in the household of Ippolito d'Este brought him in

but little, and much of his time had to be spent on special
missions and distasteful administrative detail. His industry
as a writer is no less marked than his genius. His earlier poetry
was in Latin; such of it as I have read does not rise beyond
the general level—though that was, of course, high—but it
must have been of great value in giving him the sense of
classical form. Cardinal Bembo advised him to write in Latin
if he aimed at immortality. Much later than then it was still
questioned whether poetry in Italian or any other vernacular
could reach an European audience or be in the full sense
classical. But here Ariosto dared and achieved. He eclipsed
Boiardo and his other predecessors not so much in substance
as in added lucidity, grace, melodiousness and exquisite
finish. He wrote lyrics, sonnets and madrigals, as was the
fashion; his only lyric piece which has effectively survived is
the noble canzone on Alessandra Strozzi, the beautiful Florentine, whom he loved passionately and finally married. For
her and himself he built the little country house which still,
though greatly altered, survives, and inscribed over its door
the couplet of which the three opening words have become a
proverb, familiar to thousands who do not know their author
and may hardly even have heard his name:

> Parva sed apta mihi, sed nulli obnoxia, sed non
> Sordida, parta meo sed tamen aere domus.

His *Satire* or familiar epistles on the model of Horace are
very pleasant reading, fluent, simple and racy, the work (like
Horace's) of a man of the world and a gentleman. His four
comedies (a fifth was left unfinished at his death) are of much
importance in the historical evolution of modern drama; the
earliest two, the *Cassaria* and *Suppositi*, share with the *Calandra*
of Bibbieno the claim to be the first regular comedies written
in Italian. For the later pieces he used a vehicle of his own
invention, the *iambo volgare* as he calls it himself, later known
as the *verso sdrucciolo*: a metre which, though much and
perhaps not unjustly condemned by Italian critics for monotony and lack of dignity, is not wholly unpleasing to a Northern
ear. The fragment of a heroic poem in *terza rima*, and the

Cinque Canti, which, if genuine—as to this, opinions differ—
must have been a rough draft for a continuation of the
Orlando, sketched out and laid aside by him before his great
poem received its final form, require only a passing notice.
For the world at large, and for readers other than professed
students of Italian literature, at the present day, the word
Ariosto means the *Orlando Furioso*; and to the *Orlando* (as for
the sake of brevity I shall henceforth mostly call it) we may
now turn.

Narrative romantic poetry, in the *ottava rima* which Boccaccio
had long since definitely established as its proper vehicle, had
been carried by Boiardo to its full scope. The chivalrous
romance culminated with him. Superficially, what Ariosto
undertook was the continuing of that poem, from the point at
which Boiardo's work broke off. In the opening stanzas of
the *Orlando Innamorato* the Count of Scandiano announces his
subject to be (1) the battles and glory of Charlemagne, (2) the
prowesses of Orlando achieved for love, (3) the treacherous
murder of Ruggiero by Gano. The *Orlando Furioso* does not,
in fact, complete this scheme, ending as it does with the
death of Rodomonte and the marriage of Ruggiero and
Bradamante. But the title was carefully chosen to convey the
fact that the poem was, as regards its narrative, a continuation of the *Orlando Innamorato*. Not only does it assume
knowledge of the contents of the earlier poem, to which
perpetual reference is made; but it opens, without any re-
capitulation, by plunging at once into the story just at the point
where Boiardo had stopped.

What Ariosto did, however, was more than continuing a
tradition. He greatly expanded, and, to a large degree,
remodelled its substance. The object which he aimed at and
attained was, in the words of a contemporary, "to equip a
romantic poem with dignity and magnificence." Out of the
chivalrous romance he created the romantic epic. Its predecessors had been romantic chronicles, which still, though
permeated with the humanistic spirit, preserved much of the
medieval method, with its inconsequence, its garrulity, its lack
of high tension and organic construction. Whether, or how
far, Ariosto's romance can be called an epic is a question that

has often been debated; and the discussion has generally turned
on the inquiry whether it has, in point of fact, a subject,
whether it possesses epic unity. If we seek to find that, we
must begin by throwing the title overboard. The titular hero
does not appear at all till the ninth canto. He only goes mad
in the twenty-third. The story of his madness and recovery,
though it occupies an important place in the poem, and is
adroitly interwoven with its structure, might not unreasonably
be called an episode. The leading structural motive of the
Orlando, so far as there is one, may be described as (like
that of the Iliad or the Aeneid) an incorporation of a national
with a personal human interest: the former, in this case, the
large epic motive of the Pagan invasion of France and the final
victory of Christendom; the latter, the story of Ruggiero and
Bradamante. This latter was dictated partly by an obvious
reason, the position which Ariosto held at the Ferrarese Court,
and his desire—his summons likewise—to glorify the House
of Este in the persons of its legendary ancestors. But it was
more largely chosen on artistic grounds, at the prompting of
the instinct towards the epic.

The epic proper has a beginning and an end; it rejects and
concentrates; it has a single movement, however complex that
may be in its evolution; it moves throughout at a high tension.
In this sense, the *Orlando* is only an inchoate epic. Its beginning is, as we have seen, what might be called accidental;
we are plunged at once into an intricate story of adventure,
almost unintelligible unless we come to it with previous
knowledge of the *Orlando Innamorato*. It is episodic in its
treatment in the largest and most unbounded way. Many
of the major episodes, like for instance, those of Ginevra and
Ariodante, of Olimpia, of Ullania, fill more than a whole canto
apiece, and are in no sense necessary to the poem. There are
even insets, frankly produced as such, stories told incidentally
by minor characters introduced for the purpose, and quite
detachable, like that of the Orco (canto xvii) told by the
unnamed knight to Grifone at Damascus; of Gabrina (canto
xxi) told by Ermonide to Zerbino; of Astolfo King of
Lombardy, Iocondo, and Fiammetta (canto xxviii) told by
the innkeeper on the Saône to Rodomonte as heard by him

K

from a Venetian; and of Anselmo and Argia, related by a sailor to Rinaldo on his voyage down the Po (canto xliii).

But in the ending of the poem the epic instinct asserts itself; the main narrative does not trail endlessly along as in a romance, but is concentrated, is knit up into an epic climax. The victory of Christendom is decisive and complete. Peace reigns throughout the world. Angelica, "the star that made men mad," has faded away into India; Orlando has resumed his place among the Paladins. All the loose threads of the complex story have been taken up, and it is given its place in world history by the last stroke of the enchantress Melissa when she brings the pavilion of the Greek Emperor through the air for the nuptials of Bradamante and Ruggiero. It had been made by Cassandra for Hector; it was given by Menelaus after the sack of Troy to Proteus, King of Egypt; it was captured from Cleopatra's fleet at Actium, and carried by Constantine from Rome to his new imperial capital. On it were embroidered in prophecy the name and deeds of Ippolito and the fame of the House of Este. Then, by a stroke of brilliant genius, Rodomonte, the last left, as he was the fiercest and the most terrible of the Pagan champions, arrives, released from his self-imposed penance, on the last day of the wedding festival; challenges Ruggiero; and is killed by him after a long and furious duel. The last lines of the poem,

> Sciolta dal corpo più freddo che ghiaccio
> Bestemmiando fuggì l'alma sdegnosa
> Che fu sì altiera al mondo e sì orgogliosa,

are, as has always been noted, Dantesque in language and Virgilian in substance. But they are no mere echo of the final couplet of the Aeneid; they are a touch of that epic genius by which Ariosto lifts his work into relation and community with that of his two great Italian predecessors.

To seek throughout the *Orlando* for anything like epic unity or epic structure is an idle quest. Panizzi tried hard to vindicate this claim; he sets out to do so by an analysis of its contents aimed at showing how all its incidents and episodes are causally connected with what he names as its main subject.

To follow his analysis leaves, I must confess, one's brain in a whirl. To those who read the *Orlando* for the first time, or even for the second or third, I would venture to suggest that they should abandon themselves frankly to the enchanter, follow him through a gorgeous wilderness of adventure and pageantry, war and love and magic, satire and pathos; that they should float down the great powerful stream, following it in all its windings and embranchments, its loops and divagations, and not troubling to map out the lands through which it flows. Afterwards, it is worth while, as it is fascinating, to study and analyse, to appreciate the brain-work and the genius for design which underlie the apparent inconsequence of the poem, with its "wild enormities of ancient magnanimity." We can then come to appreciate the skill and tact of the transitions, the care with which dropped threads are taken up into the structure, the certainty of hand with which Ariosto passes, not only from one character or adventure to another, but from tragic pathos to sparkling comedy or extravagant farce.

> Signor, far mi convien come fa il buono
> Sonator sopra il suo instrumento arguto,
> Che spesso muta corda, e varia suono,
> Ricercando ora il grave, ora l'acuto.

In this quality, in his unfailing lightness and security of touch, as also in the lucidity of his narrative he is unapproached by any of his successors or imitators. Beside him, Spenser seems laborious and imperfectly civilized, heavy where he is serious, clumsy where he tries to be light.

> But turn we back now to that lady free
> Whom late we left riding upon an ass—

that is Spenser attempting to handle a transition like Ariosto. The *Faerie Queene*, with all its excellencies, is monotonous; it lacks life and movement. In his set scenes, his great pageants, Spenser comes nearer his master. But, by the end of the sixteenth century, the age of humanism was over, while the new synthesis aimed at by classicism had not been yet achieved. Further, he had not wholly escaped from the medieval prison; he set out to make his great poem a sustained allegory. The allegorical figures in the *Orlando* (Logistilla, for instance, in the island of Alcina, or the monster, Jealousy, that attacks Rinaldo in his search for Angelica, and the knight, Disdain, who relieves him), are but few. Even so, they are not in tone with the full-blooded humanity of the poem; they must be admitted to be flaws in it.

When we have studied the *Orlando* in this fuller and more searching way, we shall at least understand what C. J. Fox meant, when he said that it was the "most regular and connected of all the poems he knew"; and we shall also appreciate, as a complement to that, Coleridge's, "I am for Ariosto against Tasso, though I would rather praise Ariosto's poetry than his poem." Its quality is not architectural; that is as much as to say, it is not an epic, though it is, on a large view, an equally great as it is a rarer and indeed an unique poetical achievement. It rather resembles the fabric of some amazingly rich series of tapestries, such as were in that same time being produced, from the designs of great artists, on the looms of Flanders; but preserving unimpaired at the present day (such is the special gift of heaven to poetry) not only its masterly design and crowded ornament, but the full brilliance of its colouring and vitality of its figures. "I have just read Ariosto's *Orlando Furioso*; it is all beautiful, and often miraculous." So, in December, 1517, wrote Niccolo Machiavelli; so any appreciative reader, in any quarter of the world, might write to-day. "It is perhaps," wrote a fine English scholar just a century ago, "the poetical work which is oftenest re-perused with pleasure." How few there are among educated Englishmen and Englishwomen now who can speak of re-perusing it! Surely, the change is a great loss. Is pleasure, of a high kind, so abundant that we can afford to ignore one among its amplest sources?

Perhaps I should say a word here as regards the episodes or passages which do not conform to either ancient or modern ideas of decorum. They have been, no doubt, a stumbling-block to many from the first. Some of the peccant stanzas are said to have been marked by Ariosto himself for omission or modification; some have been, in prudence or modesty, left out in translations. There are a few pages (only a few) in the *Orlando* which one would hesitate to recommend for reading. I will, of course, not indicate these. But at the opening of one canto, Ariosto himself gives his readers fair warning:

> Donne, e voi che le donne avete in pregio,
> Per Dio, non date a questa istoria orecchia. . . .
> Lasciate questo canto; chè senza esso
> Può star l'istoria, e non sarà men chiara. . . .
> Passi, chi vuol, tre carte o quattro senza
> Leggerne verso; e chi pur legger vuole,
> Gli dia quella medesima credenza
> Che si suol dare a finzioni e a fole.

These *fole*, "idle tales," are swept along in the flood of his large humanism.

The prologues to the canti, in which Ariosto speaks in his own person, were a new invention of his, handled by him with extraordinary skill and variety. Generally, they are by way of comment on, or reinforcement of, his narrative; some are moralizations, like the fine openings of canto xxxi on jealousy, of canto xliii on avarice, of canto xlv on the mutability of Fortune; in others, writing with a higher and more impassioned note, he speaks more fully from the heart, as in canto xxxiv, the apostrophe to the Furies which devastated Italy, in canto xxxvi, the exaltation of the courtesy of old time in contrast with the barbarity of contemporary warfare; and the magnificent praise of women which occupies the first twenty-three stanzas of canto xxxvii. One of the best known is the eulogy of great painters, (xxxiii), introducing the long episode of the historical pageant of the French wars in Italy painted by Merlin's demons in the great hall of the Rôcca di Tristano. That episode, which fills no less than fifty-six stanzas of canto xxxiii, shows Ariosto's constructive and descriptive powers at their full height. The painters whose names he celebrates in its introduction are, besides those of the ancient world,

> E quei che furo a' nostri dì, o sono ora,
> Leonardo, Andrea Mantegna, Gian Bellino,
> Duo Dossi, e quel ch' a par sculpe e colora,
> Michel più che mortale, Angel divino;

> Bastiano, Rafael, Tizian ch'onora
> Non men Cador, che quei Venezia e Urbino;
> E gli altri di cui tal l'opra si vede   ·
> Qual de la prisca età si legge e crede.

Of Ariosto's narrative power—unsurpassed and seldom equalled among poets—little need be said, for it is universally recognized; in lucidity and a sort of unhurried swiftness it approaches perfection. It is equally good in the ordinary course of the story and in the more highly elaborated incidents such as his great battle pieces. The *aristeia* of Rodomonte when he breaks into Paris (xiv–xvi), and the storming of Biserta (xl), are told with a verve like Scott's and a splendour like Homer's; and the same is true of his innumerable single combats; culminating in the final desperate fight between Rodomonte and Ruggiero on which the *Orlando* ends. Perhaps the highest point of all is reached in the great battle of three against three on the island (xli). I know nothing like it except in Dumas at his best; and that is prose, this is poetry.

Le cortesie, l'audaci imprese io canto, Ariosto says in his opening lines; and *cortesia*, the sense of chivalrous honour, is a dominating motive throughout, though it is always shot across by his sense of comedy and his turn for light, or serious, or even sometimes cynical, satire. The *gran bontà de' cavallieri antiqui* is always in his mind; he may not quite believe in it, but he accepts and unreservedly admires it. The world of medieval chivalry lives anew in the *Orlando* not only among Charlemagne and his Paladins, but in the heathen kings and captains. There is an under-sense even of the more mystical Arthurian romance:

> Gran cose in essa (in Scotland) già fece Tristano,
> Lancilotto, Galasso, Artù e Galvano.

Medieval too, if we should not rather call it Virgilian, is the sense of pity over fate, of the shadow that creeps across human glory.

> Hector is dead, and Troilus is dead;
> Aeneas turneth toward the waters wan;
> In his fair house Antenor hides his head;
> Fast from the tree of Troy the boughs are shred;
> And now this Paris, now this joyous one,
> Is the cry cried that biddeth him begone?

Hardly different in tone from these lines in Morris' *Death of Paris*, are the words of the King of Spain at the last council held by Agramante,

> Del nostro campo Mandricardo e scemo,
> Gradasso il suo soccorso n'ha rimosso;
> Marfisa n'ha lasciati al punto estremo,
> E così il Re d'Algier, di cui dir posso
> Che, se fosse fedel come gagliardo,
> Poco uopo era Gradasso o Mandricardo.

It is thus that, in a serious moment, he speaks of life itself in terms which might come from the lips of Dante,

> questa morta gora
> C'ha nome vita, che sì piace a' sciocchi.

But, as the converse, or complement, of this sense of melancholy and disillusionment, he is always ready to break out into a clear flame of Italian patriotism. Citations need not be multiplied; but special note may be made of canto xvii, with its noble introductory stanzas, and the impassioned call on Italy (lxxvi) to awake and shake off Spanish domination—

> Dormi, Italia imbrïaca, e non ti pesa
> Ch'ora di questa gente, ora di quella
> Che già serva ti fu, sei fatta ancella?—

the appeal to the *Tedesco* (lxxviii) to turn his arms against the Mohammedan, and to the Pope (lxxix)—*tu sei Pastore*—to defend his flock and put forth the power given him by heaven. Not less remarkable in its feeling for Italian unity is the pageant of the French invasions (one of the later insertions in the *Orlando*) which fills nearly half of canto xxxiii.

But it is in his characterization, in the warmth and fullness of life which he pours into his figures, that the large humanism of Ariosto culminates. I have spoken of the richness of his crowded and elaborate intertexture as resembling that of a tapestry. But his figures, his men and women, are not the faint or even ghostly figures, felt and expressed as elements of the design, which we associate with tapestries when that art was at its highest. We do not in the *Orlando* "in a cool green room all day gaze upon the arras giddily, where the wind sets the silken kings asway." They are live people, men and women of flesh and blood, each with character and quality of their own; we can never doubt or forget (as one is apt to do in the *Faerie Queene*) who it is that we are reading about. The high prince Orlando, the Achilles of the Paladins, always, even in his madness, bigger than anyone else; Ruggiero, that mixture of bravery and devotion with glaring weakness of character; the great broad-shouldered genial Englishman Astolfo; Zerbino, that flower-like figure of youthful gallantry; the light-hearted incorrigible Ricciardetto; Leon, the prince of courtesy; Brandimarte, the good knight, brave and a little stupid, but shining throughout in the reflected light of Fiordiligi's devoted love; the charming boy Medoro: what a gallery in which these are principal figures! and beside these have to be placed likewise the no less largely and sympathetically modelled figures of Pagan kings and captains, the splendid savage Rodomonte, Gradasso, the great warrior, the *preux chevalier* Norandino of Damascus, the finely contrasted figures of Marsilio and Sobrino. All are distinct, all are alive.

Even more wonderful is the gallery of Ariosto's women. The later Renaissance was an age of great women, great in intellect, in affairs, in arts and letters, as well as in feminine charm. "Many," in his own words, "leaving the needle and the cloth, have gone, and go, with the Muses to quench their thirst at the fountain of Aganippe"; and of other fountains they drank as well. It was under the stimulus of this highly cultured and wholly enfranchised society that Ariosto modelled the heroines—using that word in its largest sense—who live in his pages, subtly, powerfully, and (even where he gives fullest rein to the comic spirit) imaginatively drawn.

Of Angelica, the titular heroine, in a sense, of the poem as Orlando is its titular hero, a word must be said; for the delicacy of Ariosto's art here has not been enough appreciated. He took her over from the *Orlando Innamorato*, but what was

he to do with her? "He gave her a soul," says Professor
Gardner. With all submission, that is just what he did not do.
He was not going to wreck his poem on that shoal, however
alluring. His Angelica has no more soul than Helen of Troy.
Incapable of love, even in her infatuation for Medoro, she is a
sort of symbol of intangible and intoxicating beauty. She
has brains enough to make adroit use of her ring of invisibility:
but otherwise she is without soul, as she is without courage
or devotion or eloquence. She seldom speaks; some sixty
lines are all that are put in her mouth throughout the whole
poem. She is chiefly occupied in running away from her trail
of lovers; from Rinaldo, Sacripante, Ruggiero, Orlando,
Ferraù. She is essentially elusive; we do not really know her,
for there is nothing to know, behind the intoxicating power
that she has, and that she radiates rather than exercises:

> La gran beltà, che fu di Sacripante
> Posta innanzi al suo onore e al suo bel regno;
> La gran beltà, ch'al gran Signor d'Anglante
> Macchiò la chiara fama e l'alto ingegno;
> Le gran beltà, che fe' tutto Levante
> Sottosopra voltarsi e star al segno.

We are never alarmed for her in any of her adventures.
When she goes off with Medoro and disappears out of the
poem, we do not miss her, and we are not meant to do so.
Indeed, we sympathize with Ariosto's parting fling at her and
her convenient knack of slipping through people's fingers at
the end of canto xxix, as much as with the apology he makes
for it at the beginning of canto xxx.

In strong contrast with her in this respect are the other
women who are episodically introduced, or are only on the
second plane of the main story: like Ginevra and Olimpia; or
the hussy Doralice of Granada, that combination of easy
morals and light-heartedness, equally ready to take up, as
opportunity arises, with Mandricardo or Rodomonte or
Ruggiero, whom after all one cannot help liking; or the hag
Gabrina, who properly ends (like Mrs. Hearne in *Lavengro*), as
report goes, by being hanged,

Scrive l'autore, il cui nome mi taccio,
Che non furo lontani una giornata
Che per torsi Odorico quello impaccio,
Contro ogni patto et ogni fede data,
Al collo di Gabrina gittò un laccio
E che ad un olmo la lasciò impiccata:

or Beatrice of Montalbano, who hardly appears at all, yet who is so distinct and living, and so obviously the mother of all her children, unlike as they are to one another. On the second plane, too, though of the first importance in it, is the exquisite figure of Issabella, as well and widely known, perhaps, as any of Ariosto's creations. The scene in which Zerbino dies in her arms remains one unsurpassed in pathos and beauty, and hardly to be read without tears, and the famous *Vattene in pace, alma beata e bella* is her everlasting epitaph when she finds her own death at Rodomonte's drunken hands.

Then, on the first plane, and among the great women of poetry, are the three: Marfisa the virgin warrior, clear-sighted, powerful, inflexible, with a heart of gold and a temper of steel, *come un acciar che non ha macchia alcuna*; Fiordiligi the perfect wife, tender and devoted and courageous, who goes into the religious life (as Vittoria Colonna did) after Brandimarte's death in battle; and—we come to her at last—the adorable Bradamante.

On Bradamante one would like to linger. But she requires a separate study. She is the most subtly and lovingly drawn of them all. In her splendid large modelling there are many fine touches which yield themselves more as one knows her better. She is a heroic and yet a completely human figure. In handling his wonderful creation Ariosto is as tender, as sympathetic, and on occasion as delicately humorous as Chaucer. I have called her his creation; she is, of course, technically the Brandamante of the *Orlando Innamorato* and the Bradiamante of Bello's *Mambriano*. But by the slight change of name Ariosto may have wished to mark that he had in effect recreated her, given her flesh and blood and made her out of air and fire. It is in her lips that he puts his noblest and most moving eloquence; her agonized outpourings of love and doubt and jealousy (xxxii, 18–25 and 37–43) when

Ruggiero fails to come and the camp gossip reaches her that he is going to marry Marfisa; her lamentation on waking from dreams of him in Tristan's castle (xxxiii); her last and loveliest bewailings (xlv, 32–39 and 97–101) when her happiness seems just shown to be irretrievably snatched away from her, are not only Ariosto's high-water mark, but among the high-water marks of all poetry. From her first appearance flashing through the forest in white armour, to her last where the married maiden sits looking on anxiously at the desperate contest between Ruggiero and Rodomonte, she never fails to hold us. With her only does Ariosto rise to the heights of intense human passion; he carries us with her, not only where she is shown the pageant of her own posterity, or where the three Northern Kings go down one after another at the touch of her spear, or where she passes her sword again and again through the body of the coward and traitor Pinabello; but more powerfully still when she flings herself on her bed and crams the sheet into her mouth to keep herself from screaming, and where in a spasm of heart-sickness she sends her challenge to Ruggiero and in blind fury falls sword in hand on Marfisa; and again, most touchingly, in her child-like obedience to the parents whose ambition for a great marriage for her makes her so miserable.

One of Ariosto's prettiest touches is where he remembers to tell us when the *aurei crespi crini* that had to be cut off when she was wounded in the head had grown long enough again to be knotted up behind; and one of the most tenderly humorous, where he mentions that, just as the Englishman Astolfo had done before her, she honestly believed that it was her own strength and skill which made all antagonists go down before the enchanted golden lance of Argalia. Spenser's Britomartis (and Britomartis is perhaps the character in the *Faerie Queene* who comes nearest to being alive) is but a pale wavering reflection of her; and if Ruggiero has a trace of the weakness and indecision of Scott's heroes, Bradamante leaves all Scott's heroines out of sight.

There is another point worth mentioning, for it is one that may easily escape notice. Bradamante is, like Homer's Nausicaa, the one sister in a family of five brothers. But this is not all: she is the twin-sister of the light-hearted scapegrace Ricciardetto. It gives one a new insight into Ariosto's art, a new respect for the way in which he thought out and vitalized his characters, to study his treatment of the two pairs of twins in the *Orlando*, Bradamante and Ricciardetto, and Ruggiero and Marfisa; to notice how the elements of character are parted between them, their fundamental kinship working out in sharp contrasts, and one in each pair being as it were the complement to the other; most markedly, of course, in Marfisa's fierce virginity and Ruggiero's amorousness, and in Ricciardetto's light-mindedness and Bradamante's depth and passion and constancy.

In the sixteen years' revision of the *Orlando* one may trace increasing human interest, increasing depth and seriousness, the greatness of his art expanding, as it were, before the artist. But one result was to add several thousand lines to a poem which was already enormously long. Inexhaustible fluency, though personal to Ariosto, is characteristic of all the work, in art or letters, of the later Renaissance. Already, two centuries before, Dante had noted, in his *De Vulgari Eloquentia*, the *Ferrarensium vel Regianorum garrulitas*; and both in Boiardo (his estate of Scandiano is near Reggio) and in Ariosto it reaches its climax. The unfinished *Orlando Innamorato* breaks off at between 35,000 and 36,000 lines; what it would have extended to had it ever been completed, Heaven only knows. The revised and enlarged *Orlando Furioso* has close on 40,000. Our own Spenser, half a century later, when the glow of the Renaissance had already faded, "flatly professed"—so Gabriel Harvey wrote to him in 1580—that he meant to emulate, and hoped to overgo Ariosto; and if he had ever finished his gigantic scheme, the *Faerie Queene* would have run to something between 60,000 and 70,000 lines. Such was the excess of magnificence to which the sixteenth century aspired, its insatiable craving to outdo all past human achievement. *La poésie*, in Michelet's striking words, *s'en va cherchant aux terres lointaines. Que cherche-t-elle? L'infini.* Against this splendid extravagance, this excessive liberation of thought and life, this boundlessness of intellectual and artistic ambition, the reaction came. That vaporized sphere rapidly chilled and contracted; the counter-Renaissance reverted towards sobriety and clarity, precision and succinctness. It is an index of the process that the *Gerusalemme Liberata* extends to little over 15,000 lines, and the *Paradise Lost* to between 10,000 and 11,000 only. There was clear gain to set against the loss of the magnificent Renaissance ideal. But loss it was. "It seems to be a law," writes a fine critic, "that the highest works of art can only be achieved when the forces which produced them are already doomed and in the act of disappearance. Those who would contemplate the genius of the Renaissance, consummated and conscious of its aim, upon the very verge of transmutation and eventual ruin, must turn to the *Orlando Furioso*."

If space allowed, it would be pleasant to say something here of Ariosto's style, and of particular beauties in his poetry. He gathered up into himself all the great tradition of his predecessors. It has been long remarked that the first and last lines of the *Orlando* are suggested by, indeed, closely and consciously modelled on, lines in the *Divina Commedia*; and in many other passages he borrows largely from Dante and Petrarch as well as from the romance poets. His general vocabulary, the management and rhythm of his stanza, he took over complete from Boiardo. But he infuses into them a new suppleness and splendour, a higher technical skill, a more melodious movement. His ornate similes, his landscapes (like the lovely description of Alcina's island, vi, 20–22), his vivid single touches of which scores might be cited, are all incomparable. And not less masterly are his swift and subtle strokes of psychology. But this is a field that I can only mention and commend to study.

Nor can I enter on the interesting ground of the English translations of the *Orlando*, with the light they throw on the history both of Italian studies and of poetic appreciation in this country, over a space of two centuries and a half. The earliest, Harrington's (1591), was, according to the tradition, a task commanded by Queen Elizabeth; and bears all the marks of an exercise, undertaken with inadequate scholarship and small poetical gift. It is slovenly, often grossly unfaithful, and (in the severe, but just, censure of Rose) always omits what is best worth preserving. Yet it secured, with all its faults, a wide and long-continued popularity, and was not replaced during the seventeenth century. The next version by Croker (1755), revised and annotated by Huggins, and published with a dedication to George II in 1757, had from the first no vitality, and little influence. The popularization of Ariosto in English was effected a generation later by Hoole. His translation (1783) passed through nearly twenty editions. One of the most curious criticisms to which it gave occasion may be quoted here. In John Wesley's *Journal*, under the date 19th February, 1784, we read:

On Saturday, having a leisure hour, I made an end of that strange book, *Orlando Furioso*. Ariosto had doubtless an uncommon genius, and subsequent poets have been greatly indebted to him; yet it is hard to say which was most out of his senses, the hero or the poet. He has not the least regard even to probability, his marvellous transcends all conception. Astolpho's shield and horn and voyage to the moon, the lance that unhorses every one, the all-penetrating sword, and I know not how many impenetrable helmets and coats of mail, leaves transformed into ships, and into leaves again, stones turned into horses and again into stones, are such monstrous fictions as never appeared in the world before, and one would hope never will again. O who that is not himself out of his senses can compare Ariosto with Tasso!

Considering that Hoole, though a competent versifier, was not a poet; that the heroic couplet which he employed is ill calculated to carry Ariosto's undulating movement; and that the translator now and then quite misunderstands his Italian, the immense popularity of Hoole's version is remarkable testimony of the appeal of Ariosto to the romantic temperament of the period. It was during the next half-century that Italian poetry was most widely read, and influenced taste most, in this country. That period culminated during the Regency; soon after, it was swept away by the flood of the new romanticism.

Rose's translation marks the apex of the curve and its rapid fall. The eight volumes of which it consists were successively published, one a year, between 1823 and 1831. It is graceful and scholarly, and far excels its predecessors; but it came just too late for the market. Mr. John Murray has kindly looked into the old accounts of his firm and tells me that the final adjustment showed a considerable loss on the whole work. A reprint in two volumes was brought out in 1858 in Bohn's Illustrated Library, and is, I believe, still purchasable. No one else, so far as is known to me, has since endeavoured to produce a fresh rendering. Probably no one ever will; which is neither surprising nor regrettable. We need no translations while we have, ready to our hands, the incomparable original.

THE PILGRIM'S PROGRESS

*[A Lecture at the Royal Institution of Great Britain,
14 March, 1924]*

THE book about which I am going to speak is one of the
great English classics. If, as I think is the case, it is less
largely read now than it once was, this is a temporary obscura-
tion, in which, from time to time, all classics share. Fashion,
in the art of letters as in all arts, is capricious, but there may
be traced in it, if we extend our survey widely, a certain
periodic movement. The masterpieces appeal to fresh generations in different ways and aspects, and in virtue of different
qualities. Some of their qualities are temporary and accidental,
for all classics, even the greatest, were produced at a particular
time and place, in a particular environment. "Kingdoms fall
and climates change and races die," and not only so, but
language alters. I use the term language in its widest sense,
as meaning any medium, of words or forms or colours or
sounds, in which the thought and emotion and aspiration of
man can express themselves, become articulate, and leave
permanent record. The language of men in this wide sense
alters, and the historical sense has to be invoked to translate
its import into some fresh code of symbols which has displaced
those earlier in use. I shall have something to say on this
later in relation to *The Pilgrim's Progress*. But the effort
required to bring the mind and imagination and language of
the seventeenth century into touch with our own is not great,
and in this case, at least, will be amply repaid.

I have used the word "classic." That is the highest claim
that can be made for any work of art. Its meaning is fairly
obvious, but should anyone be disposed to press for some
closer definition I would say, without going into technicalities,
but only giving a working criterion, that any product of
literature or art is a classic, whatever be its date or place of
origin, to which we find ourselves continually returning, and

144

which we continually find on returning to it even greater than we had realized.

This claim in the case of *The Pilgrim's Progress* hardly needs vindication. It is now nearly a century since it was formally made by Macaulay in his well-known Essay. That essay did not, of course, create the fame of the work, any more than Addison's papers in the *Spectator* created the fame of the *Paradise Lost*; what it did was to register that fame as an accepted thing; in Macaulay's own words, "to pay homage to the genius of a great man." But it was only more recently that either the artistic quality of *The Pilgrim's Progress* or its importance in the history of English literature was adequately appreciated. Three names in this process of increasing appreciation must specially be mentioned. Froude, in his monograph on Bunyan in the "English Men of Letters" series, published in 1880, may be said to have handled the matter for the first time with fully intelligent sympathy. The late Mr. Hale White (better known under the name of Mark Rutherford) did so again five-and-twenty years later with an even finer touch, and with that lucidity of which he was an unequalled master. And more important for the present purpose than either of these is the introduction written, for an edition of *The Pilgrim's Progress* published in 1898, by Sir Charles Firth, Regius Professor of Modern History at Oxford, the foremost authority upon England of the seventeenth century, and an accomplished man of letters. It would be an impertinence to praise his introductory essay, whether for the width and depth of its knowledge, for the completeness of its appreciation, or for its literary skill. It is my easier and pleasanter task to follow in his footprints when I invite you to renew your acquaintance, if it needs renewal, with this unique product of the English genius.

The Pilgrim's Progress—I speak now of the first part, to which the name properly applies—was begun by Bunyan in the winter of 1675–6 while he was in prison for a few months in the county gaol at Bedford, after Charles II had been obliged by parliamentary pressure to revoke his Declaration of Indulgence, and the persecution of Nonconformists had been reinstated. This, not the town gaol in the gatehouse on the

L

bridge over the Ouse, was the "den" in which Bunyan laid him
down to sleep, and as he slept dreamed a dream. He resumed
and finished his work after his release, some time in the spring
or early summer of 1676. The break occurs about three-
quarters of the way through the story, and is marked by the
author with his curious accuracy by the interjected sentence,
"So I awoke from my dream, and slept, and dreamed again."
It was published early in 1678 at the price of eighteen-pence.
Its success was immediate and complete. A second edition
followed almost at once, and new editions thereafter were
called for every year.

During that short imprisonment Bunyan had found out by
accident his real genius. It is true that he had developed one
side of it ten years earlier when he wrote *Grace Abounding*, the
greatest of all spiritual autobiographies. But that is a thing
by itself. It does, no doubt, suggest, and to some degree anticipate, the narrative and dramatic qualities which are so consummate in *The Pilgrim's Progress*, but its scope was strictly
limited and its modulations were confined to one key. It
would not, by itself, place Bunyan among the masters of literature. *The Pilgrim's Progress* unsealed new springs not only for
the author, but for the world.

It was in its inception a by-product. Bunyan himself, in
the versified preface or apology which he prefixes to it, has
told the story of its origin and growth with perfect candour
and vivid clearness. One cannot begin to quote from that
without the temptation to go on, but you will remember
how he begins:

> When at the first I took my pen in hand
> Thus for to write, I did not understand
> That I at all should make a little book
> In such a mode; nay, I had undertook
> To make another; which when almost done,
> Before I was aware, I this begun.
>
> .   .   .   .   .
>
> Neither did I but vacant seasons spend
> In this my scribble; nor did I intend
> But to divert myself in doing this
> From worser thoughts which make me do amiss.

Thus I set pen to paper with delight,
And quickly had my thoughts in black and white;
For, having now my method by the end,
Still as I pulled, it came; and so I penned
It down; until it came at last to be,
For length and breadth, the bigness which you see.

"Faster than springtime showers" came thought on thought, image on image, incident on incident, and one may well believe that in putting them down on paper he, like Shakespeare, hardly blotted a line. He dropped his pen when he did, partly because the book had already grown to a size beyond all his expectation, partly however—and this is a more important point—from the artist's instinct which developed in him from the moment when he first allowed it exercise. The pressure of matter behind his pen was as strong as ever, but he knew where to stop. Nor, indeed, had he realized the importance of his new achievement, or shaken himself quite free from the feeling urged on him frequently enough by some of his brothers in religion, that creative romance was a thing which it was unbecoming or even dangerous for a Christian to handle:

Some said, It might do good, others said, No.

But he had taken a decisive step at a single stroke. He had not only produced a masterpiece, but had created the English novel. He had no suspicion, as Macaulay observes, that he was doing the one; still less was it possible to have the faintest idea that he was doing the other. If he was at all conscious that he had become—the words are Macaulay's again—"the most popular religious writer in the English language," it was the religious side of his work to which he attached all the importance. He would have been perplexed and probably pained if he could have been told that after two hundred and fifty years his theology would be regarded as obsolete, that the truths upon which he anchored himself would be either disbelieved or translated into new terms wholly beyond his comprehension. It would have been little comfort to him if he had been told that he would be looked back to

and looked up to as an initiator, or almost as the creator, of
the form of literary art which has bulked more largely, and
exercised more influence, over life than any other. Yet he was
so open-minded that one might be doing him an injustice by
this suggestion. In good sense, tolerance, charity, he was in
advance of his time. He shared the national hatred and fear
of Popery, but his only other religious antipathy is, oddly,
for the Quakers. His Puritanism was intense. There is for
him no neutral ground between truth and falsehood, between
right and wrong. The way is, like the way in *The Pilgrim's
Progress*, inflexibly straight; a single step off it is dangerous,
a divergence from it is fatal. But his large humanity
was even more remarkable, and it kept expanding as his life
advanced.

Modern readers, at all events, approach *The Pilgrim's Progress*,
as it were, from the other end; not so much for edification,
for the sake of the religious and ethical doctrine set forth in it,
as for its narrative and dramatic excellence, its unsurpassed
power of characterization, its humour, its mastery of terse
and lucid English. Only when we get behind these qualities
we can still realize—and if it costs us an effort to-day so much
the better—that his "message"—that is to say, those truths or
realities which are behind his picture of life, and give it
consistence—is fundamental. They remain truths, however
differently we express and envisage them now. The ethical
and spiritual import of *The Pilgrim's Progress* is more fundamentally valid than that of the *Paradise Lost*, and the kingdom
of the classics is so large that there is room in it for two works
so completely different in kind and yet that suggest a strange
affinity. They represent between them the national character
and the spiritual belief of a great age.

The English novel was, of course, no sudden growth due
to any single inventor. Tentative approaches to it had been
made a century earlier by Greene and Lodge and Nash, but
these had at the time come to little or nothing. The inchoate
novel was swallowed up by the predominance of the drama,
and during the period which followed literature went astray
in the wilderness of those enormous heroic or sentimental
romances, the fashion for which did not collapse under its

own insufferable weight until nearly the end of the seventeenth century.

The Pilgrim's Progress is generally called an allegory. That is a word used by Bunyan himself: "I fell suddenly into an allegory." But, on the title-page, the description of the book given is, "The Pilgrim's Progress from this world to that which is to come, delivered under the similitude of a dream." It is in effect, like all works of art, a dream in the deeper sense of the word. Allegories, if they are nothing more than allegory, are always tedious. For proof of this we need not go beyond Bunyan's own *Holy War*, written four years later. In the *Faerie Queene* the allegory is only in the way. Allegorization was an obsession of the medieval mind; the age of its universal and disastrous popularity was already over, and in *The Pilgrim's Progress* it has become merely one form or medium of art, a particular framework which serves to give shape and definition, to give structural quality to material which it would otherwise be difficult to set out. It is the absence of this structural quality which prevents *The Life and Death of Mr. Badman*, Bunyan's next work after *The Pilgrim's Progress*, which is in effect a realistic novel, from being a work of art in the highest sense. In *The Pilgrim's Progress* the allegorical quality does not fetter him, it rather gives him wings. The words he uses himself in speaking of it are many and various: metaphor, parable, figure, shadow, similitude, fable, romance. "I make bold to talk thus metaphorically, for the ripening of the wits of young readers," he says in Part II. But he keeps falling back on the word dream as what comes nearest to the truth. He begins by saying, "As I slept I dreamed a dream," and ends with the words, "So I awoke, and behold, it was a dream."

All art is in a sense allegorical, because it is not a record but an interpretation of facts. This applies to fiction just as much as to anything else. Forty years later Defoe incorporated in *Robinson Crusoe* an allegory of his own life and his spiritual experience. We should hardly know this unless he had told us so, but the fact is just one reason for its singular and arresting charm. With both Bunyan and Defoe, the point is that they projected their own life—and that is as much as to say the life of mankind, for life is one thing—into a book, and so the book is alive.

There is a prevalent idea that, for a hundred years or more, *The Pilgrim's Progress* was a book only read by the vulgar. This is so exaggerated as to be in effect untrue. From the first it was eagerly read and enjoyed by all ranks and classes, not in England only, for it was very soon translated into French and Dutch, as it has since been into nearly all the languages of Europe. In the verses prefixed to the second part Bunyan, who always told the exact truth, says as much as this:

> My Pilgrim's Book has travelled sea and land,
> Yet could I never come to understand
> That it was slighted, or turned out of door,
> By any kingdom, were they rich or poor.

And later he adds quaintly:

> Brave gallants do my Pilgrim hug and love;
> Young ladies, and young gentlewomen too,
> Do no small kindness to my Pilgrim shew.

It was in the small but well-selected library in Lady Wishfort's dressing-closet in 1700, and Lady Wishfort was in the first flight of fashion.

The only exception taken to it, in fact, was by the ultra-religious. "Romance they count it," Bunyan says, the only place I think where he uses the word romance, and he devotes himself at some length to arguing against this criticism. Depreciation of the book as vulgar did exist, no doubt, during the period of strong classicist reaction known as the Augustan Age; though even then, if disparaged in a paper which has been wrongly attributed to Addison, it received praise from Swift which is the higher because it is put in studiously quiet words. But, after that, disparagement is confined to the few people who would now be called "highbrows," thin pedants like Mrs. Montague. Johnson's appreciation is a typical no less than a splendid tribute. It is, he says, "of great merit both for invention, imagination, and the conduct of the story, and it has had the best evidence of its merit, the general and continued approbation of mankind." And he said of it even

more strikingly that it was one of the only three books ever
written that are wished longer by their readers. The idea that
it was either long or largely disparaged is mainly due, I think,
to misapprehension of Cowper's well-known couplet, the
date of which is 1784—more than ten years after Johnson's
eulogium:

> I name thee not, lest so despised a name
> Should move a sneer at thy deserved fame.

In this couplet both the existence of its fame and the actual
merit on which its fame was based are expressly stated. What
Cowper hints at is, that the name Bunyan was a little ludicrous,
like other words which it is difficult to hitch into poetry.
There are other instances of this: Sprat, one of the most eminent
men of his time both in letters and science, or Flatman,
Dryden's contemporary, whose unlucky name has in fact
done much to obscure the real excellence of his poetry. Yet
it is curious that the plebeian name of Bunyan is Anglo-
Norman. The Buingnons or Boynuns who held it were a
family of standing in Bedfordshire as early as the thirteenth
century.

Macaulay's essay was written just at the full tide of the
Evangelical movement, when *The Pilgrim's Progress* was exalted
by that school, and was correspondingly depreciated by their
opponents, as a manual of theology. It is, in fact, just about
this time that the most hostile criticism comes. Dunlop a
few years earlier, in his *History of Fiction*, had called it coarse
and inelegant, and another critic, a little later, mean and weari-
some. The immediate occasion of Macaulay's essay was a
sumptuously printed edition of *The Pilgrim's Progress* with a
Life by Southey prefixed to it, the appearance of which (though
Southey was himself a High Churchman of the old school)
was in fact an Evangelical manifesto. It was part of the boom
in revived Puritanism just then at its height. But Puritanism
is deeply rooted in the national character in one form or
another. We may be sure that it will reappear; the eternal
antithesis between Puritanism and Art will be raised once
more, and will again, as it does in Bunyan's work, arrive at
some synthesis. For Bunyan's glory is that he was at one and

the same time a Puritan of burning conviction and an artist
of irrepressible genius, and that in him the two elements
for once coalesced. The tendency of the fiction of our own
day is, in its pursuit of impressions, to lose touch with reality.
It does not penetrate below the surface, and, having no roots,
has no permanence. It is an impression of impressions, which
fades away and is forgotten. We do not find ourselves returning to it, and if we do return to it, there is even less in it than
we thought.

To enlarge on the qualities of *The Pilgrim's Progress* as a work
of art would be delightful but endless. I will just single out a
few points.

The first thing perhaps to notice is the author's certainty
of touch, the completeness with which he has his mechanism
in hand. The really accomplished artist may be known by
the way in which he begins. The first half-dozen lines of
The Pilgrim's Progress give an example of a perfect beginning:

As I walk'd through the wilderness of this world, I lighted on
a certain place, where was a Den; and I laid me down in that place
to sleep: and as I slept I dreamed a Dream. I dreamed, and behold
I saw a man clothed with Rags, standing in a certain place, with
his face from his own House, a Book in his hand, and a great burden
upon his back.

In these few words, as in a few strokes by some master of
etching, the atmosphere is made, the movement is launched,
the effect is got for the whole narrative. But even more
remarkable is the skill with which he brings it to an end:

Now I saw in my Dream, that these two men went in at the
Gate; and lo, as they entered they were transfigured, and they
had Raiment put on that shone like Gold. There was also that
met them with Harps and Crowns, and gave them to them; . . .
Then I heard in my Dream that all the bells in the City rang for
joy.

This by itself would be a fine conclusion, and perhaps almost
anyone else, even were he possessed of narrative instinct and
dramatic power of a high degree, would have stopped here.
But Bunyan with a more subtle and accomplished art goes on:

Now just as the Gates were opened to let in the men, I looked in after them; and behold, the City shone like the Sun, the Streets also were paved with Gold, and in them walked many men, with Crowns on their heads, Palms in their hands, and golden Harps to sing praises withal. There were also of them that had wings, and they answered one another without intermission, saying, Holy, Holy, Holy, is the Lord. And after that, they shut up the Gates: which when I had seen, I wished myself among them.

Notice the beautiful cadence of these last words. They give the quiet ending which was insisted upon by Greek art, and which is so conspicuous in Milton at the close both of the *Paradise Lost* and of the *Samson.*

But even this is not all, for to Bunyan art is not everything, art indeed is nothing. He is an artist only because he cannot help being one. He has had throughout the sense of his message resting on him heavily, and the sort of happy ending which would suit comedy or romance will not satisfy him here. And so by instinctive force of genius he triumphantly transgresses all rules, and knits up his work, before letting it go, with the most tremendous passage in the whole book.

For other failures or backslidings Bunyan has some touch of sympathetic pity, or at the worst, a certain passionless contempt: for Pliable at the Slough of Despond, for Simple, Sloth, and Presumption laid by the heels asleep at the foot of the Hill Difficulty, for Formalist and Hypocrisy who were born in the land of Vainglory and were going for praise to Mount Sion, even for the irrepressible Talkative and the ingenious By-ends. To Ignorance alone he is merciless:

Now while I was gazing upon all these things, I turned my head to look back, and saw Ignorance come up to the river side; but he soon got over, and that without half that difficulty which the other two men met with. For it happened that there was then in that place one Vain-hope, a ferryman, that with his boat helped him over; so he, as the other I saw, did ascend the hill to come up to the gate, only he came alone; neither did any man meet him with the least encouragement. When he was come up to the gate, he looked up to the writing that was above; and then began to knock, supposing that entrance should have been quickly administered to him. But he was asked by the men that looked over the top of the gate, Whence came you? and what would you have? He answered, I have eat and drank in the presence of the King, and he has taught in our streets. Then they asked him for his certificate, that they might go in and show it to the King. So he fumbled in his bosom for one, and found none. Then said they, Have you none? But the man answered never a word. So they told the King; but he would not come down to see him, but commanded the two Shining Ones that conducted Christian and Hopeful to the City, to go out and take Ignorance and bind him hand and foot, and have him away. Then they took him up and carried him through the air to the door that I saw in the side of the hill, and put him in there. Then I saw that there was a way to hell even from the gates of heaven, as well as from the City of Destruction.

Alike for substance and for style this cannot be surpassed in his, or indeed in any, writing. Then, the instinct of the artist again rising in him, he adds the dying fall of one more brief sentence :

So I awoke, and behold, it was a dream.

The next thing on which stress may be laid is his extra-ordinary power of characterization. This applies not only to the main figures, but to all those incidentally introduced. Each one of them has only to be mentioned in order to become fully alive. Mrs. By-ends, for instance, though she does not appear in person, we know as well as if we had been familiar with her all our lives from her husband's incidental words, "My Wife is a very vertuous Woman, the Daughter of a vertuous Woman. She came of a very Honourable Family, and is arrived at such a pitch of Breeding, that she knows how to carry it to all, even to Prince and Peasant." In the most celebrated instance, perhaps, (it is in the second part), the personality is given complete in seven words, "A young Woman her name was Dull." "Of this young woman," Mr. Hale White says, "it is much to be regretted that Bunyan did not give us a further account." I do not think so. The account is entire and perfect as it stands, in its significant vacuity. It requires no addition, and no comment, except to note, for it is worth noticing, that the seven words form only a single phrase. Most modern editions have done their best to spoil it by inserting a comma after the words "young Woman."

This power is equally conspicuous in the relation of incidents and even in the description of scenes and landscapes. In the fewest words he makes us see things happen just as they did, and gives us their setting with a clearness which stamps them on the mind once for all. The way to the Celestial City can be followed from one end to the other with the precision of a map. The vignettes of the sights shown in the House of the Interpreter are all perfect in their clearness as well as large in the variation of their range. They include household pictures like those of the dusty parlour, the two children on their chairs in the little room, the fire against the wall; and along-side of these, romantic or tragic pieces such as the Achievement of the Palace and the Man in the Iron Cage. But all alike get their effect in the fewest possible touches, and all alike once read are unforgettable. This is·in sharp contrast to the usual method of allegory, which is conventional and not precise.

His sensitiveness to nature is like Wordsworth's. Christiana hears "in a grove a little way off, on the right hand, a most curious melodious note." "They are our country birds," is the comment: "they sing these notes at the spring, when the flowers appear and the sun shines warm, and then you may hear them all day long. They make the woods and groves, and solitary places, places desirous to be in.".

Bunyan's power as a landscapist has hardly been recognized enough. He might be called one of the originators of the English School. Take one instance out of a hundred, the view from the House Beautiful:

When the morning was up, they had him to the top of the house, and bid him look south, so he did; and behold at a great distance he saw a most pleasant mountainous country beautified with woods, vineyards, fruits of all sorts, flowers also, with springs and fountains, very delectable to behold.

It is interesting to compare this with the landscape work of another great English writer, who was as serious-minded as he

was romantic, William Morris. This is the landscape seen by
Michael in *The Man Born to be King*:

> Long time he rode, till suddenly
> When now the sun was broad and high,
> From out a hollow where the yew
> Still guarded patches of the dew,
> He found at last that he had won
> That highland's top, and gazed upon
> A valley that beneath the haze
> Of that most fair of autumn days
> Showed glorious, fair with golden sheaves,
> Rich with the darkened autumn leaves,
> Gay with the water-meadows green,
> The bright blue streams that lay between,
> The miles of beauty stretched away
> From that bleak hill-side bare and grey,
> Till white cliffs over slopes of vine
> Drew 'gainst the sky a broken line.

In a way no two methods could be more unlike, but
the point is to notice how the one with its exquisite minute
detail does not lose breadth of effect, and how the other
in its few large swift touches gets an effect almost equally
vivid. I do not mean to suggest that the two methods
should be set against one another or put into competition:
for there are many kinds of perfection; but these are two
kinds.

Then, again, what is very remarkable in *The Pilgrim's
Progress* is the author's conspicuous fairness, the largeness of his
dramatic sympathy. His religious belief is, of course, inflexible;
it admits no doubt and no compromise, but he thoroughly
understands, he even, we might say, humanly sympathizes
with, the irreligious point of view, and in particular he sees
the humorous side both of his hero—if Christian may be
called the hero of the work—and of life itself, however grave
and even awful a thing life is. It is this sense of humour which
makes Christian a thoroughly living character. Look at the
conversation between him and Evangelist when he has got
into such trouble by taking the advice of Mr. Worldly
Wiseman:

Then said Evangelist, Art not thou the man that I found crying without the walls of the City of Destruction?

Yes, dear Sir, I am the man.

Did not I direct thee the way to the little Wicket Gate?

Yes, dear Sir, said Christian.

How is it then that thou art now out of the way?

I met with a gentleman as soon as I had got over the Slough of Despond, who persuaded me that I might, in the village before me, find a man that could take off my burden.

What was he?

He looked like a gentleman.

What said that gentleman to you?

Why, he asked me whither I was going, and I told him.

When the Shining One has disentangled Christian and Hopeful from the net "he asked moreover, if the Shepherds did not bid them beware of the Flatterer? They answered, Yes: but we did not imagine, said they, that this fine-spoken man had been he."

Or again, after the sights had been shown to him in the Interpreter's House, we come to an inimitable touch, when Christian begins to feel what is known to all of us as the museum headache, and timidly suggests, "Sir, is it not time for me to go on my way now?" Even in the colloquy between Christian and Apollyon there is a dash of mingled candour and humour, for Bunyan is determined to treat even the devil fairly. When reproached by Apollyon with quitting his service, Christian's answer does not take any spiritually high ground; it is apologetic rather than defiant. "Your service," he says, "was hard, and your wages such as a man could not live on, therefore I did as other considerate persons do, look out if perhaps I might mend myself." Or when he has asked Faithful to tell the whole story of his experiences, notice the way that he keeps interrupting with some experiences of his own, so that Faithful has to protest feebly, "But, dear brother, hear me out."

In the discussion between Faithful and Talkative, Talkative's manners are much the better of the two, and his complaint that Faithful "lies at the catch" and that "this is not for edification" is perfectly true. And not only in *The Pilgrim's*

Progress, but in all Bunyan's later work, there is this wonderful fairness, this appreciation of what may be said on the other side, and this frank recognition of the difficulties, and even, as it may seem, the impossibilities connected with orthodox belief and with Christian practice. As good an instance of this as any occurs towards the end of that very noble discourse, *The Heavenly Footman*. Bunyan has had occasion to mention Lot's wife, and his comment is this: "His wife looked behind her, and died immediately, but let what would become of her, Lot would not so much as look behind him to see her. I have sometimes wondered at Lot in this particular." Few preachers would be as frank as this.

Mr. By-ends, with whose wife we have already made acquaintance, is treated in almost a loving way. In some respects he is amazingly like Shakespeare's Falstaff; both have to be turned down in the end, but they have had a full run for their money. The adroitness and fertility with which Mr. By-ends meets the criticism made upon him are hardly less than Falstaff's own:

Is not your name Mr. By-ends of Fair-speech?
That is not my name; but indeed it is a nickname that is given me by some that cannot abide me, and I must be content to bear it as a reproach, as other good men have borne theirs before me.
But did you never give an occasion to men to call you by this name?
Never, never! The worst that ever I did to give them an occasion to give me this name was, that I had always the luck to jump in my judgment with the present way of the times, whatever it was, and my chance was to get thereby. But if things are thus cast upon me, let me count them a blessing; but let not the malicious load me therefore with reproach.

Shakespeare might have written that.

We can see the grave face with which Christiana pretends to taste the nauseous concoction made up by Mr. Skill (the doctor who evades a direct answer to the inquiry what he charges, only saying, "Nay, I hope I shall be reasonable"), when her boy has made himself ill with eating fruit from the garden of the man who keeps the barking dog; we can hear her voice as she says, "Oh Matthew, this potion is sweeter than honey." We can see the pert little toss of her head with which Mercy remarks, after Mr. Brisk has ceased calling, "I might a had husbands afore now, though I spake not of it to any; but they were such as did not like my conditions, though never did any of them find fault with my person."

And once more, though it is idle to multiply instances of what meets us at almost every other page of the work, there is a stroke of almost malicious humour in the middle of the long religious conversation between Christian and Hopeful on the Enchanted Ground. That was a region "whose air naturally tended to make one drowsy," and the drowsiness is creeping into the discussion. Bunyan perfectly realizes this. "I believe you have said the truth," Hopeful interjects, and we can feel him smothering a yawn as he says so; "are we now almost got past the Enchanted Ground?" "Why, are you weary of this discourse?" Christian a little testily asks. "No, verily," answers Hopeful meekly, "but that I would know where we are." "We have not now above two miles further to go thereon," Christian replies: "but let us return to our matter."

And there is another point also to be noticed, the sense of romance, and even of romantic beauty, which only appears in *The Pilgrim's Progress* shyly and fitfully, but very remarkably. The finest instance of the romantic thrill is the dream within the dream, which is the last incident in the pageants shown at the House of the Interpreter. For mingled splendour and terror it bears being set alongside of the *Ancient Mariner* or the *Belle Dame sans Merci*:

So he took Christian by the hand again, and led him into a chamber, where there was one a rising out of bed; and, as he put on his raiment, he shook and trembled. Then said Christian, Why doth this man thus tremble? The Interpreter then bid him tell to Christian the reason of his so doing. So he began, and said, This Night as I was in my sleep, I dreamed, and behold, the Heavens grew exceeding black; also it thundered and lightened in most fearful wise, that it put me into an agony. So I looked up in my dream, and saw the clouds rack at an unusual rate; upon which I heard a great sound of a trumpet and saw also a Man sit upon a cloud, attended with the thousands of heaven; they were all in flaming fire; also the heavens were on a burning flame. I heard then a voice saying, Arise ye dead, and come to judgment; and with that the rocks rent, the graves opened, and the dead that were therein came forth; some of them were exceeding glad, and looked upward; and some thought to hide themselves under the mountains. Then I saw the Man that sat upon the cloud open the book, and bid the world draw near. Yet there was, by reason of a fierce flame that issued out and came from before him, a convenient distance betwixt him and them, as betwixt the judge and the prisoners at the bar. I heard it also proclaimed to them that attended on the Man that sat on the cloud, Gather together the tares, the chaff, and stubble, and cast them into the burning lake; and with that, the bottomless pit opened, just whereabout I stood; out of the mouth of which there came in an abundant manner smoke and coals of fire, with hideous noises. It was also said to the same persons, Gather my wheat into the garner. And with that I saw many catched up and carried away into the clouds; but I was left behind. I also sought to hide myself, but I could not; for the Man that sat upon the cloud still kept his eye upon me; my sins also came into my mind, and my conscience did accuse me on every side. Upon this I awaked from my sleep.

The simpler sense of romantic beauty is found sometimes in scenes and episodes, but more frequently in a mere passing touch here and there, like that of the "grave and beautiful damsel" who comes out of the door of the House on the Hill, or that of "the meadow curiously beautified with lilies, and it was green all the year long."

"He was illiterate," Macaulay says of Bunyan, "but he spoke to illiterate men." This needs careful qualification. Illiterate in the sense of not being widely read he certainly was, but illiteracy in its more accurate sense does not depend so much on the quantity of a man's reading as on the quality of mind which he has brought to it. He knew his Bible thoroughly, and that is in itself a literary education. He had read quantities of the political or religious treatises which were produced in immense volume at that period. As regards works of pure literature, the books which we are certain that he knew may be counted on the fingers of one hand. We cannot go much beyond Foxe's *Martyrs*, Quarles' *Emblems*, and the *Seven Champions of Christendom*—if this last may be called literature. It is all but certain that he had never read, and probable that he had never heard of, the numerous books which have been suggested as origins or suggestions for *The Pilgrim's Progress*, from the fourteenth-century *Pilgrimage of the Soul* down to the *Faerie Queene*. No doubt with his quick intelligence and his great receptive power he must have picked a great many things up incidentally just as Shakespeare did, but his genius he had direct from nature, and it is this incalculable genius, not education, and not study of models, which made him a master of prose. That same genius did something even more wonderful: it let him recapture, alone in his age, and for once only, the authentic note of the great lyric period. The copy of verses in Part II beginning:

> Who would true valour see,
> Let him come hither,

if they came to us without any indication of their origin, would certainly be called Elizabethan; for their actual date they are unique. It is as though he had taken up the torch just where Nash, nearly a century before, had laid it down. They are in the rhythm, and no doubt were meant to be sung to the tune, of "Phyllida flouts me," that lovely air which was a "new tune" in 1612, which was sung by the milkmaid and her daughter on the riverside in Walton's *Compleat Angler*, (1653), and which throughout the century, as indeed since, had unbroken and immense popularity.

The exaggerated notions about Bunyan's illiteracy are like the exaggerations about his belonging to the lowest class of the people. That was not the case. Whether as a boy he went to Bedford Grammar School, as Shakespeare to the Grammar School at Stratford, is uncertain. The status of the family was not much lower than that of Shakespeare's. His father was not a tinker in the modern sense of the word, but a brazier or whitesmith, quite a reputable occupation. The whole thing rests on a misconception of some expressions of his own which are of elaborate, even ostentatious, humility: "I never went to school to Aristotle or Plato, but was brought up at my father's house in a very mean condition," and elsewhere, "My father's house being of that rank that is

M

meanest and most despised of all the families of the land."
The accent is precisely like that of Gideon in the Book of
Judges: "Behold, my family is poor in Manasseh, and I am the
least in my father's house." That humility is a sort of inverted
pride. It was in both cases an assertion of spiritual dignity
independent of rank or wealth.

The other two books which, according to Johnson, were
the only ones which their readers wished longer are *Robinson
Crusoe* and *Don Quixote*, and this triad have resemblances to
one another which are very remarkable. All three were written
in mature or even advanced age. Bunyan was fifty, Defoe
fifty-eight, Cervantes fifty-seven at the time when they produced their masterpieces. It is a curious coincidence that this
holds good likewise for Bunyan's greatest contemporaries.
Dryden, had he died at fifty, would only be known as a
minor poet; and Milton, had he died at fifty-five, would
indeed hold a very distinguished place in English letters, but
as a lyrical poet whose great poetical gift had dried up early.
All three were subsequently followed up by their authors with
a second part or continuation. In the case of *Robinson Crusoe*
the second part followed almost immediately, but there was
an interval of six years in the case of *The Pilgrim's Progress*,
and of ten years in the case of *Don Quixote*. All three stand
quite alone among the voluminous and multiform products
of their authors; so much so, that when the author's name is
mentioned, it is the single book that is instinctively thought
of. All three have had circulation and fame, not only in their
native country but throughout the world; and all three owe
little to any predecessor (except in so far as Defoe has to be
regarded as carrying on the tradition of Bunyan), while they
have been a source of inspiration to whole schools of subsequent
writers.

The parallel between Cervantes and Bunyan in particular
is very striking. It is not only in their mixture of satire with
high idealism. It is not only in their humane and splendid
wisdom—for of *The Pilgrim's Progress* also might be said what
the late Sir Walter Raleigh finely says of *Don Quixote*, "It is a
mine, deep below deep." It is so close as to suggest the notion
that Bunyan may have read *Don Quixote* in Shelton's transla-

tion. This is within the limits of possibility, but is very unlikely.

Continuations are notoriously dangerous, but these two are exceptions. In both there is a curious feature of which there is hardly a third example, that the first part is treated in the continuation as a known work, familiar not only to the readers of the second part, but to the characters in it. This device, and the intricate humour with which it is treated, have always been noted in *Don Quixote* as marks of the unique genius of Cervantes, but they are equally conspicuous here. "There are but few houses," says Mr. Sagacity, "that have heard of him and his doings, but have sought after and got the records of his pilgrimage." On the Delectable Mountains the shepherds tell Christiana and her companions of the man whom they see tumbling the hills about, "That man was the son of one Great-grace, of whom you read in the first part of the record of the Pilgrim's Progress. Then said Mr. Great-heart, I know him."

Later on, one Mr. Tell-true is reported as having told Mr. Valiant-for-truth how Christian had killed a serpent that did come out to resist him in his journey. That serpent, in fact, we only hear of now for the first time: it is not mentioned in the first part. Valiant-for-truth then goes on to give a summary sketch of the main incidents of Part I, as they had been told to him by his father and mother. It includes the surprising information that, according to some authorities, Christian "after all his adventures was certainly drowned in the Black River and never went foot further, however it was smothered up."

The immediate occasion for a second part was in both cases the flood of imitations and spurious continuations of the first part which its popularity had let loose. It is only in the second part of *Don Quixote* that the powers of Cervantes are fully manifested. This is not so with *The Pilgrim's Progress*. The second part is at a lower temperature than the first. It has not the same tension, it has not the same elevation, it has not the same dramatic unity. But it marks a further step of great importance in the development of prose fiction. There is much freer handling. There is greater variety and multiplicity

of incident. It takes in a larger field of human nature. Not
only are there many more characters but they are of much
more varied kinds. Indeed, this second part might almost be
called the first example in England of the picaresque novel on
a large canvas. In it Bunyan even seems now and then to
forget his moral purpose, throwing allegory for the moment
completely overboard and abandoning himself to the delight
of realistic portraiture and of romantic incident or sentiment.
Its movement from first to last is very leisurely, in strong
contrast to the swiftness of the first part. There are many
digressions, which are only kept from spreading quite beyond
bounds by what may be called the geographical framework,
the map of the route and its stages, taken over from Part I.
But even there the secularization or humanization of the whole
outlook on life was beginning occasionally to break in. Some
scandal was caused among purists by phrases and passages in
both parts where Bunyan wrote more like a man of the world
than like a Nonconformist minister. The sentence in which he
mentions that the lock of the gate of Doubting Castle "went
damnable hard" was actually altered by scrupulous editors. A
like exception was taken to the passage where Great-heart
applauds Mr. Honest as "a cock of the right kind." Cock-
fighting was one of the pastimes to which Bunyan, in his
autobiography, deplores that his own youth had been addicted.
But evidently his taste for it had not wholly disappeared.

But in Part II we feel the breath of the open air throughout.
Never, except in the noble conclusion (to which I shall return),
is the tension acute. The road, like the story, unrolls itself in
a leisurely fashion. It is pleasantly diversified by adventures
with giants, by prolonged visits at the houses of friends, by
frequent junketings, and by little episodes of no particular
relevance, except that they make the story more interesting
and more of a picture of common daily life. We move gently
through a country "made green with the running of rivers,
and gracious with temperate air." We are never in any anxiety
about the travellers, for we have complete confidence in Mr.
Great-heart, who is indeed no other than Bunyan himself;
and he makes fun of them upon occasion inimitably.
Christiana's loss of her pocket-flask at the arbour on the Hill

Difficulty is almost like a deliberate burlesque of Christian's loss of his roll there, and his bitter remorse over it. The scene of Christian's fight with Apollyon has already become a tourist resort, with an inscription carved on a monument at the roadside giving an account of the battle, and with stains of Christian's blood, like those of Rizzio's on the floor of Holyrood Palace, carefully preserved, while the comment of the guide is that Christian in that battle "showed himself as stout as Hercules himself." The Valley of the Shadow of Death has ceased to be awful and has become only disagreeable or frightening. Vanity Fair is quite a desirable place to live in. The townspeople have an esteem and respect for the Pilgrims; and the Pilgrims in their turn grew acquainted with many of the people of the town, and "did them what service they could." Instead of being put in the cage or killed they make up a party to kill a serpent "that came out of the woods and slew many of the people of that town and would also carry away their children." The whole company stay for more than a month at the house of Gaius, "who keeps an excellent table," which the Pilgrims thoroughly appreciate. And they stay apparently for several years at Mr. Manson's, where—note the delicacy of the distinction—there is "a very fair dining-room." Christiana tips the porter half a sovereign when she leaves the Palace Beautiful. Mercy sets her heart on the great looking-glass that hangs up in the dining-room at the House of the Shepherds. Christiana asks what ails her, for she does not look well, and when told, says at once that she will mention it to the shepherds. "Then, Mother," says Mercy, "if you please, ask the shepherds if they are willing to sell it." Of course she gets it, and of course she gets it for nothing. It is a good world that we are in, and a cheerful one. After Giant Despair has been killed ("he struggled hard," Bunyan tells us, "and had as many lives as a cat"), the Pilgrims are very jocund and merry.

Now Christiana, if need was, could play upon the viol, and her daughter Mercy upon the lute; so, since they were so merry disposed, she played them a lesson.

The lesson she played was very likely by Blow. Purcell's sonatas had been published the year before. But Bunyan may perhaps have been thinking back to his own youth and the music of Byrd or Lawes.

And Ready-to-Halt would dance. So he took Despondency's daughter Much-afraid by the hand, and to dancing they went in the road. True he could not dance without one crutch in his hand, but I promise you he footed it well; also the girl was to be commended, for she answered the music handsomely. As for Mr. Despondency, the music was not much to him; he was for feeding rather than dancing, for that he was almost starved. So Christiana gave him some of her bottle of spirits for present relief, and then prepared him something to eat; and in a little time the old gentleman came to himself and began to be finely revived.

It is a pretty picture of Puritan England; and perhaps not a misleading one.

Further on, the Enchanted Ground, only lightly sketched in in Part I as a "sleepy place," becomes here a romantic fairy-land, with secret arbours in tangled briar thickets, with a mist (like that round about Camelot in Tennyson) that settles down strangely and as strangely drifts away, and with a witch-woman in the heart of it, "by virtue of whose sorceries this ground is enchanted."

It is through this episode with its imaginative or romantic treatment that Bunyan leads up from the common daylight of the earlier scenes to his magnificent conclusion. Here we are in some Land East of the Sun, where there is no earthly night and day. The Shining Ones walk in it. The bells so ring, and trumpets continually sound so melodiously, that they could not sleep, and yet they received as much refreshing as if they had slept never so soundly. "Here also all the noise of them that walked the streets was, More Pilgrims are come to town." The words and their musical cadence are both almost an exact reproduction of the famous *Lenten is come with love to town*, the loveliest of English lyrics of the earlier fourteenth century. Children go into the King's garden to gather nosegays, and the post comes in daily from the Celestial City.

It is in this setting that Bunyan ends his work, with the dispersal of the company and the farewells of Christiana to all her companions. There is a wonderful touch here, the delicacy and beauty of which are seldom quite realized. One hardly likes to speak of it, so poignant is it in its reticence and depth of meaning, and yet it would be a pity to miss it. To the others Christiana has words of comfort or encouragement or exhortation, very practical and very beautiful; to one alone among them she says nothing. "But she gave Mr. Stand-fast a ring."

In his last words Bunyan makes a half promise to continue the story. He did not do so, and he was right. His work was rounded off and concluded. It was for other hands in later times to take up, and handle after their own fashion, the art which he had created. But he had unlocked the door. He had made the English novel, with its large, searching treatment of actual life, possible. He had given it method and aim, and a consciousness of both. The pilgrimage of life has received a thousand interpretations since; this one remains unique in truth and beauty.

The two parts of *The Pilgrim's Progress* might almost be called an English prose Iliad and Odyssey. To weigh one work of art against another is not a very profitable occupation. But by the common judgment of mankind, in both these cases the earlier work of the two is also the greater. It is more concentrated and more elevated; not perhaps more interesting, but more majestic and impressive. Bunyan, in fact, inserted a few additional episodes in the second edition of Part I. He did well to insert no more: but a considerable amount of the contents of Part II might be called spare material from Part I, which would have overloaded its structure. Or one might say without insisting on its accuracy, that Part I is an epic, Part II a romance. It is in virtue of its epic quality, its sustained nobility, that Part I takes its place in literature. To more modern taste, its theological discussions, like the battle-scenes in the Iliad, have seemed to bulk disproportionately, and to deal with matters that have lost their interest and their relevance to actual life. But, in both cases, to remove these would be fatal. The artist's control over them is secure; they belong to, they are inseparable from, they are alive in, a single organic structure. Nor, perhaps, are we so inclined now to slight or discard them as we should have been twenty or even ten years ago.

Bunyan was more than an artist; and *The Pilgrim's Progress* is more than a work of art. The "similitude of a dream" is also the clear vision of one who had probed life to its depths. It is the statement of and the appeal to truths which, under whatever form they may be expressed from one age to another, are unchangeable: that there is but one way; that the difference between right and wrong, between good and evil, is fundamental; that the laws of God are inflexible and inevitable; that ignorance, so far from being a venial error, still less a flaunted merit, is a vice and a sin, the root of all other sins and vices. Implicit on every page is the doctrine formally laid down a generation later by Bishop Butler: "Things are what they are, and their consequences will be what they will be; why then should we seek to be deceived?" That is a truth which, simple as it seems, has continually to be restated.

Bunyan held, as part of his deepest conviction, the doctrine of predestination. But the argument that predestination carries with it absence of human responsibility was to him not so much false as meaningless. Responsibility was an abstraction. It did not trouble him; it did not even interest him. Sin, and the consequences of sin, were facts. So, too, was the forgiveness of sin. But here we touch on deep matters; and in these, no less than as a work of art, *The Pilgrim's Progress* may be left to produce its own impression. "If a man was to come here as we do now, he might see that that would be delightful to him. Some have wished that the next way to their Father's House were here, that they might be troubled no more; but the way is the way, and there's an end."

HENRY BIRKHEAD AND THE FOUNDATION OF THE OXFORD CHAIR OF POETRY

[A Public Lecture delivered in the Examination Schools, Oxford, on 19 October, 1908]

TWO hundred years ago to-day, on Tuesday, the 19th of October, 1708, the first Professor of Poetry in the University of Oxford delivered his inaugural lecture. We are much overdone nowadays with commemorative celebrations in various multiples of centuries; but the occasion is fitting to say something, among ourselves here and not as part of any public ceremonial, about the founder of the Professorship and the circumstances in which it was founded. The name of Henry Birkhead is almost forgotten; nor, but for this foundation of his, would it have any particular claim on our regard or remembrance. But some duty of piety is owed, by the wholesome tradition of this University, to the memory of its founders and benefactors; and while there is little to say about Birkhead himself, he is, in a way, the type or average representative of his period; and his period is one of no little importance in the history of English poetry; for it was that of Milton.

In the first place, then, I propose to say what little there is to be said about the founder himself; next to give an account of the foundation of the Professorship of Poetry, and in connection with that to consider the circumstances in which it was founded as illustrating (which they do in a very interesting way) the attitude of the academic mind towards poetry at the end of the seventeenth century, and the point in its secular progress which poetry had then reached.

With regard to the life of Henry Birkhead I find little to add to the facts which have been collected by the industry and research of Mr. A. H. Bullen in the *Dictionary of National Biography*. The Birkheads, Bircheds, or Birketts, were a Northumbrian family, of whom there are many records in the registers of Durham Cathedral and of different parishes in that county during the sixteenth and seventeenth centuries. Of our founder's father nothing seems to be known except that he was, or became, a Londoner, and, according to Aubrey, "kept the Paul's Head" near St. Paul's Cathedral. Henry Birkhead was born there, in 1617, according to the most probable statement. His father must have been a thriving man, for he gave him the best education which London then provided. This was at Farnaby's famous school in Cripplegate—the school which for a whole generation educated hundreds of eminent Englishmen. It was then at the height of its fame, the first classical school in England, and known throughout Europe. Its size was almost double that of the neighbouring foundation of St. Paul's; three hundred boys attended it, of whom a large proportion were of high birth and many became distinguished in after life. Farnaby himself was reckoned one of the foremost scholars of his age.

From school, Birkhead proceeded to Trinity College, Oxford, where he was admitted a commoner in 1633—at the age of sixteen according to Aubrey's chronology, of twenty, if Anthony Wood is right in dating his birth in 1613—and was elected a scholar in 1635. The next that we hear of him is interesting; it gives evidence that he was a scholar of fine parts, and perhaps also that the accusation made against him in one of the few notices that there are of him after his death, of weakness and conceitedness, may have had some foundation. Under Jesuit influence, then working strongly if secretly in Oxford, he joined the Church of Rome, and left Oxford to enter as a student at the great English Jesuit College at St. Omer. As often happened in that age of fluctuating religious opinions, his conversion to Catholicism was brief. Within a year or two he rejoined the Church of England; and on the recommendation of Archbishop Laud, the Visitor of the College, was elected in 1638 a Fellow of All Souls. He was an Anglican and Royalist, but accepted things as they came, and submitted quietly to the Cromwellian Commissioners. While at All Souls he sustained his reputation as a scholar and man of letters, and also studied law and medicine. He associated on friendly terms with other Oxford scholars of both parties; for one of his friends, and joint author with him of a volume of Latin poems which ran into a second edition during the Commonwealth, was Henry Stubbe, a violent opponent of authority in Church and State, who was expelled from Christ Church and from his keepership of the Bodleian Library for scandalous attacks on the clergy, but had the reputation of being "the best Latinist and Grecian in Oxford." Birkhead himself remained at All Souls for nineteen years. In 1657 he resigned his fellowship and went to live in London, where he had chambers in the Temple. At the Restoration he became Registrar of the Diocese of Norwich, a post which he continued to fill for the next twenty years. Of his later life we know nothing: he lived, says Wood, in a retired and scholastical condition. Two volumes of Latin poems, and a few contributions to miscellanies of English and Latin verse, all included within the period of his residence at All Souls, are the sum total of his published works. A MS. play, written by him, and entitled *The Female Rebellion*, is among the collections in the Bodleian. Mr. Bullen, who is probably the only person alive who has read it, reports that it has little or no merit: I have not had an opportunity of verifying this judgment, but it may no doubt be accepted as right.

He died at his house in Westminster at a very advanced age in 1696, and was buried in St. Margaret's Church, as I find from the parish records, on the 30th September of that year. It was a year of capital importance in English history, the year of the renovation of the currency and the restoration of public credit which opened for England, after a century of distress and confusion, that long era of commercial prosperity under which the Empire was created.

The will under which this Chair was founded had been made by him three years before his death. It is a document of much human interest; and as it is brief, and has never been published, I make no apology for quoting it in full, omitting only the parts of it which are common form.

I give and bequeath unto Mrs Margaret Jones my niece because I think she is well provided for five shillings Item I give and bequeath to her brother John Donaldson if he be alive one shilling Item I

give and bequeath to Stephen Donaldson the younger brother of
the said John Donaldson if he be alive one shilling Item I give and
bequeath to Jane Stevenson whom I have formerly called and
written to as my wife to save her credit in the world though I was
never married to her nor betrothed to her or did she ever so much
as desired me to marry her or be betrothed to her. She is of Monkwearmouth in the County of Durham I write this in the presence
of God who knowes she has been extream false and many wayes
exceeding injurious to me. And therefore I bequeath to her but
one shilling Item I give and bequeath to Mrs Mary Knight *alias*
Geery my sister five shillings
   Item I give and bequeath to Henry Guy of Westminster Esq
[The sum is left blank in the original document.]
I doe hereby nullify and revoke all wills formerly by me in
any wise made particularly one last Will and Testament made by
me to my best remembrance in the yeare of our Lord 1688 and in
the moneth of December I constitute and appoint hereby the forenamed Mary Knight and forenamed Henry Guy executrix and
executor of this my last will and testament, to whom I bequeath
and give all my lands tenements and hereditaments whatsoever
with their appurtenances scituate in the parish of Sutton or there-
abouts near Abbington in Barkshire and my lease of lands scituate
in the parish of Monkwearmouth in the county of Durham with
its appurtenances held by me of the Reverend Dean and Chapter
of Durham with all the rest of my goods and chattells of what kind
soever In trust to maintain as far as it can for ever a Publick Professor
of Poetry in the University of Oxford

There is something pitiable, and almost tragic, in the hot
spurt of anger that breaks here from the lonely old man of
eighty. From the specific allusion to the previous will of five
years before, the natural inference is that the miserable story
had reached its climax then, and was the case of an old scholar
and recluse fallen into senility and become the prey of a
woman who looked forward to inheriting his property, but
played her game badly.
   The Henry Guy named as co-executor with his sister, and
described in the letters of administration as *armiger*, was no
doubt the politician of that name, a member of Christ Church
and of the Inner Temple, and Member of Parliament for
Hedon in Yorkshire. He was Secretary to the Treasury when

the will was made, and probably a neighbour of Birkhead's in Westminster. It is not surprising, in view of the terms of the will, that both he and Mrs. Knight declined to undertake the executorship. Mrs. Knight very probably regarded the legacy of five shillings as little short of a direct insult. Guy, a short time before Birkhead's death, had been removed from his post at the Treasury and committed to Newgate for accepting bribes; he was presumably in no state of mind to undertake an onerous and unremunerative duty, and is not known to have felt the least interest in poetry. Letters of administration were consequently granted in the ensuing December to the Syndic General of the University of Oxford.

The delays of legal procedure were in any case then great; Jane Stevenson had very possibly made some such havoc in the property as Becky Sharp did later with that of Joseph Sedley, and there appears in particular to have been some long negotiation with the Dean and Chapter in regard to the Durham property. In the inaugural lecture of the first professor they are spoken of as themselves benefactors to the University in the matter, and almost as co-founders. How this exactly was I have not been able to discover. The present Dean, who takes an interest in the matter as it affects both Durham and Oxford, has very kindly had search made for me in the Chapter Records. From the Receiver's books it appears that the rent of certain property which had been paid by Birkhead for 1696-7 was paid by the University for 1697-8, and that in 1698 the University was mulcted in the customary fine on renewal of the lease. But from that point the records become defective: "Our Chapter clerk in Queen Anne's day," the Dean writes to me, "was a neglectful rascal." It would seem that at some time within the ten years 1698-1708, the Dean and Chapter gave up the rent and made a present to the University of the estate. In any case, the University acquired the estate in some way, for they afterwards sold it. Had this not been done, it is possible either that the endowment of the Chair would be much larger than it is, or, and this is perhaps more likely, that it would have been before now dealt with by statute, whether by the University itself or by a Commission, and its application varied. For, as we shall see presently,

Professorships of Poetry do not seem to be in consonance with modern ideas about the organization and staffing of universities.

At all events, it was not until eleven years later that the statute establishing the Chair was framed. It passed Convocation on the 13th July, 1708. The preamble of the statute is in the following terms: I quote from an old translation of the original Latin:

Seeing that the reading of the old poets contributes not only to give keenness and polish to the natural endowment of young men, but also to the advancement of severer learning whether sacred or human; and also forasmuch as the said Henry Birkhead hath, for the purpose of leaving with posterity a record of the devotion of his mind to literature, founded a poetical lecture in the University of Oxford, to be given for all future times; and hath by his last will bequeathed a yearly income for its support; we decree, &c.

The provisions of the statute itself, which are in main substance still those in force, are as follows:

1. The Reader is to be either M.A. or B.C.L., or holder of some higher degree in the University.

2. He is to be elected in full Convocation, and at the end of five years may be elected afresh or some other person appointed, provided that no Reader is to be continued in office beyond ten years, and that no other person of the same House is to succeed him without interval.

3. He is to lecture in the Natural Philosophy School on every first Tuesday in full term (with arrangements for postponement if that Tuesday should be a Saint's Day) at 3 p.m., and also in the Theatre at the Encaenia, "before the philological exercises commence."

4. The income of the foundation is to be received and accounted for by the Vice-Chancellor, and a fine of £5 to be deducted from the Reader's salary on each occasion when he neglects to lecture, and applied to the uses of the University.

When the terms of the statute were being debated, a proposal was made, by no less a person than Dean Aldrich, that there should be Encaenia terminally, for the recitation of compositions in prose and verse by young gentlemen, and that on each of these occasions the Professor of Poetry should make a speech. The proposal was fortunately negatived.

This statute remained unaltered till 1784, when the hour of lecturing was altered from 3 to 2 p.m., and the regulation as to the additional lecture at Commemoration omitted. In 1839 the precise regulation as to the day and hour of the terminal lectures was dropped, and it was enacted in more general terms that the professor was to read one solemn lecture every term. The more recent changes by which reappointment for a second term of five years was forbidden, and the inconvenient regulation which did not allow two successive professors to belong to the same college was repealed, are modern and familiar. A ten years' occupancy of the Chair had up till then been the rule; of the twenty-one professors who successively held the Chair until the power of reappointment was abolished a few years ago, all but four were re-elected for a second term. The new rule, whatever may be thought of it by the occupant of the Chair for the time being, is probably in the interest both of poetry and of the University. That the foundation should have, but for this single change, remained practically the same in its terms for two centuries may be taken, if we like, partly as an indication of the sagacity of its founders when they drew the original statute, partly as an instance of the innate conservatism of Oxford, and of her far from deplorable tendency rather to make the best of existing institutions than to cast them into the melting-pot.

Of the particular aims which Birkhead had in view in his foundation we have no evidence. Thomas Smith, of Magdalen, writing at the time of the foundation of the Chair, says that he knew Birkhead, and that the current story after his death was that he had left considerable sums to the Society of Poets: "of which," he adds, "I know no such formal establishment." His general ideas, however, may probably be taken as substantially represented by the preamble of the statute of 1708. Poetry was then, from the academic point of view, one of the liberal arts. The inaugural lecture of the first Oxford professor laid it down as a sort of axiom that instruction in the art was both possible and desirable: "artem poeticam institutionem et

admittere et mereri." There were similar Chairs or lecture-
ships in other European Universities. I do not know whether
this was at all generally the case, and have come on but few
actual instances. In 1705, there is a record of a visit to Oxford,
and admission while there "to the privileges of the Publick
Library," of one "Mr. Bergerus, Professor of Poetry in the
University of Wittemberg." This must have been J. W. von
Berger, one of three brothers who were all professors, each
in a different faculty, at that University. The title of his Chair
is, however, given in the *Biographie Universelle* not as Poetry,
but as Eloquence.

  · The title is fancifully suggestive. One can hardly help
wondering whether the lectures of some predecessor of his
were attended by Hamlet, and whether their influence re-
appears in that able and wayward scholar's tendency to drop
into poetry and his keen interest in dramatic criticism. But
the University of Wittenberg itself, Chair of Poetry and all,
has long since disappeared. Still the most flourishing of the
Universities of Protestant Germany till well on in the eighteenth
century, it fell into decay during the Napoleonic wars, and
was merged in 1816 in that of Halle. The Vereinigte Friedrichs-
Universität Halle-Wittenberg has no Chair of Poetry. Indeed,
in the possession of such a Chair Oxford stands, as far as I can
ascertain, alone. There is no Chair of Poetry, other than ours,
in the British Empire. There is none at Athens or Rome, at
Bologna or Berlin. There is none in the many Universities,
with their multifarious professorships, which have been
founded in the United States of America. At the Sorbonne
there are Chairs of Latin Poetry and of French Poetry; but
that is a different thing. The nearest and the sole approach to
a Chair of Poetry like ours is in the University of Budapest,
where there is half a one; at least there is, among the ordinary
professorships, one of *Aesthetik und Poetik*. With these exceptions, if they be exceptions, the Oxford Professor of Poetry
has no colleague in the two hundred and twenty Universities
now catalogued, and spread over the whole civilized or
partially civilized world.

  Two hundred years ago the foundation of a Readership in
Poetry was a sort of symbol of the generally accepted view

that the laws of the art had become fixed, and its principles
had become a matter, as one might say, of international agreement in the republic of letters. The *Poetics* of J. C. Scaliger
had, ever since its publication in 1561, after Scaliger's death,
been received throughout Europe as a sort of textbook of the
art. The seventeenth century had gone on building on these
foundations; and what was expected of a Professor of Poetry,
here or elsewhere, was the same sort of work, in comment
and consolidation, that was being done in France by the joint
labours of the two Daciers. But in England poetry had taken
a course of its own; and the immense and splendid production
of a century had been followed by a body of poetical criticism
which included work of great excellence and value. Sidney's
Apology and the treatise attributed to Puttenham belong to the
Elizabethan age proper. Through the whole century of the
transition there was a constant stream of discussion on the
principles and practice of the art; Dryden, who died in the
last year of the seventeenth century, was the first critic of his
age. Soon after this Chair was founded, Addison began in the
Spectator the series of literary papers, which remained for
more than half a century, until the appearance of Johnson's
Lives of the Poets, the last word in English poetical criticism.
Within the limits which it had then assigned itself, poetry
settled down, during that half-century and longer, into an art
of fixed rule. The new Renaissance of poetry first fore-
shadowed in the writings of Gray, Percy, and Warton, did not
rise in its full splendour until the last years of the eighteenth
century. Coleridge, its inaugurator, also opened up the new
Renaissance of poetical criticism. But Oxford was then and
for years afterwards still firmly rooted—or, shall we say, fast
stuck?—in the old tradition.

In Oxford itself poetry, and poetical criticism as we should
now understand that term, were two hundred years ago at a
low ebb. There was no nest of singing-birds here then such
as there had been earlier, and was to be again more than once
later. Among the Oxford versifiers of Queen Anne's reign
no one attained immortality; the thin but delicate piping of
Tickell, a poet best remembered now as Addison's devoted
pupil and panegyrist, is the only note that remains audible now.

N

He was deputy-professor of Poetry during the third year of
the existence of the Chair, when Trapp, according to the easy-
going fashion of those days, had gone off to Ireland as chaplain
to the Irish Lord Chancellor. Henry Felton of Edmund Hall
might perhaps be still remembered as a poet if he had written
many things like these two melodious stanzas, "occasion'd by
a Ladies making a copy of Verses:"

> In Antient Greece when Sappho sung
> And touch'd with matchless Art the Lyre,
> Apollo's Hand her Musick strung
> And all Parnassus form'd the Quire.
>
> But sweeter Notes and softer Layes
> From your diviner Numbers spring,
> Such as himself Apollo plays,
> Such as the Heavenly Sisters sing.

The lines have something of the purity and sweetness of an
early Blake. But Felton, unlike Crabbe, appears to have said
farewell to the Muses when he became domestic chaplain to
the Duke of Rutland. Other Oxford poets of the period can
hardly be mentioned but in a spirit of levity. A single typical
instance may suffice; the entry in Hearne's diary in May, 1710,
where he notes that "Mr. Stubbe of Exeter, an ingenious
Gentleman, has publish'd a Poem called *The Laurell and the
Olive*, inscrib'd to his dear Friend and Acquaintance Mr.
Bubb, who is likewise an ingenious Gentleman, and has a
Copy of Verses before this Poem in two pages to Mr. Stubbe."
Such were then, and such with allowance for difference of
fashion still are, the frail blossoms of the flying terms. But it
had not then become the fashion that a young man should stop
writing poetry when he put on his Bachelor's gown. Poetry
was at least regarded as an art to be practised by grown men,
not as an exercise or amusement to be outgrown with boyhood.
In such a change of fashion there may be both loss and gain.

Among the English poets of the preceding generation,
Cowley still retained his curious pre-eminence, though now he
shared it with Dryden. Milton, as a republican and regicide,
was an abomination to all orthodox Anglicans; and in Oxford

any praise bestowed on him was faint and grudging, while eager credence was given to an absurd legend that he had died a Papist. Pope only became known after the appearance of his *Pastorals* in 1709. The older poets were, however, becoming the subject of critical study. One of the first acts of Atterbury when he became Dean of Christ Church in 1712 was to give his countenance and assistance to Urry in preparing the edition of Chaucer which, with all its faults and imperfections, was the first attempt made at forming a satisfactory text of the poems, and was only superseded by that of Tyrwhitt more than half a century later. Perhaps a fair judgment may be formed of the way in which poetry was generally read and studied in the University by looking at the names mentioned in the published lectures of the first professor. His inaugural lecture makes no mention of any but Greek and Roman poets; in the other lectures the English poets named are, except for Spenser and Shakespeare, all those of his own age or that immediately preceding it, of the period, that is, when poetry in this country had been attacking and achieving the task of becoming fully civilized, of throwing off its insular and national character, and joining—one might almost say, merging in— the general international current of European letters. The knowledge of our older poetry, with but few exceptions, did not extend beyond students and antiquarians.

It was the age of poetical translations; and these were not only translations into English of foreign masterpieces, but translations into Latin of English originals. Fanshawe, half a century earlier, had started the fashion by his translation of Fletcher's *Faithful Shepherdess* into Latin verse. Sir Francis Kynaston, about the same time, had made a Latin translation of Chaucer's *Troilus and Creseide*: it was dedicated, like the second edition of the volume of Milton's Latin poems, to Rouse, the principal librarian of the Bodleian. Henry Bold, of New College, translated the *Paradise Lost* into Latin verse within a few years after its publication. All this work was on the same lines and directed towards the same object, the testing of English poetry by a universally recognized classical standard, and the vindication for it of a certain classical quality and international value.

It would be a mistake to suppose that the Professorship of Poetry was generally thought of at the time as an institution of high importance, or one which might exercise a powerful influence over thought and taste: still less was there any idea that the interpretation of poetry should be in the hands of its chosen exponent nothing short of the interpretation of life. The statutory lectures of the professor either were rhetorical exercises, or dealt with the laws of poetry regarded as a formal code, and with the art of poetry in a narrowly technical meaning. The extraneous duties which he was expected to undertake were of a trivial kind: to write a prologue to be spoken before the theatrical performance in Oxford of some play by Betterton or Vanbrugh, or a set of complimentary verses on some public occasion. A little while before he was elected to the Chair of Poetry, Trapp had been desired by the Vice-Chancellor to write encomiastical verses upon the new English edition of Spanheim's treatise *De Nummis*, a copy of which had just been presented by the author to the Bodleian. Pegasus had been got well into harness; and it was the Professor of Poetry's function to keep him there, and see to it that the harness fitted. It is clear enough from all the indirect evidence, of which there is abundance, that this was what was meant. It is clear enough too that this was what actually happened, so far as the earlier Professors of Poetry refrained from following the notorious Oxford fashion of totally neglecting their duties. Of one Oxford professor of that time a contemporary notes that "having got the place by a Corrupt Interest among the Electors" he turned out "so dull a Reader that after a few Lectures he could get no Hearers, and so makes the Place in a manner a *sine-cure*, as most other Publick Readers do." The last words are venomous, but seem not to be wholly untrue. But as regards the estimation in which the Chair of Poetry was held at its foundation we have direct and tangible evidence. The first professor was elected without competition; and this was not, we are told, because of any striking or supereminent fitness on his part, but because others "did not stir for it on account of the smallness of the salary." The salary was £25, which would represent, I am told, something like £75, or rather more, perhaps nearly £100, at the present day.

Poetry and poetical criticism cannot of course be weighed in terms of money; but in a salaried appointment, the importance of the office generally bears some kind of relation to the amount of the stipend. It is a further fact, which may induce various reflections according as one looks at it, that the first Professor of Poetry received, for the copyright of a volume of the lectures given by him during the first two years of his tenure of the Chair, just twice the sum that Milton received for the copyright of *Paradise Lost*. But poets, with a few remarkable exceptions, have not been good men of business.

Ample materials exist from which, without going deeply into records, one can form a picture in one's mind of the Oxford of two hundred years ago, alike in its material, its social, and its intellectual aspect. The general impression that one receives is of an Oxford not so very unlike the Oxford of the present day. Like the present time, it was an age of building here, in a new manner and on an imposing scale: we owe to it many of the buildings which are now among the most striking and characteristic of those which adorn the city. "Lord Arundell's Stones," as they were called, were still lying in the Theatre yard, but the building in which they were housed until a few years ago was in preparation. Peckwater quadrangle was rising in Christ Church; the stately Church of All Saints on the site of an old and ruinous Gothic predecessor in High Street; and, further down, the massive and dignified façade of Queen's, even then the subject of great controversy, and called a "great staring pile" by those who held by the smaller and richer Jacobean architecture which was then, as it still remains, predominant in Oxford. It was while that last building was in progress that, one November evening, the Provost—known familiarly in the University as Old Smooth-boots—fell into one of the open cellars "and was like to have broke his Neck." He was popularly supposed to have been drunk at the time: for hard drinking was then common even among Heads of Houses and other high officials. When one Fletcher, a scholar of University, was expelled for abusing and striking the Proctor, Harris of Wadham, in the open street, "there are not wanting credible witnesses," we are told, "who say that Harris was more in drink himself than Fletcher." But

University was a difficult college to keep in hand. As an illustration of undergraduate life in Queen Anne's time, and its remarkable likeness to that of our own day, the following account of an incident which took place there in 1706 is worth recording. A newly appointed Bursar of University had entered on his duties full of zeal for reform. "Amongst these laudable undertakings," says the chronicler, "is chiefly to be mention'd the College Garden which having been almost ruinated and quite out of Repair, he order'd to be cover'd with Green Turff, planted with Trees and Flowers, and the Walks to be gravell'd, to the great Beauty of the Place and Satisfaction of the rest of the Fellows: and there was no one of the College appear'd at present displeas'd with it but the Master: which perhaps being known to one Robinson (a commoner of that House, and Nephew to Mr. Smith, lately Senior Fellow and now in London, who it seems was always averse to this Reform) a day or two after it was finish'd with two or three more of the College, got into the Garden in the Night time, pull'd up some of the Ews spoil'd others, and did other Mischief, to the no small Grief of the Doctor and the rest of the Fellows; it being such a piece of Malice as one would think could not enter into the thoughts of any person of common Breeding, and indeed seldom or never heard of in the University, but in this College, where they have had some other Instances of the same Nature, and have had some lads noted for this Diabolical Wickedness; and without doubt 'twas from them Mr. Robinson was instructed, he being reckon'd at first a civil modest Youth, and to be very good natur'd. One reason which instigated him I hear is because the Doctor and the rest of the Society had taken care that all the undergraduates and Bachelors should dine and sup in the Hall, or to undergo a penalty for it, which it seems had been neglected before, to the disgrace somewhat of the College, this being a proviso in all College and Hall Statutes, and if kept up redounds much to the Honour of the University."

Only a little before this, the Master of University, Dr. Charlett, together with the President of Magdalen and the Provost of Queen's, had been dining with the Warden of New College, "where they staid till 9 of the clock," says the letter-writer who tells the story, "but 'tis highly scandalous to say they drunk to excess, the Warden of New College being not in a very good State of health, and neither of the other noted for being hard Drinkers." When the dinner-party broke up, Dr. Charlett's boy lighted him home with one of the New College silver tankards instead of a lantern; "which was not perceived till they came home, because"—here our authority seems to be blowing hot and cold—"because the President of Magdalen and Provost of Queen's accompany'd him." However this may have been, the incident "made a great Noise in Town." The boy was turned off, and disappears from history. "But I am heartily sorry," the narrator goes on to say, "any one should hence take occasion to blacken the Doctor's character, who (notwithstanding some Failings, to which all are subject) is a man of several excellent Qualifications, and if he had Abilities would be one of the Greatest Encouragers of Learning that have appeared of late."

But it would be an entire mistake to suppose, from incidents like these, that Oxford was a place entirely given over to idleness and good living. It was full of scholars of wide erudition and vast industry. It was eminent in the study of law and medicine, and of the physical sciences as they were then understood, as well as in its own peculiar field of classical scholarship and theology. Research into the history and antiquities of England was pursued zealously and actively. Rent asunder and half crippled as it was by the furious political and theological controversies of the time, it found even in these a stimulus to the study of ecclesiastical and constitutional history. The University Press was continually bringing out treatises and editions which at least showed no lack of labour and of learning. And it was a subject of regret then, as it has so often been in later times, that many of the finest scholars in Oxford contented themselves with amassing knowledge without communicating it, and carried it all to the grave with them when they died.

Yet, when all is said, it is true that Oxford had then entered on the long period of quiescence, almost of stagnation, which lasted until the early years of the nineteenth century, and the reputation of which still clings to it after almost another century of progress, reform, and revolution. But all through that period it bred fine scholars and accomplished critics; it remained a seat of learning which, if often narrow, pedantic, and insular, was solid and unostentatious. It kept within itself the springs of intellectual life, and the potentiality of reform and advance, the power of adapting itself, though slowly and cumbrously, to new conditions imposed on it by an altered world. It slept, but was not dead; and thus it is that it is still alive now.

What may be said of the University of Oxford generally may also be said of the Chair of Poetry during the eighteenth century. It slept, or at least dozed: its occupants are names now forgotten, with the exception of Warton, and, to some degree, of Spence and Lowth. It clung hard to its academic and conservative traditions. The great renaissance of poetry at the end of the century was long in reaching it, and reached it at last in the dimmed or distorted form that it took when passed through the absorbent and refractive medium of Anglo-Catholicism. Until Arnold, fifty years ago now, gave the Chair a higher importance and spoke from it to a wider audience, it is to other sources that we must go to trace the progress of poetical criticism, whether such criticism be regarded as the technical exposition of an art or as the appreciation of poetry as a living thing and a power over life. The reading of the old poets, named in the original statute as the object towards the promotion of which the Chair was founded, had sunk into a matter of routine, into a branch of scholarship in the narrower meaning of that ambiguous word. But the greater part of all life is routine; and the reading of the old poets, in whatever spirit it be pursued, at all events ensures that they shall be read. They themselves, not what is said about them, must do the rest. Yet what can be said about them is endless, and endlessly interesting. Poetry itself, like all organic functions of life, may be incapable of exact definition. The works of the great poets cannot receive any final and conclusive appreciation; each age, one might almost say each individual mind among their readers, must appreciate them for itself, and find in them what it brings the power and the will to find. But in the art of poetry, as in other arts, it is possible to distinguish, to disengage, to illuminate, to pass on to others something of the meaning and beauty that otherwise might not reach them. There are a thousand ways of doing this; for art like nature is inexhaustible; and the foundation of this Chair "for all future times" requires no justification, since for all future times the need of this elucidative and constructive appreciation will remain, and the instinct towards it be part of human nature. The progress of poetical criticism means the progress of the study of poetry; and that follows endlessly the endless progress of poetry itself. So long as there is a University of Oxford, so long is it permissible to look forward to a succession of occupants of this Chair of Poetry, who one after another will set themselves to realize, in the terms of their own time and in the communication of their own experience, the object which, after his manner and in consonance with the ideas of his age, was in the mind of the Founder: who one after another will be commissioned by the University herself to speak, in her name, of poetry as a function, interpretation, and pattern of life.

BENTLEY'S MILTON

[*Warton Lecture at the British Academy*, 1924]

THE foundation on which this annual lecture is delivered
gives a large scope to successive lecturers; and in the
fourteen years over which its history now extends there has
been correspondingly wide variation among the subjects
chosen. I need not, I think, offer any apology for the limited
field of inquiry which the title of this lecture suggests. It is
one which opens up ground of great and not merely occasional
or obsolete interest. The relations between poetry and scholarship, the function and use of the trained scholar in criticizing,
elucidating, or interpreting the work of a poet, are intricate,
and worth studying. The questions which their examination
raises, the conclusions to which their study leads, have not
only a historical interest, but are fertile both for guidance and
for warning. Even after nearly two hundred years, it is not
useless either to professional scholars or to the appreciators
and interpreters of poetry to examine somewhat closely what
the first European scholar of his age did with the greatest of
English poems, and to draw from that examination lessons
with regard to the methods, the apparatus, and the effective
results of the science of criticism when applied to the art of
poetry.

The study of English literature, in poetry and in prose alike,
now occupies a very important place in our Universities. It
has successfully surmounted its initial difficulties; it has
organized itself, and is no longer liable to the attacks once made
on it as, on the one hand, a soft option, a dabbling in merely
belletristic pursuits, or on the other, an over-specialized study
of Early English and the cognate Teutonic languages. The
continuity of English literature, and its intimate association
with the national history and the development of English
civilization, are fully grasped. But the need still remains of
preserving for the study of English a high standard. The study

of English literature, as of the English language, must be incomplete, unless it deals with both by the methods and standards of accurate scholarship, as these have been wrought out, and still continue being wrought out further, through the organized work done on the Greek and Latin classics. The study of our literature, in particular, if it is to be solid and fruitful, involves the application to it of the principles and methods of textual criticism, and the handling, with the full armament of scholarship, of the constructional, the verbal, and as regards poetry the metrical, technique of language. English literature is, no less than the English language, a field for accurate and exacting work. This is fully realized by all who have to deal with its teaching. But it must be more fully realized in larger circles, if its study is to surmount the risk, which still exists, of dwindling into merely aesthetic appreciation, or of being degraded into a technical training for professional journalism.

Of poetry as the highest form of human language, and of English poetry as the chief glory of our national literature, this is more specially true. Poetry, more than prose, raises all the problems of critical scholarship; and it does so in a concentrated form when we are dealing with poetical masterpieces, among which the *Paradise Lost* is in the highest rank. Towards its study, Bentley's celebrated edition gives preliminary training. It shows, in large letters, the application and the misapplication of critical method. What is more valuable still, it shows very clearly the width of the field which the application of scholarship to poetry covers, and the mass of knowledge, of insight, and above all of judgment (the fusion, that is to say, of imagination and common sense) which it demands.

The story of the inception and execution of the luckless work is well known. It may be read at large in Monk's *Life of Bentley*; and I need not do more here than very briefly recapitulate the main facts.

When Bentley first directed his attention to the text of the *Paradise Lost* is a matter of dispute, but not of much importance. There seems little or no reason to reject the tradition that it was soon after the publication of Fenton's edition of Milton in 1725, in which for the first time the suggestion was made that a certain number of mistakes had crept into the original text either through blunders of Milton's amanuenses, or through his inability from blindness to ensure correction of the proof-sheets. No date is assigned for the alleged suggestion (the equivalent of a command) made to Bentley by Queen Caroline that he should undertake a complete revision of the poem. It is borne out by the last note (xii, 648) in Bentley's volume, where, speaking of "the Censure I must expect to incur, who have presum'd to make so many Alterations," he adds, "*Non injussa cecini*." In any case, Bentley's own words in his preface are precise, and there is no reason why he should have told a deliberate falsehood: "I made the Notes *extempore*, and put them to the Press as soon as made." As we shall see, the copy of the *Paradise Lost* on which he made his manuscript notes fully bears out the statement.

Rapidly done, indeed done with impetuous haste, the "new edition" was published by Bentley in January 1731/2, in a handsome quarto. The date was timed to coincide with the opening of a fresh session of Parliament, and the resumption of the proceedings in the House of Lords for reversal of the judgment of the previous year in the Court of King's Bench, which had practically decided the thirty years' conflict between Trinity College and its imperious Master in Bentley's favour. According to his habit on other occasions, he desired at this juncture to attract public attention, to win further Court favour, and to give a striking proof of his powers. In vain did his nephew and secretary, Richard Bentley the younger, urge him to suppress publication. The sheets were printed off at top speed, without even revision of notes which sometimes are in flat contradiction to others on later pages. Tonson and his associate booksellers paid, it is said, one hundred guineas to Bentley for the edition. If so, that was the first and last success which it had. It was received, first with a feeling akin to stupefaction, and then with an universal roar of anger or derision.

But Bentley's reputation was so great, his genius so undoubted, that it could not be ignored. A year later, Zachary Pearce, himself a former Fellow of Trinity, and afterwards

Bishop of Bangor and of Rochester, issued (without attaching his name to it) a volume which may still be studied with much interest and profit: *A Review of the text of the twelve books of Milton's "Paradise Lost": in which the chief of Dr. Bentley's Emendations are consider'd; And several other Emendations and Observations are offer'd to the Public.* For the first time, he paid real attention to punctuation, often (as for instance in vii, 422; viii, 504; x, 580) with highly illuminating results. Both where he defends the received text against Bentley's stricture, and where he suggests, though this he does sparingly, emendations of his own, he always shows both insight and good sense; and it is further to his credit that he had studied the vocabulary and the sentence-structure of Milton's prose works.

Contemporary with, but independent of, Pearce's *Review*, is the volume of *Explanatory Notes and Remarks on Milton's "Paradise Lost," By J. Richardson: Father and Son. With the life of the Author: and a Discourse on the Poem. By J. R. Sen.* It was published in 1734, but represents the loving study of many years, carried on in concert by the father and son, whose lives extended jointly over a full century beginning with the date of the original publication of Milton's poem. By profession portrait-painters, they were both of them highly cultured men of letters, well acquainted with the Greek, Latin and Italian classics as well as with English poetry. Richardson's strictures on Bentley are severe, but undeniably just. Speaking of "Suggestions and assertions that we have [*Paradise Lost*] not as the author gave it, but as corrupted by presumption, folly, carelessness, and I know not what," he goes on, "Presumption, folly, or something worse has been at work in suggesting or believing such things, which is the more dangerous because founded on a specious probability." "We have reverenc'd our text, have handled it as something which it would be a sort of prophaneness, as well as a ridiculous presumption in us, to aim at improving, by adding or diminishing. If any man could do it, 'tis not his business; 'tis his author's thoughts, not his own, which the publick expects from an expositor, and such only we pretend to be." "I leave the reader to judge . . . whether this book affords any pretence or excuse to a new editor, who shall dare to change, though it were with the utmost deliberation and taste. He may indeed honestly say, thus and thus the author should have thought or said, but let him not palm himself upon us as a genuine Milton." Bentley's own "It is a pretty poem, but you must not call it Homer" is turned upon him here with crushing effectiveness.

When he brought out his *Paradise Lost*, Bentley was just seventy. Forty years had passed since the *Epistola ad Millium* which had made his reputation; thirty-three since the enlarged Dissertation on the Epistles of Phalaris which had established it throughout Europe. Since then much of his life had been spent on the epic struggle which he carried on for a full generation with his College and with the University authorities. It was carried on by him with every weapon of intimidation and chicane. Its fluctuations make a drama which even now cannot be followed without breathless interest. He had been formally degraded by the University, and restored to his degrees by the Court of King's Bench: it still remained for him, after exhausting every legal artifice but one, to receive sentence of deprivation; then to play his final card and win trick and rubber, and to spend his last years in quiet possession of the battlefield where his antagonists were dead or exhausted. It is easy to suggest, and it has often been suggested, that his Milton is the work of a scholar in his dotage. But this contention will not bear examination. Age had added to his imperious arrogance; conflict had exacerbated his temper. But neither his body nor his mind was in decay. It was seven years later that he brought out the edition of Manilius which remains one of his titles to fame. The old lion was as formidable as ever; and as contemptuously indifferent as ever to hostile criticism. Probably even the brilliant and highly amusing parody by Arbuthnot of his style and method in the *Virgilius Reformatus* of 1727 had left him wholly untouched. Pope, always cautious in his malice, did not venture to publish his immortal attack on Bentley (in the fourth book of the remodelled *Dunciad*) until years after; it only appeared when Bentley was on his death-bed.

Nor, on the other hand, is it allowable to relieve him of the charge of reckless haste by fixing on him the heavier stigma of considered and long-matured wrong-headedness. An anonymous charge was made at the time that Bentley's preface was mendacious, and that he had in fact been working at the text of the *Paradise Lost* for six years or more. A statement made in the *Grub Street Journal* over the signature A.Z., on the authority of another gentleman "who was ready if called on to give his name," as to what had been said in conversation by a third person years before, is negligible. But an examination of the copy of *Milton* annotated for the new edition by Bentley's own hand proves it to be baseless.

For his textual work Bentley used a copy of the large quarto *Paradise Lost* which, together with a reprint of Addison's famous articles in the *Spectator*, constituted the first volume of the sumptuous edition, generally known as Tickell's, of Milton's poetical works published by Tonson in 1720. At Bentley's death in 1742 it passed, with the rest of his library, to his nephew Richard. By him it was given in 1754 to a Mr. Warren, from whose possession it passed (whether mediately or immediately does not appear) into that of a Mr. Clementson, Deputy Serjeant-at-Arms to the House of Commons. Mr. Clementson in turn presented it in 1804 to John Mitford, then a young man of twenty-three. Mitford mentions it in the Preface to his own edition of Milton (1832), and notes that it contains many alterations beyond those incorporated in Bentley's published edition. Since then the volume appears to have been unknown to or neglected by editors. On the sale of Mitford's library after his death in 1859 it was purchased by a notable book-lover and collector, Mr. John Rhodes of Potternewton House, Leeds, and is now in the library of his' son, Colonel Fairfax Rhodes, of Brockhampton Park. By Colonel Rhodes's courtesy, and the kind offices of his kinsman, Mr. Henry Broadbent, the Librarian of Eton, I recently had the opportunity of going through it with some care. It is of much, even of fascinating interest because it shows Bentley actually at work, jotting down tentative suggestions and striking them out or replacing them by others, and adding caustic notes at the foot of the page. There are additions or alterations in a different ink, apparently made in running through the poem a second time. But the volume entirely bears out Bentley's own statement to which allusion was made above: and makes it clear further, that the notes in the published work were written by him, or perhaps dictated to his nephew, straight from the manuscript notes in this volume, which are sometimes expanded, but often copied verbally. In a number of cases he has noted emendations of lines which he afterwards, with a slash of his desperate hook, struck out bodily. In one case (i, 240) where he was dissatisfied—it is not easy to see why—with the words "by their own recovered strength," he has put down in the margin, all at the same time, not only "self-recovered" for "own recovered," but no less than five alternatives—revigorate, resumed, recovering, reviving, self-raised—for the word "recovered."

Bentley's Milton has never been reprinted. For the reasons I have given, it might be worth while to do so, for use as an historical document of no little value for students of English literature. If so, it would be essential to take this other volume into account. What would we not give for the autograph notes on Virgil of a Latin grammarian (even one of much less eminence than Bentley and with equal defects of temperament and of imaginative sympathy) written little more than sixty years after the publication of the Aeneid! As it is, Bentley's Milton is seldom studied, seldom, I suppose, even looked at. It is chiefly known from a few colossal absurdities which have been picked out of it, and used over and over again by biographers or editors of Milton. "It verified the truth," Monk quite justly observes, "of his own maxim that no man was ever written out of reputation but by himself." After the first storm of condemnation and ridicule was over, it sank into practical oblivion. Even those editors of Milton or biographers of Bentley (like Jebb or Masson) who have been obliged to deal with it, have done so with a curious reluctance and distaste, and seem to have been glad to hurry away from the subject. Monk indeed had gone into it carefully, and some of his observations are of much interest both for their fairness and as showing the curious insensibility to Milton's distinctive poetical qualities which still existed then, at a time just half-way between Bentley's work and the present day.

"If any unprejudiced judge," he writes, "were to try the experiment of considering Bentley's remarks on Milton's text divested of the absurd fiction of an interpolating editor, the flippant and unseemly language of his notes, and all his own proposed emendations, he would be surprised to find himself frequently compelled to acknowledge the justice of his strictures; and even when he dissented, would recognize the ingenuity of the critic." In other words, Bentley always makes us think. It should be needless to say, but it is not, that unless we think, we shall never either understand or appreciate.

"Had similar strictures been communicated to the poet," Monk continues, "he would probably have accepted many of the hints; he would have changed or omitted many flat and inharmonious verses, and removed those inconsistencies and improprieties which cannot be denied to be blemishes."

Monk lays his finger here, without perhaps fully realizing it, on one of the principal snares which always beset poetical criticism, that of considering not what the author wrote, but what the critic thinks he ought to have written. No good comes of this. But it is a thing against which scholars still have to be and will always have to be on their guard.

It would be tedious to follow down the stream of criticism. I may just mention the two pages devoted to the subject in De Quincey's elaborate and very readable review of Monk; the pained account given of Bentley's work by Masson, in which, while admitting occasional acute criticism, he speaks of the "utter monstrousness" of the whole thing; the slight but judicious comments of Jebb in his monograph on Bentley; and the discussion by Dowden, in a paper on *Milton in the Eighteenth Century*, read to the British Academy fifteen years ago, of the vexed question how far the phantom "editor" on whom Bentley concentrates his attacks was, or came to be, believed in by Bentley himself, how far he was from first to last a deliberate fiction. This is a problem of considerable psychological interest, but of small importance otherwise. The allegation given currency in the well-known words of Johnson that Bentley "as is said, in private allowed it (the supposition of editorial tampering) to be false," cannot be traced beyond Lauder's *Essay* of 1750, and before accepting it we should want better security than Lauder's. In fact, Bentley plays with his phantom editor, not caring whether he existed or not.

o

Anyone can read his notes with their manifold inconsistencies
in this matter, and form his own judgment. The arrogance
which had for many years, in fact from the first, marked all
his work, only reaches its climax here; he had become quite
careless either of the decencies of scholarship (if there are any)
or of his own reputation.

To pick out special fatuities in Bentley's treatment and hold
them up for amazement or ridicule is easy; and I need not
waste time on doing again what has often been done. But
one remark may here be made; that it is essential in all these
cases not only to look at Bentley's alteration of text, but to read
his own note. If this be done, what is otherwise only a poor
amusement may be converted into a quite profitable study.[1]

What is more profitable is to attend to larger considerations:
to (1) the point which the attitude of mind towards poetry
had reached in England two hundred years ago in the course
of progressive evolution; (2) the position which the *Paradise
Lost* then held; (3) the conditions affecting knowledge of
historical development in the English language, of metrical
and rhetorical structure, and of literary tradition; (4) the place
held by English poetry as a factor in European movement and
inter-connected with the whole Commonwealth of letters;
and (5) the aims and methods of technical scholarship as applied
to the art of poetry in its concrete embodiments.

The romantic revival, a phrase of which no exact definition
is possible, is generally thought of as having begun about or
after the middle of the eighteenth century. The dates assigned,
so far as exact dates in such a matter are assignable, range from
"about 1740" according to Dowden, down to the capital
point marked by the publication of Percy's *Reliques* in 1765.
But that period only marks the culmination of a movement
which had begun a good deal earlier. A landmark in the
"return to Nature" which, together with the return to the
past, marked the opening up of the clogged springs of poetry,
is the issue in 1724 of Allan Ramsay's *Evergreen*. That collection, with all its defects—which include a total absence of

[1] As good instances one might select, from among many others, his notes
on ii, 274, 937; iv, 24, 177, 555, 810; v, 198, 217, 293; vi, 391, 513; vii, 15;
viii, 653; xii, 648.

critical scholarship—set the stream of romanticism flowing. Two years later, Thomson's *Winter* and Dyer's *Grongar Hill* launched the movement in England.

Bentley, both by age and temperament, never felt its effect. His mind, his attitude towards literature, remained what they had been at five and twenty. Milton's recognition as a classic had then begun, but it was as a classic in the narrower sense of the term. The classicist reaction against the literary anarchy of the earlier seventeenth century was then growing; it came into power (as one says of a government in the political world) with the end of the century and the death of Dryden. It is interesting to observe the stages of that recognition.

It was not immediate; it was, in fact, very slow. The first edition of the *Paradise Lost* was put on the market in successive instalments: not less than six of these are traced by differences of title-page; and it took two years before 1,300 copies had been sold, and Milton received the second payment of five pounds provided for in the contract with his publisher. The second edition, in which the division into twelve Books was made, came out in 1674. The commendatory verses prefixed to it by Marvell are apologetic and uneasy; those by Barrow make a higher claim, and for the first time assert Milton's equivalence to Homer and Virgil. But Barrow, though no doubt a worthy medical man and a pretty scholar, was not one whose judgment in literary matters carried much weight.

It was Dryden himself, on whom Marvell in the verses just mentioned had made a petulant attack, who gave the first authentic testimony. This was after Milton's death, when it had become possible to praise the official apologist of regicide without exciting political prejudice. Yet even if full allowance be made for this, Dryden's words, in his preface of 1677 to his own unacted dramatization of the Fall of Man, are as generous as they are sincere: "Undoubtedly one of the greatest, most noble, and most sublime poems which either this age or nation has produced." They established, by the sanction of the first of living poets and critics, the position of Milton as an English classic. Yet even after this, the circulation of the *Paradise Lost* was so limited that the publisher compounded in full with Milton's widow for eight pounds down to obtain the entire property in the poem. In 1688 the established place which Milton had by then secured was registered by the publication of a sumptuous folio edition of his poems, printed by subscription, at the instance, or with the active subsidy, of Somers and Atterbury, with a list of over 500 subscribers; it is said to be the first instance of this method of publication. It was for this edition that Dryden wrote the well-known lines in which he claims, or seems to claim, as Barrow had less ably and less authoritatively done fourteen years earlier, a supremacy for Milton in the world's poetry as high as if not higher than that of Homer or Virgil. "In lapidary inscriptions," Dr. Johnson reminds us, "a man is not upon oath," and in such tributes extravagance of laudation was the common practice. Yet one cannot but be struck by the immense difference between what he says here and what, with more tempered praise, he had written in 1677. Then he asserted a place for Milton among the highest either of his own contemporaries or of other English poets; now he advances the claim to cover the poetry of all times and of the whole world.

A subsidiary indication of Milton's recognized position as a classic is found in the immense success, a few years later, both of John Phillips's masterly burlesque of the Miltonic style and phrasing in *The Splendid Shilling*, and of his *Cyder*, which launched the long list of serious imitations of the Miltonic diction and versification. A few years later still, we come to the series of papers by Addison in the *Spectator*, from January to May 1712, which did not make the reputation of the *Paradise Lost*—that was already made—but diffused and popularized it among the whole reading public. It will be noticed throughout that the tendency of appreciation was towards the classic side of Milton's poetry; towards the claim, not unjustly made, that it gave English poetry a standard of accomplishment, of classical perfection, which placed England alongside of Greece and Rome.

It was Milton's classicism, the attainment in his work, and in the *Paradise Lost* particularly, of the supreme technical quality exhibited in the work of the ancient classics, which Bentley understood. He was wholly untouched by the romantic reaction which had begun in his own mature life.

To pre-Miltonic poetry, including the whole output of the Elizabethan age, he had given little study; he regarded it as barbarous, or at least imperfectly civilized. Consequently, he treated the *Paradise Lost* as an isolated phenomenon, and took no pains to master its antecedents and surroundings or to examine the soil out of which it grew. The doctrine from which he started, as simple as it is amazing, was that if the *Paradise Lost* was to be accepted as a classic, it must be cleared completely of what he called "romantic rubbish." It was probably to give some colour of sanity to this mad clearance that he invented his interpolating editor. And once that grim phantom had taken substance in his mind, he found in him the temptation—or I should rather say, the occasion, for against a temptation there must surely be some little struggle—to ascribe to that hand, and cut out from the poem, everything in it which Bentley himself did not like. His editor becomes "an injudicious smatterer in Astronomy, Geography, Poetical Story, and Old Romances." Bentley will have none of these. The desperate hook slashes right and left; and as he plies it, "brightness falls from the air." Out go, one after one, Milton's most splendid and most inimitable beauties. It would be tedious to multiply instances. The largest single excision is that of the whole passage of fifty-five lines (iii, 444–98) describing the Paradise of Fools; this is not, to be sure, one of Milton's happiest or most inspired passages, though few are more essentially Miltonic. But the three lines in the same book (557–60):

> From eastern point
> Of Libra to the fleecy star that bears
> Andromeda far off Atlantic seas
> Beyond the horizon;

the eight lines in Book i, 579–87:

> And what resounds
> In fable or romance of Uther's son,
> Begirt with British and Armoric knights;
> And all who since, baptized or infidel,
> Jousted in Aspramont or Montalban,
> Damasco or Marocco or Trebisond,
> Or whom Biserta sent from Afric shore
> When Charlemain with all his peerage fell
> By Fontarabbia;

the seventeen lines in Book iv, 268–85, one of the best known
and most magnificent passages in the whole poem:

> Not that fair field
> Of Enna, where Proserpin gathering flowers
> Herself a fairer flower by gloomy Dis
> Was gathered, which cost Ceres all that pain
> To seek her through the world; nor that sweet grove
> Of Daphne, by Orontes and the inspired
> Castalian spring, might with this Paradise
> Of Eden strive; nor that Nyseian isle
> Girt with the river Triton, where old Cham,
> Whom Gentiles Ammon call and Libyan Jove,
> Hid Amalthea, and her florid son
> Young Bacchus, from his stepdame Rhea's eye;
> Nor where Abassin kings their issue guard,
> Mount Amara, though this by some supposed
> True Paradise, under the Ethiop line
> By Nilus' head, enclos'd with shining rock
> A whole day's journey high, but wide remote
> From this Assyrian garden;

all these, with many others, are violently and contumeliously
struck out. They were romantic; and for Bentley, that was
enough. In the first three Books alone, 147 lines fall to his
hook—"the pruning knife—zounds!—the axe!"—and of
these the greater number are not only exquisitely beautiful
but characteristically Miltonic.

This insensitiveness to the romantic temperament, this
attitude of dislike or contempt for romance, was the weak
side of the classicist period in English literature: it was the price
that had to be paid, and a heavy one, for reaching the object
which that whole movement had in view, the complete
civilization of a national literature which till then had been
insular, had been undisciplined, and had not fully established
itself as part of the great body of European culture. During
the seventeenth century, English poetry had become chaotic;
it had to be reduced to order, disciplined, retrieved from
byways and extravagances. But in this effort both its own
continuity and the historical forces which had moulded its
development were obscured and neglected. In particular,

touch was lost with the great body of Italian poetry which
had not only interpreted and conveyed the recovered classics
to England, but had been a direct inspiration of the first
importance. Milton drew as much from the Italian as from
the Greek and Roman poets. "My younger feet," he tells
us, "wandered among those lofty fables and romances which
recount in solemn cantos the deeds of knighthood." He had
read and assimilated the great mass of Italian poetry from
Dante down to his own contemporaries. He knew the *Divina
Commedia*, with an intimacy of knowledge rare then; for
already Dante had fallen into his long eclipse; from it as much
as from any other source external to himself he drew the
rhetorical evolution of his thought, the loftiness of his style,
his management of diction and phrasing. He had saturated
himself with Boiardo and Ariosto; to the *Orlando Furioso* the
debt of *Paradise Lost* is even greater than to the more obvious
sources of Tasso's *Gerusalemme Liberata* and *Sette Giornate*.
The exploration of these sources belongs to a later period. It
was hardly opened in the middle of the eighteenth century
by Newton; it was carried out fully towards its end by Todd
(who, it is interesting to observe, was like Bentley one of the
King's chaplains, and was Librarian at Lambeth as Bentley
had been Keeper of the Royal Libraries from 1693 until his
death).

Now with Italian poetry Bentley had only a superficial
acquaintance; even his knowledge of the Italian language was
evidently slight. His notes on the *Paradise Lost* make this quite
clear. He does indeed remark on iv, 506 that Milton's
"imparadised" is the Italian *imparadisato*. But he did not know
so common a word as *adorno*: "What's *adorne*?" is his note on
viii, 576, "but that may be a misprint for *adorn'd*." "'Tis an
Italianism. *Adorno* for *adornato*" is Richardson's terse and
sufficient note. And similarly in i, 543 he alters *reign* to *realm*,
neglecting, from ignorance, as his note clearly shows, not only
the older English sense of the word, still preserved in the
French *règne*, but the regular Italian meaning of *regno*. He does
cite Ariosto once, the well-known *cosa non detta in prosa mai nè
in rima*. This citation, even if not made at second hand,
would only prove that he had read the first ten lines of the

Orlando. But it should be observed, in connection with his celebrated alteration of "sounding alchemy" into "sounding orichalc" in ii, 517, that *oricalchi* are repeatedly named in the *Orlando Furioso* as instruments of music employed first for this purpose. In the tournament at Damascus in canto xvii, the combatants are let loose, and the victor proclaimed, *al suon de gli oricalchi.* Todd's note, "Alchemy here means any mixed metal," and Masson's, "i.e., trumpet: this use of alchymy for any metal being not uncommon in poets," while they are correct so far as they go, miss this point.

So with Dante: Bentley's attack on the passage in *Paradise Lost* about the spots on the moon (v, 419–20) shows that he did not know canto ii of the *Paradiso,* just as his violent alteration of "falsities and lies" in i, 367 shows the same ignorance of Virgil's *dei falsi e bugiardi* in the first canto of the *Inferno.*

This point is worth noting; for the moral to be drawn from it is that the scholarly study of English poetry in the sixteenth and seventeenth centuries (and indeed beyond that period both before and after), is crippled without collateral study of Italian poetry. The revival of Italian studies in our Universities at the present day is to be welcomed and encouraged not only for their own sake, but as a powerful and necessary reinforcement to the scholarly study of our own literature.

But English studies themselves were, in Bentley's time and for long afterwards, not organized, and only pursued imperfectly and sporadically. Perhaps it was only after the apparatus and methods of such study had been wrought out by generations of work on the Greek and Latin classics that its application to our own language and literature became possible. Even now, the interconnexion of classical and English studies is of vital importance for both. When Bentley set about reforming the text of the *Paradise Lost,* his recklessness came largely from sheer ignorance. Such ignorance was then explicable and in a sense excusable; it would not be excusable now, and the danger-signals set up by his treatment of the text may therefore be of less importance: yet even now they are not without value.

His knowledge of Milton's English predecessors was but slight. In his notes he cites Chaucer occasionally (*Troilus and*

Creseide, and the *Legend of Good Women*) and Spenser frequently; here it may be remarked that he shows familiarity not only with the *Faerie Queene*, but with the minor poems also; the *Epithalamium*, the *Hymns to Earthly* and *Heavenly Beauty*, *Mother Hubbard's Tale*, *Muiopotmos*. But when to Chaucer and Spenser are added Sidney's *Arcadia* and Fairfax's *Tasso*, the list is almost, if not quite, exhausted. There is no indication of his having even known Sylvester's *Du Bartas*; or of his having given any study to those post-Elizabethan poets among whose output, and subject to whose pervasive influence, Milton grew up.

Further, he in common with nearly all his contemporaries had not mastered, had not even studied, the vocabulary, accidence, and syntax of the English language. The means for doing so were still lacking. In all these matters he attempts to regularize or modernize Milton's usage. Wherever he finds the pronoun *his* referring to a neuter noun he alters it to *its*. He thinks the so-called *nominativus pendens* is an ablative absolute as in Latin (it is fair to add that Milton himself sometimes copies the Latin idiom) and actually alters the text accordingly; altering "thou looking on" to "thee looking on" (ix, 312) and "he descending" to "him descending" (xii, 228). When he comes on a strange word, he generally tries to eject it. "I do not remember," runs his note on vi, 93, "ever to have met with the word *hosting* either in verse or prose," and he accordingly—a most ingenious suggestion and one which might still be argued—alters it to *jousting*. Even now, the *New English Dictionary* does not cite any other instance of the world *hosting* in English poetry, though it occurs both in Elizabethan and in post-Elizabethan prose. By a more unaccountable lapse, he notes on the "faith and realty" of vi, 115, "our Author would not have said *realty* but *reality*," and alters it to *fealty*. This use of *realty* (realitas) survives as a technical legal word; but throughout the seventeenth century its wider meaning, "reality" or "sincerity" was quite common. In ix, 353 he quite wantonly changes "bid her well beware" into "bid her well be aware."

Equally defective—and this is a more serious matter—is his grasp of English metrical structure. Partly this came of ignorance, partly of wrong-headedness. The former is not creditable, but is pardonable; indeed it was not until Mr. Bridges took it in hand that Milton's prosody was analysed and the rules of its practice clearly laid down. What is inexcusable is the absence of perception with which Bentley approaches the matter; and more inexcusable still in a professional scholar is the carelessness with which he handles it and his frequent inaccuracy on matters of fact. One instance of this carelessness, if it should not be called by an even severer name, may serve; it is typical.

In the syllabization of names like Michael and Raphael, Milton makes them disyllabic or trisyllabic as suits him, and as accords with the cadence of the verse in which they occur. On mere theory divorced from observation of the facts, Bentley creates a law that they are disyllabic only, then asserts that this law must have been obeyed by Milton, and then proceeds to alter the text accordingly wherever it does not fit into his doctrine. In his rash haste he has left the traces of his procedure quite apparent. When the trisyllabic use first occurs (ii, 294) his note is "Our Author generally pronounces *Michael: Raphael*, &c., with Two Syllables. How comes it then here with Three?" When he has got on to Book vi (l. 202) he comments more curtly, "*Michael* makes but two Syllables." And when he reaches the end of the poem, having by that time (as he trusts) destroyed the evidence to the contrary, he comes forward with his alleged law and his supposititious editor: "Our Author always gives *Michael*, *Raphael*, &c., in two Syllables" (xi. 466); "the Editor here gives *Michael* three Syllables, which the Author had here and elsewhere pronounc'd with two only" (xi, 552). For those who are familiar with modern Homeric criticism it is needless to say that this way of tampering with the evidence is not an obsolete vice, or that it is still often applied to matters of substance as well as of form. It is the more dangerous in its effects because those who practise it seldom give themselves away with the transparency which was the redeeming offset against Bentley's arrogance. This comes out perpetually in his metrical emendations. Of the principles of English metre so far as they differ (and they differ fundamentally) from those of Greek and Latin metre, he is almost wholly ignorant. Inverted feet (as he probably would have called them, and the term may be used for convenience without claiming for it any accuracy) he is perpetually attempting to get rid of: yet even here he flounders among inconsistencies. One striking instance is the way in which he deals with the beautiful line (vi, 906),

As a despite done against the Most High.

Three of the five "feet" in this line do not conform to his canon. He leaves two of them alone, and regularizes the third by writing "God Most High."

The same careless precipitance comes out where study ought to have been given, and was not, to the changes in stress-accent which historically took place in many English words. When he finds "the supreme King" in i, 735, he makes the note, "He must have given it *the King supreme* as he does everywhere else." Less than 300 lines further on (ii, 210) he comes on "our supreme foe." Any other human being, one would suppose, would have turned back at this and altered or struck out his previous note. Bentley does not. He leaves it as it stood; and notes here, with a change of tone that would be laughable if it were not a little painful, "Better accent, *our foe supréme.*"

Finally we must notice what in a professional scholar was as inexcusable then as it would be now, his slipshod inaccuracy in collation. At the first place where the 1674 second edition of the *Paradise Lost* varies in text from the first, he pours contempt on the altered wording, and goes on to say, "The Editor has made three or four more Changes from the first Impression, and every one for the worse." Thenceforward he seems to have got it into his head, as an ascertained and unassailable fact, that there were but three more. Where each of these occurs (v, 639; xi, 485; xi, 551) he in substance repeats this assertion, and finally in his preface speaks once more of "these four and sole Changes made in the second Edition." Whether these changes, or any one of them, be what Bentley calls them, "manifestly for the worse," is a matter on which he, or any one, may have his own opinion. But the changes of text in the second edition are not four; they are thirty-three.

So far we have been dealing with the danger-signals which Bentley's *Milton* holds up for the warning of commentators or critics; they show, and it is well that it should be shown, of what a great scholar may be capable. But Bentley's critical work has more than this dubious negative value; it has a value which is real and positive. He applied to the *Paradise Lost*, for the first time that this had been done with any English poem, the standards of scientific scholarship and of classical quality, testing it by these standards line by line and word by word. It is this which makes his mistakes and even his absurdities instructive. The rigorous application of scientific tests was his aim. Merely to fix this as an aim, and to transmit it as such to posterity, meant the vindication of English studies as a branch of the higher scholarship; and Bentley may be called in some sense the founder of these studies, which are now so large and so fertile a field.

To pursue this into detail by examination of his methods and results would be to travel beyond the limits of one lecture, or indeed of several. But it may be possible, in a very brief and rather tentative summary, to class Bentley's emendations, or what he put forward as such, under five heads. The classification will not be wholly uninstructive.

1. Two, and two only, have been expressly accepted by most subsequent editors, and have found their way into the received text. They will be found by those who are curious in vii, 321 and 451. It may be remarked here, that in each case they represent alteration only of a letter or two in a single word; and that it is just in this sort of case that the genius of a textual critic shows itself most conspicuously. In each case they may be legitimately considered as misprints which had escaped notice both in the original proof-correcting and in the revision for the second edition. Bentley may indeed have the credit for two others, in xi, 344 and 583. Here he restored the true text. But the credit for his acuteness has to be set against it the discredit of his carelessness; for in both passages the first edition gives the correct reading.

2. Several others, not fewer I think than five, and probably not more than ten or a dozen, though they have not been formally accepted, are convincing and all but certain. These five, like the others just mentioned, are alterations in a single word. I will mention them. Three are: ii, 90, *vessels of his anger* for *vassals of his anger*; ii, 256, *lazie yoke* for *easie yoke*; and xi, 694, *glory won or triumph* for *glory done of triumph*. Stillingfleet's desperate attempt to defend *glory done* by making it equivalent in meaning to *glorious deeds done* is far from convincing, and even if it were, *deeds of triumph* hardly makes sense. The two others are more interesting, because they raise questions of general principle.

The text of vi, 578–81 reads:

> At each behind
> A seraph stood, and in his hand a reed
> Stood waving tipt with fire, while we suspense
> Collected stood.

Bentley alters the second *stood* to *held*. Here, as in similar instances of repetition of a word, he hardly pays sufficient attention to Milton's habitual usage in this respect, which is so marked that it is almost a feature of his diction (as, in a less degree, it was of Virgil's). Many of these repetitions or echoes Bentley alters very rashly. But here the threefold repetition is almost intolerable.

The text of x, 328–9 reads:

> Betwixt the Centaur and the Scorpion steering
> His zenith, while the sun in Aries rose.

This is astronomically incorrect. The angle of right ascension from Aries to Sagittarius is more than 90°, and to a point between Sagittarius and Scorpio more still.[1] Bentley, without giving his reason, but no doubt that was his reason, alters *rose* to *rode*. It is a beautiful emendation. Yet it must be borne in mind that Milton's astronomy, while amazingly accurate, is not wholly impeccable. An actual blunder which he makes

[1] It should be borne in mind that the description here relates to a time when, according to Milton's theory, the Zodiac lay along the celestial equator, the obliquity of the ecliptic being brought about by special angelic action after the Fall.

elsewhere strangely enough eluded Bentley's notice. It is in one of the most famous and most splendid passages in the whole poem, ii, 706–11:

> On the other side
> Incens'd with indignation Satan stood
> Unterrified, and like a comet burn'd
> That fires the length of Ophiuchus huge
> In the Arctic sky, and from his horrid hair
> Shakes pestilence and war.

Ophiuchus is huge; but it is not in the arctic sky. It stretches along close by the celestial equator. There can be little if any doubt that Milton for the moment confused the two constellations of *Anguitenens* and *Anguis,* the Serpent-bearer and the Serpent, and that this is simply one of his very rare mistakes. The well-known "Hermione and Cadmus" (instead of Harmonia and Cadmus) in ix, 506 is not a mistake of Milton's, but of the authorities on whom he in common with his contemporaries relied. Professor D. A. Slater has pointed out to me what was, with practical certainty, the immediate source of Milton's *Hermione.* It was one of the editions of Ovid's Metamorphoses then current containing the *Narrationes* or arguments of each book attributed to Lactantius Placidus. Most of these editions until Muncker's of 1681 printed the name as *Hermione* following the erroneous reading of the Florence MS. Marcianus 225; and even in later editions the false reading occasionally survived. In the text of Ovid himself, it may be added, the name does not occur. A tragedy, *Cadmus et Hermione,* "représentée pour la première fois en 1674 devant le Roy," held its place on the French stage for more than half a century, and was printed in 1737. The error did not, and could not, escape Bentley's notice; but with his normal impatience, he takes the opportunity to eject the whole passage of six lines in which it occurs as an interpolation by the "smatterer," his imaginary editor.

3. Many more are plausible in varying degree, and sometimes both acute and suggestive. These cannot, except in a minute detailed study, be cited and arranged in order of their attractiveness or probability. But this study deserves and repays the attention of students who propose to become textual critics

or to appreciate the science of textual criticism. Each student must do this for himself, so far as he finds it profitable to do it.

4. Another type, also useful for study, is that of Bentley's false emendations due to his (a) following or adopting a misleading punctuation; or (b) failing to trace Milton's intricate syntax and the elaboration of his periodic structure; or (c) misunderstanding Milton's use of certain words.

Punctuation is a rough-and-ready notation for indicating phrasing. A delicate ear is needed both for punctuating and for interpreting punctuation. It was this that Bentley lacked. Sometimes he was misled (of course he ought not to have been) by the punctuation of the printed text before him. A good instance is the line (viii, 264):

> Creatures that lived and moved and walked or flew.

Bentley found a semicolon after *lived* in the copy of the *Paradise Lost* on which he was working: and so, with the observation that "Moving is common both to walking and flying," he arbitrarily alters the latter part of the line into "crept or walked or flew." But in the first edition the line is properly punctuated,

> Creatures that lived, and mov'd, and walk'd, or flew,

and no difficulty arises.[1]

Closely connected with this (for very careful punctuation is required to bring it out clearly) is the complexity of Milton's syntactic and periodic structure: and more particularly, the elaborate parentheses in the use of which he followed in some measure the example of Virgil, and largely also the usage of his own immediate English predecessors, very notably of Massinger. One passage may be cited in illustration (iii, 344–9):

> No sooner had the Almighty ceas'd but all
> The multitude of angels with a shout
> Loud as from numbers without number, sweet
> As from blest voices uttering joy, Heaven rung
> With jubilee and loud hosannas fill'd
> The eternal regions.

[1] Other instances of the same kind will be found in 1, 191; ii, 1039; iii, 498, 719; ix, 1063.

"Here's a sentence without a verb," Bentley joyously cries; and he alters *with a shout* to *gave a shout*. If he had only thought a little more (or perhaps rather, felt a little more) he would have realized that the words from *all the multitude* down to *uttering joy* are one of Milton's long magnificent parentheses, and that the syntax is faultless. But the amplitude of Milton's phrasing was (which is strange) beyond the critic's grasp.[1]

The personal equation in the usage of, and force attached to, particular words by a poet is a factor of obvious importance towards appreciation of his meaning; and when we are dealing with one of the great masters cannot be studied too carefully. Here, too, Bentley's precipitance is very marked. As an instance may be cited the passage (ix, 64–6):

> Thrice the equinoctial line
> He circled, four times cross'd the car of night
> From pole to pole traversing each colure.

Taking it for granted that *traverse* must mean, and that it meant to Milton, *move across*, Bentley says quite truly, "He could not traverse the Four Colures by going from Pole to Pole; that's done by circling the Aequinoctial." And accordingly he rewrites the whole passage (incidentally making the brilliant and all but convincing emendation of *cone* for *car*) thus:

> Four times cross'd the cone of night
> From pole to pole, thrice the equinoctial line
> Circled entire, traversing each colure.

If he had held his hand until he had read down a little further he would have found in the same Book (l, 434):

> Nearer he drew, and many a walk travers'd
> Of stateliest covert.

In Milton's usage, that is to say, *traverse* does not mean *move across*, but *move along*.

5. On the last type of Bentleian emendations, and the worst, it is needless to enlarge. Some of the more glaring instances are matters of common knowledge; and others may be found

---

[1] For similar instances see viii, 500–7; xi, 495–9; xi, 802 f., and Bentley's note on 807.

by the hundred if any one chooses to look for them. These are alterations in the text made from want of taste and want of poetical instinct.

Bentley's intelligence was acute, but his mind was essentially prosaic. In textual matters, he had wonderful powers of divination, but he was without the imaginative touch, and without the thrill which responds to it where it gives life to poetry. Imagination is no doubt a dangerous weapon; "we must temper it with judgment" as Keats, in the vein of the hermit of Prague, justly observes. But in dealing with works of art, there is a very narrow space between common sense and obtuseness, as there is between imagination and nonsense. The greatest works of art bear every test alike.

Appreciation of Milton, in the often quoted saying of Mark Pattison's, is the last reward of a consummated scholarship. It was certainly a reward to which Bentley never attained. Yet from study of Bentley we may, as I have endeavoured to point out, enlarge our own appreciation of Milton. For that study will aid us to form a trained judgment in the art, or science, or practice of criticism, and to see more clearly how hard the task is, and how it calls for the exercise of all our faculties at their highest pitch. In all great works of art, in those which seem simplest as in those which are most patently complex, there is deep beyond deep. Bentley fell short or went wide of the mark because, in the last resort, with all his great powers, he was beyond his depth. The science of Milton's art, alike in structural quality and in the handling of language and metre, was more delicate and more profound than that which Bentley brought to bear on its criticism. And this is a lesson which applies to the study of poets other than Milton, and to the treatment of them by scholars inferior to Bentley.

P

ALLAN RAMSAY AND THE ROMANTIC REVIVAL

[1924]

L ET me begin with a reminiscence.

Sixty years ago, Edinburgh was still a city of enchantment. The expansion into a vast overgrowth of suburbs, with the consequent loss in vividness of life and concentration of impression, had then only begun. The romance of the Scottish capital was still massed within well-marked limits; and among its lesser romantic features which, together with the greater, kindled the active imagination of childhood, was Allan Ramsay's house on the Castle Hill.

It had no beauty beyond that of its superb situation. "My Bower on the Castle Bank," Ramsay's own fond description, was a title belonging to the dawning era of "sensibility." The name of the Goose Pie, by which it had been familiarly, and in some measure affectionately, known for more than a century, suited it better. "Now I see you in it, Allan, I think the name very proper," is said to have been the comment made on it in early days by Lord Elibank. Yet it did not misbecome its surroundings, splendid as these were; for they dominated it and gave it character. It had insensibly become a national monument, a note in national history.

West Princes Street Gardens were then the jealously guarded preserve of a few favoured householders. The thin railway line sunk in the valley was hardly noticeable. The steep, sparsely grassed hillside flung from the towering basalt cliffs, and the shrubbed slopes below it, might still be fancied a primitive solitude. The grey house keeping vigil on the hill-brow, in sunlight and starlight or swathed in the sea fog, seemed a symbol that carried the mind back, not only to the times of the Porteous Riots and the Forty-five, but beyond them into medieval Scotland.

Steel's statue of Ramsay, down in the Gardens, has nothing

romantic about it. It is the presentment of the sleek little tradesman of the Luckenbooths, burgess and *bon vivant*, and the presentment is true to life. But it is incomplete. Here, as often elsewhere, a man stands in the history of his country and of his art not merely for what he obviously was and consciously did, but also for what he in effect, and perhaps unconsciously, originated; for the turn he gave, recognizable only in the backward perspective of distance, to the movement of a whole age. Portrait and biography have to be supplemented by a larger and more searching interpretation.

Thus with Allan Ramsay; his importance in letters is less in respect of his own poetry, vital and even excellent as some of it is, than as having given the first clearly assignable impulse to the romantic movement of the eighteenth century. That movement is generally thought of as having begun much later. Its effective development is dated from the publication of Macpherson's *Ossian* in 1762, and of Percy's *Reliques* in 1765. But these, important and decisive as their influence was, appeared when the soil was already prepared and the new growth was well started. Quite twenty years earlier, the re-emergence of romanticism is clearly marked in the two Wartons. No less remarkably, though more confusedly, does it appear at about the same date in the *Castle of Indolence*. That was the work of a Scotsman, though one denizened in England and hardly counting as a Scottish poet. But for its first beginnings we have to go earlier still, and to go to the northern kingdom. We shall find them (so surprising and unexpected are the ways of the Muses) in the little Edinburgh wig-maker; and not so much in his idylls and lyrics, or in the pastoral drama by which his name is chiefly known, as in *The Evergreen*, that collection of older Scottish poetry which holds in germ, forty years before the *Reliques*, the rediscovery of romance and the recapture for poetry of the submerged or dormant lyrical instinct.

Ramsay's original poetry is not negligible. It had a wide fame even beyond his native country; and it retained for a full century a hold not merely on the partial judgment of Scottish critics but on the heart of the Scottish people. It is true that much of it is not original, and a good deal of it is not poetry. *The Gentle Shepherd* itself is an amorphous structure. The absurdities which are so easy to find in it are perhaps no greater, though they are more patent, than those of the *Aminta*. The point to be emphasized is that they arise in the course of a real attempt to rescue the pastoral convention from classicism and re-connect it with life. This was what had been the unique triumph of Theocritus; but with the instinctive Greek tact, Theocritus kept within the manageable field of the detached idyll. The idyllic drama of Guarini and Tasso was only made possible by narrowing the convention. *The Gentle Shepherd*—and the courage, even the daring, of the attempt is remarkable—aimed at widening it. Success was not attained, and was not attainable; the return to nature had to be made through other channels.

Praise may be given, with little or no qualification, to several of the distinct and still separable idylls which were pieced together as scenes in one idyllic drama. This holds good for the originating idyll of *Patie and Roger*, with its beautiful opening lyric of *My Peggy is a Young Thing*, which now stands as Act I, scene i, of *The Gentle Shepherd*; it had in fact been printed as a separate piece years before. It holds good even more fully of the two idylls of *Peggy and Jenny* (now Act I, scene ii) and of *Roger and Jenny* (now Act III, scene iii). It is in the former of these that the beautiful lines come,

> Gae farer up the burn to Habbie's How
> Where a' that's sweet in spring and summer grow;
> Between twa birks out ower a little lin
> The water fa's and makes a singan din;
> A pool breast-deep beneath, as clear as glass,
> Kisses wi' lazy whirls the borderin grass:

which give perfect expression to the native quality of the North, the "delicate spare soil," the "slender and austere landscape" where "through the thin trees the skies appear." Nor would it be easy to overpraise several of the interposed songs, of which there are more than twenty in the whole piece. The one, for instance, beginning:

> O dear Peggy, love's beguiling,
> We ought not to trust his smiling;
> Better far to do as I do
> Lest a harder luck betide you:

or the other beginning:

> Hid from himself, now by the dawn
> He starts as fresh as roses blawn,
> And ranges o'er the heights and lawn
> After his bleating flocks:

or one which may be given in full:

> Jock said to Jenny, "Jenny wilt thou do't?"
> "Ne'er a fit," quoth Jenny, "for my tocher-good;
> For my tocher-good I winna marry thee."
> "E'ens ye like," quoth Jocky; "ye may let it be.
>
> "I hae gowd and gear; I hae land eneugh;
> I hae seven good owsen ganging in a pleugh,
> Ganging in a pleugh and linkan o'er the lea;
> And gin ye winna tak me, I can let ye be.
>
> "I hae a good ha' house, a barn and a byre,
> A peatstack fore the door, will mak a rantin fire.
> I'll mak a rantin fire, and merry sall we be;
> And gin ye winna tak me, I can let ye be."
>
> Jenny said to Jocky, "Gin ye winna tell,
> Ye sall be the lad, I'll be the lass mysell.
> Ye're a bonny lad, and I'm a lassie free;
> Ye're welcomer to tak me than to let me be."

But the group of idyllic sketches lose a good deal of their effectiveness by embodiment in the cumbrous framework of a regular drama constructed according to rule, "the time of action within twenty-four hours," and with a conventional plot. The historical or quasi-historical setting for the action in this queer stageland Arcadia is preposterous. To a generation for whom the Killing Time was well within living memory, the representing of the Restoration as inaugurating an era of peace and happiness could only, one would think, be an unconvincing and repellent fiction. Sir William Worthy is a figure whose only possible place is in the naked and shameless innocence of melodrama. But even in that atmosphere he is not much of a success. It is curious that the name "Sir

William" is, throughout the fiction of the eighteenth century, whether in prose or verse, a danger-signal to the reader. Sir William Thornhill in *The Vicar of Wakefield*, Sir William Honeywood in *The Good-Natured Man*, are no less than Ramsay's Sir William, in the apt phrase of Sir Robert Ayton's, "fond impossibilities." But more largely, it was the weakness of Ramsay's "return to nature" that it sought expression here in the vehicle of the *favola boschereccia* which had gone hopelessly out of date. Just so, in his production on the wedding of the Duke of Hamilton, he had attempted with even scantier success to revive the Elizabethan Masque which had expired in a blaze of splendour with Milton's *Comus*.

But the artistic defects of *The Gentle Shepherd*, no less than its real excellences, just hit popular taste. It made him a popular poet in the most genuine sense of the term. The assertion made in 1800, that "there is not a milkmaid, a plough-boy, or a shepherd of the lowlands of Scotland, who has not by heart its favourite passages and can [*sic*] rehearse its entire scenes," was no doubt a flight of rhetoric; but it was the exaggeration of a substantial truth. Sir Archibald Geikie, when making a geological survey of the Pentland range in 1856, "was much interested to find that the custom still prevailed among the peasant population of acting Allan Ramsay's pastoral play of *The Gentle Shepherd* in the midst of the very scenery which had inspired the poet. The Scottish language of the dialogue was given by the rustic actors with full Doric breadth, and even sometimes with creditable dramatic power. That the poem which was published in 1725 should survive in the affections of the peasantry is strong evidence of the force and fidelity of its picture of Scottish rural life. Its survival in this form has probably kept much of the old Scots tongue still in use throughout the district."[1] But when a later editor wrote, as recently as 1877, that "to this day it is as much read and as often quoted by many of the peasantry as any of the poems of Burns," the exaggeration is excessive. For the Lothians it may have had a grain of truth; *The Gentle Shepherd* no doubt remained alive longest among its native Pentlands, though the occasional performances of recent

[1] Sir A. Geikie, *A Long Life's Work*, p. 55.

years have only been artificial antiquarian revivals. But as regards Ayrshire, which that editor specifically mentions, it cannot be accepted. Allan Ramsay's name was a lingering household word there, but that was about all.

It is, however, with full truth that the same editor claims for Ramsay that he "was the pioneer of a new era, and gave an impulse to the study and cultivation of the poetic art." He was a germinal force. His own lyrical gift, though genuine, was slender. His dramatic sense, notwithstanding that devotion to the theatre which got him into so much trouble with the Edinburgh Town Council and very nearly ruined him financially, was weak. When he "gets to his English," he is only a minor and provincial Augustan. Only in his admirable *Fables and Tales* can he take rank beside those Southern contemporaries of whom he writes, that

> Swift, Sandy, Young, and Gay
> Are still my heart's delight.

With Swift he had little or nothing in common. With Gay, that thin but sweet voice of poetry (himself too connected with Scotland through the fostering friendship of the Queensberrys), he had much. There is a certain kinship between *The Gentle Shepherd* and *The Beggar's Opera*; and Gay and Ramsay are the two best British fabulists. Their debt to La Fontaine and La Motte is of course, in both, patent and confessed, but their own skill of handling was much alike and was very great. Gay's own *Shepherd's Week* (1714), though primarily a burlesque, touches here and there, in virtue of his delicate and never fully disengaged poetical instinct, the authentic Theocritean note. "Though only half intending it," a fine critic says in words which, though with some hesitation, may be accepted, "he produced a genuine work of pastoral art, the nearest approach to a realistic pastoral which our literature had yet seen."[1] But he lacked the intention; his touch on those strings was light and transitory.

It was presumably through Gay, whose acquaintance he made in Edinburgh, that Ramsay came to the knowledge of

[1] Chambers, *English Pastorals*, p. xlvii.

the other members of the group. It should be borne in mind that it was the Young of the *Satires*, not the later and more famous Young of the *Night Thoughts*, in whom he delighted. And Sandy likewise—one cannot help wondering how Pope liked being called Sandy—is the Pope of the *Pastorals* and *Windsor Forest*, not the Pope of the *Essay on Man* and *The Dunciad*. It brings the whole eighteenth century into closer perspective to remember that the Countess of Eglinton, to whom, then in the prime of her age and beauty, *The Gentle Shepherd* was dedicated, lived on to receive the homage of Dr. Johnson during his tour in Scotland half a century later.

But Pope's known and recorded admiration of *The Gentle Shepherd* shows how "the return to nature" was a real motive, a sincere aim, even at the time and among the circle in which poetry was most artificial, and most heavily fettered by a classicist tradition. And to many readers Ramsay's *Evergreen* must have come, when it appeared in 1724, as something like a new revelation. His texts are deplorable; the liberties he took with his originals are monstrous; and he had little flair for distinguishing genuine antiquity from recent or contemporary forgery. Yet, in the words of his Preface, "the groves rise in our own valleys, the rivers flow from our own fountains, and the winds blow upon our own hills." With all its defects, a collection which begins with *Christ's Kirk on the Green* and ends with *Hardyknute*, and thus traverses the whole field of Scottish poetry for nearly three centuries, is memorable as having reopened the springs of poetry. Though the released stream ran turbid, it had not lost its quickening and refreshing power. And as it ran on, it cleared itself, as streams do, in the open air.

It was in the generation after Ramsay's that Edinburgh first put forward the boast of being the modern Athens, and that Scottish writers took a leading place in British letters. But the most famous of these were writers of prose; historians, essayists, or philosophers. Among Edinburgh poets, Allan Ramsay may still claim the foremost place but one; and indeed, if we set Scott apart as belonging less to Edinburgh than to Scotland, and less to Scotland than to the world, he might claim the foremost; for Fergusson's fame rests more on he generous and over-generous praise of Burns than on his own substantive merits. Ramsay when still a young man was made poet-laureate of the Easy Club. He became in effect for the rest of his life poet-laureate of the city. He received no public honours; in the eyes of authority he was only one of "the playhouse comedians who debauch all the faculties of our rising generation"; but he had a secure place in popular affection, and his wreath still remains green. His house has for many years been merged in a students' hostel; a better use, one may judge, than to be preserved like Abbotsford as a show-place filled with ghostly memories. Something of his gay spirit, of his love for nature and for books, of his devotion to the national poetry of his country, may still linger there to inspire new generations of students.

HURDIS AND THE POETRY OF THE TRANSITION

TO most modern readers, other than professional students
of English poetry, Hurdis is unknown even as a name.
In his own day, he had popularity and a certain degree of
fame. But the flame of poetry burned faintly in him, and he
left little or nothing in his work which can raise a claim to
immortality. It is still worth while, however, to study him as
typical of the age of transition. The work of poets of the second
or even the third rank, it has often been noted, is an index to
the prevalent taste or fashion of their time; and in this respect
Hurdis claims attention. His period of production was the
last decade of the eighteenth century. He belongs to the school
of Cowper; and the recent rediscovery of Cowper by the
younger generation makes it appropriate to trace Cowper's
own influence as it extended into and even beyond the age of
the full romantic revival.

It does not appear that Hurdis' poems were ever reprinted
after the collected edition of 1808. By that time, Scott and
Byron had taken possession of the field; the two volumes of
Poems by William Wordsworth, Author of the Lyrical Ballads
had appeared in the previous year; Crabbe and Southey were
at their zenith. It was not until 1835 that Southey brought out
his complete edition of Cowper; to meet a demand which
was still as wide as ever among an important section of the
nation, though Keats, Shelley, Byron, Scott and Coleridge
had meanwhile, in both senses of the term, put off mortality.

In Anthologies however, Hurdis long retained something
of a footing. There are a number of extracts from his work
in the *Beauties of British Poetry*, a collection which, first issued
in 1801, passed through a large number of editions in the early
years of the nineteenth century, and which also includes three
pieces by Coleridge, and one by Wordsworth. So late as

1857, one piece of his, an extract on Rural Sounds from the poem of *The Favourite Village*, was included in Willmott's *Poems of the Nineteenth Century*, a volume which had also a large popularity and was repeatedly republished. It is placed there between Hayley and Charlotte Smith, contemporary names which retain some faint reputation. After that his name seems to disappear: he is not represented in the *Oxford Book of English Poetry*, nor, so far as I am aware, with one exception which I shall mention, in any of the numerous modern anthologies. His memory chiefly lingers in Cowper's letters. Those—about a dozen in all—which Cowper wrote to him in 1791–3 were preserved and placed in Southey's hands for the collected edition of Cowper's Life and Works. Hurdis' own letters to Cowper were returned to his family after Cowper's death; they, or some of them, were afterwards printed in the *Sussex County Magazine*; and they were recently republished in an inconspicuous little volume printed at Eastbourne in 1927. The whole collection, giving both sides of the correspondence, is pleasant and interesting reading. It was broken off abruptly by Cowper's mental collapse in 1794, which lasted until his death six years later.

A short sketch of Hurdis' uneventful life may here be given as a framework or background for some account of his writings. Their value is less from their own quality than as an index to the taste and fashion of his age, and to the place which the school of Cowper, as it may be called, holds in the evolution of English poetry. They have also a further interest in relation to what may be called the Sussex tradition. That county, largely cut off until modern times from the main body of southern England, had, as to some extent it even now retains, a distinct provincialism both racial and cultural. There may be traced in the work of Sussex poets, from Otway and Collins downwards, a marked affinity in a certain quality of *morbidezza* both in the technical and in the etymological sense of the word; the *mollities*, the delicacy and tendency to pass into pulpiness or lack of fibre, of the classical terminology. It reappeared two generations later in the poetry of that fine scholar and sensitive critic W. J. Courthope, who like Hurdis held the Chair of Poetry at Oxford, and whose own poems *The*

County Town and *The Hop Garden* draw from the same sourc
as Hurdis' *The Village Curate* and *The Favourite Village*, an
show a striking continuity of spirit and tradition. Both o
the two were born and died in East Sussex and to each of then
Sussex was, in the fullest sense, both mother and nurse.

James Hurdis was born in 1763 (four years after the deatl
of Collins) at the tiny hamlet of Bishopstone near Seaford. I
consists now, as it did then, of the church with its exquisit
Norman tower and some half-dozen houses, hidden in a cu
of the downs where they sink into the flats of the Ouse valley
Of his father, the squire of the place and belonging to an ol
Sussex family, little or nothing seems to be known; he die
when Hurdis was a child; and the boy was sent to school a
Chichester, where his uncle, Thomas Hurdis, was a residentiar
canon. In the diary of Thomas Turner of East Hockley there i
an entry under date of 22nd April, 1759, "we had a sermo
preached by the Rev. Mr. Thomas Hurdis, and in my opinio
he is as fine a churchman as almost I ever heard."

From Chichester he proceeded to Oxford, first as
commoner of St. Mary Hall and subsequently as a Demy o
Magdalen. Neither his delicacy of health nor his addictio
to poetry and his passion for music appear to have at all stoo
in the way of his happiness in the College where Gibbon
generation earlier had found his surroundings so distasteful
The publication by Lord Sheffield in 1799 of Gibbon's auto
biography with its venomous attack on the University an
on his own College, in fact drew from Hurdis, who had the
become a Fellow, a pamphlet entitled *A Word or two i
vindication of the University of Oxford and of Magdalen College i
particular from the posthumous aspersions of Mr. Gibbon.* T
Routh, that remarkable figure who bridges the whole interva
between Hurdis and Courthope, he records himself as indebte
for much kindness and encouragement, given by him first as
Fellow and afterwards in the early portion of his sixty-thre
years' Presidency. Hurdis took orders in due course: for som
time he was private tutor at Stanmer, not far from Bishop
stone, to the Hon. George Pelham, who afterwards held thre
successive bishoprics, and was in the acid words of the *Dictionar
of National Biography* "notorious for his greed of lucrativ

office," and of whom his young tutor rather ambiguously wrote that "it cannot be long before he obtains what his good qualities cannot fail to adorn, a mitre." After this he accepted the curacy of Burwash, taking the parochial duties of the non-resident Rector.   At Burwash he remained for six or seven years (1785–92). In 1786 he was elected to a Fellowship at Magdalen, which he held till he vacated it by marriage in 1799. Burwash, or Burridge as it is locally pronounced, is widely known now as the residence for many years of Rudyard Kipling; and in *Puck of Pook's Hill* the descriptions of the neighbourhood and its South Saxon inhabitants form an interesting comparison and contrast to those of Hurdis in his first published poem, *The Village Curate.* . This appeared in 1788: it at once secured wide popular favour; a second edition was called for almost at once, and it was repeatedly republished thereafter, both separately and together with other poems written later. I shall have to return presently to some further considerations of it as regards both its substantive quality and its place in what may be called the Cowperian tradition.

He followed this up in 1790 by a more ambitious but less successful poem, *Adriano, or the First of June*, where descriptive poetry is set in a rather feeble narrative framework. The scene of action in it is not Burwash and the Rother Valley, but his own native Sussex coast between Newhaven and Beachy Head. To this he returned in 1792, having been presented to the living of Bishopstone the year before by the Bishop of Chichester, at the instance of Lord Chichester, the father of his former pupil George Pelham. His house there, still existing though enlarged and altered, now goes by the name of Little Hallands; it was in the early years of the present century the country home of a distinguished scholar, W. G. Rutherford the head master of Westminster, and is again, though in a different sense, the "mansion of repose and ease," the "nurse of letters" which is the character given it by Hurdis. He destined it for his permanent home, and the rest of his brief life was in fact passed between it and Oxford. I have mentioned the association of Burwash, a century later, with Kipling; and it is a curious little coincidence that Kipling himself had previously lived for a good many years at Rottingdean, only a few miles from Bishopstone on the other side of the Ouse Valley, and had there engrafted himself, as it were, on the Sussex country and the Sussex local life of which he became so able an interpreter.

Hurdis' literary ambitions grew with easier circumstances and with the success of his first publications. The historical play of *Sir Thomas More*, over which he spent much labour and a good deal of historical research, is not without merit, and may be read with interest, but has not the dramatic quality for successful stage production, for which indeed it does not seem to have been meant. It is however of interest to notice that it is practically contemporary with the early dramatic efforts of both Wordsworth and Coleridge. *The Borderers* was written in 1795-6, *Remorse* in 1797. *Remorse* was produced at the Theatre Royal, Drury Lane, in January 1813, not unsuccessfully; *The Borderers* was never staged, and was not published until 1842.

It was in connection with *Sir Thomas More* that Hurdis came into touch with his own poetical master. Through the printer Joseph Johnson, who prided himself, a little excessively, on his own poetical taste and critical ability, the MS. of Hurdis' tragedy was submitted to Cowper, who received it with his habitual courtesy, and offered detailed advice for its improvement. The first extant letter of the series which passed between them is from Hurdis at Burwash, 25th February, 1791, conveying his thanks to Cowper for his "ingenious remarks" on the tragedy, and speaking of the "success which has attended me in starting as an ardent but incorrect imitator of your manner." A year later, Cowper, to whom repeated drafts of the play had since been submitted, consented that, if published, it should be dedicated to him. Fastidious as in some ways he was, Cowper never failed in kindness to young authors; and in Hurdis he recognized not only an admirer but a sincere friend. Perhaps the moderate praise of *Sir Thomas More* which he gave to Lady Hesketh after having read it twice, in the words "it will do him credit," expresses his real opinion of it most accurately. But he invited Hurdis to come and visit him at Weston, and cheerfully accepted his help towards his own translation of Homer, not only in detailed criticism and suggestion, but in collecting subscribers towards its publication. In the autumn of 1792 Cowper was staying with Hayley at Eartham, and a joint invitation was sent to Hurdis to visit them there, which he did. "Mr. Hurdis," Cowper wrote to Lady Hesketh on 9th September, "is here. Distressed by the loss of his sister, he has renounced the place where she died for ever, and is about to enter on a new course of life at Oxford. You would admire him much. He is gentle in his manners and delicate in his person."

The death, a week before this letter was written, of Hurdis' sister Catherine after a long illness, was in truth a blow from which he took long to recover if he ever recovered completely. It is clear from what he says about her that she was unusually gifted, and fully shared all his interests and pursuits. *The Tears of Affection*, a poem written by him in memory of her, may be read even now with a real thrill, and incidentally it gives a picture, as clear in its outline as it is convincing in its truth, of the life they led happily together at Burwash, a life of simplicity and high culture, of unostentatious piety combined with love of books and music, with study and recreation, and with a large share in the social life of the neighbourhood. It is very much the sort of life which Miss Austen sketches incidentally with her fine and sure touch as that in which Elinor Dashwood and Fanny Price were destined to find abiding happiness.

But there were other reasons which turned Hurdis' mind back to Oxford. His name was already known there as that of a poet and scholar and began to be mentioned in connection with the Chair of Poetry. The period of tenure of the Chair by Robert Holmes of New College—afterwards Dean of Winchester, and best known, so far as he can be said to be known at all, by his work in collating MSS. of the Septuagint —was drawing to an end. It can hardly be doubted that it was in view of offering himself as Holmes' successor to the electorate, then as now consisting of the whole governing body of the University, that Hurdis now wrote and published two very dissimilar treatises. One was *Select Critical Remarks on the English Version of the first ten Chapters of Genesis*. I have never seen it; there is no copy of it in the British Museum.

But from other sources we know that Hurdis studied Hebrew, and was something of a Hebrew scholar; and the poetry of the Old Testament, which Lowth had made the main if not the entire subject of his Professorial lectures half a century before, was accepted as one of the most important subjects with which a Professor of Poetry could deal. The other *ballon d'essai* which he launched a little later is significant both in the subject and in its treatment. It is a pamphlet—it hardly claims to be, and certainly is not, anything more—entitled *Cursory Remarks upon the Arrangement of the Plays of Shakespeare; occasioned by reading Mr. Malone's Essay on the Chronological Order of those celebrated Pieces.* It was published by Johnson, and dedicated to Alderman Boydell. He can have read Malone's famous essay, the foundation-stone of scientific Shakespearian research, with little profit. His ignorance of the whole subject is only equalled by the fatuity of his original criticisms. At the end, he gives a list of the plays of the Canon in what he supposes to be the chronological order of their composition. "I do not," he ingenuously observes, "offer it as faultless. It is at least probable that many readers will differ from me." Did any reader, one is inclined to ask—whether the readers were many or few—ever agree with him? As regards his appreciation it may be sufficient to quote one or two critical remarks which even for that age, when dawn was only beginning to break over the long night of the Ignorance, are astounding. On *A Midsummer Night's Dream* he says, "its observations are accurate and judicious. All its fictions are elegantly introduced." On *As You Like It*: "there is so much ease in the versification, and so much weight in the morality, that it must be esteemed one of his latest and best plays." On *Hamlet*: "the conduct of this piece exposes it in many instances to just reproof from the discerning critic." On *Antony and Cleopatra*: "there perhaps never fell from the pen of our immortal bard a piece written with less spirit and less knowledge of his art."

What is equally amazing is that the pamphlet not only appears to have satisfied the Oxford electorate, but was commended by Cowper, though he guards himself by adding that he is not competent to judge. Cowper interested himself in canvassing on Hurdis' behalf among the out-voters for the election to the Chair of Poetry. There was another candidate for it, Kett of Trinity, as to whom I have not been able to ascertain anything. On the voting, 31st October, 1793, Hurdis was elected by a narrow majority, 201 against 180 for Kett.

There is a pleasant little glimpse of him at Oxford in the previous summer, when the Duke of Portland was installed as Chancellor of the University. Mrs. Siddons, then at the full height of her powers and fame, was among the brilliant company collected for the occasion. She dined with the Hurdises one day, and after dinner "sang several little ballads" —among them was *Barbara Allen*—"in a stile which was very chaste and agreeable." No doubt she was enjoying herself. It brings Hurdis very close to us when we find that after the bustle and excitement of Commemoration week he went off for a rest, as he would do nowadays, to the Cotswolds.

His Professorial lectures were, according to the old tradition which survived down to the middle of last century, delivered in Latin. Little or nothing is ascertainable as to their contents. Writing from Magdalen soon after his election, he mentions that he is trying to acquire a good Latin style, and that he has made an immense collection of Biblical Beauties. That his lectures consisted chiefly of extracts with running comments may be inferred from a substantial quarto volume of twenty-one lectures (in English and dealing entirely with English poets) which he printed at his own press at Bishopstone. It was published, i.e. put on sale, by Johnson at his shop in St. Paul's Churchyard in 1797. This volume is in effect an anthology of passages arranged under different heads; aspects of nature, the seasons, trees, plants and flowers, the sea, animals, the stages of human life, characters, professions and passions of mankind, and so forth. It was probably a good deal used as a commonplace-book by essayists and sermon-writers.

Hurdis now divided his time between Bishopstone and Oxford, where he had a house in Cowley. He took the degree of B.D. in 1794 and proceeded to that of D.D. in 1797. He married Harriet Minet in 1799. On 21st December, 1801 he was attacked by a violent shivering fit, collapsed, and died

Q

two days later, in his thirty-eighth year. He was buried, at
his own desire, in the family vault at Bishopstone beside his
dearly loved sister Catherine. A memorial tablet in the church
is inscribed with some rather commonplace verses by Hayley,
laying stress on his "tender sanctity of thought" and his
unsurpassed fraternal love.

Cowper had died the year before. The fame which he
had won fifteen years earlier by the almost contemporary
appearance of *The Task* and *John Gilpin* was at its height: it
remained uncontested, and even was increased, during the
next decade. "Nay, mama, if he is not to be animated by
Cowper!" Marianne Dashwood's outburst in *Sense and
Sensibility*, expresses a wide and almost a universal feeling.
The age of sensibility was at its climax. It was reinforced in
the body of the nation by the growing predominance of the
Evangelical school both within and beyond the Church of
England. To both, Cowper and his school offered exactly
what they wanted in poetry; and Hurdis, Cowper's professed
pupil, had a considerable share in his popularity.

The collection of his poems in three volumes printed at the
Oxford University Press in 1808 has several points of interest.
When Queen Charlotte heard that it was in preparation, she
spontaneously gave permission, equivalent of course to a
command, that it should be inscribed to her. It was seven
years later that a similar compliment was paid to the author
of *Emma* by the Prince Regent. The poems were, like
Cowper's *Homer*, according to the custom which had been
initiated a century earlier by Pope, published by subscription.
The list of subscribers contains nearly 1,300 names. It opens
with the Queen, all the five Princesses, and the Princess
Charlotte of Wales: she was only ten years old, but was
already beginning to carry on her small and ill-fated shoulders
some of the burdens of prospective royalty. It includes the
Archbishop of Canterbury, eight bishops, and sixty-three
peers, peeresses and Privy Councillors. About 250 copies were
subscribed for in Oxford; ten each were taken by the Chancellor
of the University (the Duke of Portland) and the President
of Magdalen. A bridge over several generations is made by the
name of E. V. Cox, Esquire Bedel, who lived until 1875. That

of Mrs. H. L. Piozzi, Streatham Park—why this should be given as her address when she had left it for over a dozen years I do not understand—carries one back as far in the other direction. The name which stands highest in English letters out of the whole list is that of Walter Landor, Esq., Clifton: for Scott's name does not appear, though that of his intimate friend Charles Kirkpatrick Sharpe does: Sharpe however had only recently left Christ Church, which is still given as his address. Another name of interest is that of Mr. George Courthope of Whiligh; he was the grandfather of the W. J. Courthope who, as I have already mentioned, was in time to be the holder of the Oxford Chair of Poetry: and it is not a little curious that a portrait of Hurdis, copied from what must have been a very good miniature which is, or quite recently was, in the possession of his grand-daughter Mrs. Bowden-Smith, is in face and feature strikingly like Courthope as I knew him intimately for many years.

In the inevitable comparison between Hurdis and Cowper as pupil and master, two reservations must be made. One is, that Hurdis had no share whatever in the lyrical gift which forms an important element, perhaps the element of most assured permanence, in Cowper's title to fame. The few lyrical pieces among his collected poems—we must suppose that they were chosen as his best—are totally undistinguished and hardly even second-rate. The other is that there is no trace in Hurdis of Cowper's gift of demure and exquisite humour. These points must be borne in mind no less than the fact that he died at thirty-seven, an age at which Cowper had produced but little poetry. It does not seem probable—though one can never tell with certainty—that if he had lived longer he would have developed greater poetical powers.

His interest for modern readers, and for students of English poetry as an index to the social, intellectual, and imaginative movement of English history, rests mainly and almost wholly on the two poems already mentioned, *The Village Curate* and *The Favourite Village*, to which on a somewhat lower plane may be added *The Tears of Affection*. The love of nature, the eye and ear for all rural sights and sounds, the quiet but impassioned delight in the life of field and garden, woodland

and river-valley, no less than the melodiously modulated blank
verse, carry one back perpetually to Cowper: but they are,
however imitative, and they are often glaringly so, the outcome of genuine affinity. Where he falls short is partly in the
academic pedantry from which he never wholly shook himself
free; Cowper, it must be remembered, had neither the advantage nor the disadvantage of a University education. Partly it is
in some failure of instinctive tact in selection and distillation.
Cowper, whose theories on education as set forth in *Tirocinium*
may still be read with much interest as applying *mutatis mutandis*
to problems of the present day, would never have written, as
Hurdis did—

> What time Vacation 'gan his airy dance
> And left Tuition nodding o'er his books
> In Academus' shades:

for at the Temple "he acquired," as Mr. Birrell long ago
observed with just insight, "what never left him, the style and
manner of an accomplished worldling." It was partly from
this introduction into the larger world, but mainly from
native instinct, that his descriptive passages are satisfying. In
the younger poet, while showing the same quickness of perception and fineness of appreciation, they tend to run into mere
catalogues. He has not mastered the art of saying much in
little, of suggesting more than his words convey, of implying
background and conveying atmosphere. His lists of wild
flowers in *The Village Curate* and in *Tears of Affection*, while
all closely observed and accurately described, become tedious.
The difference in handling, the drop in temperature, may be
illustrated by one instance. Here is a well-known passage
from Book VI of *The Task*. Cowper is speaking of the
forecast, in the season of

>   naked shoots
> Barren as lances, among which the wind
> Makes wintry music, sighing as it goes.

of full spring and its wealth of garden blossom,

                                        Laburnum rich
In streaming gold; syringa ivory pure;
The scented and the scentless rose, this red
And of an humbler growth, the other tall
And throwing up into the darkest gloom
Of neighbouring cypress or more sable yew
Her silver globes, light as the foamy surf
That the wind severs from the broken wave;
The lilac various in array, now white
Now sanguine, and her beauteous head now set
With purple spikes pyramidal . . . the broom,
Yellow and bright as bullion unalloyed
Her blossoms; and luxuriant above all
The jasmine, throwing wide her elegant sweets,
The deep dark green of whose unvarnished leaf
Makes more conspicuous and illumines more
The bright profusion of her scatter'd stars.

And here is Hurdis, in *The Favourite Village*, trying to do the
same thing.

Now sends the garden all its glories forth;
With many a nodding pyramid of flowers
Or pale or purple-hued her varnished leaf
The lilac decks. Laburnum at her side
Weeps gold, sweet mourner! From behind appears
And tosses high in air her frothy globes,
Her unsubstantial roses, light as foam
Of new milk bubbling in the cowherd's pail,
The beauteous guelder-shrub. How sweet to sense
How delicate the breeze that lades its wings
With odours from the hawthorn! To the spot
Where dwells the sweet allurer, decking late
Her crowded foliage with abundant flowers
Turns the fond eye to gaze, and, smit with love,
Marks here the swelling bough's expanded bloom
And there a host of beauties yet unborn,
Globules unnumber'd the prolific branch
Besetting thick around, ere long to unfold
Their milky petals to the enamour'd bee.

Or, as one more illustration, take the justly celebrated lines at the opening of *The Winter Walk at Noon*:

> How soft the music of those village bells
> Falling at intervals upon the ear
> In cadence sweet! now dying all away,
> Now pealing loud again and louder still
> Clear and sonorous as the gale comes on:

and place beside them the work of the copyist in *The Village Curate*:

> Then let the village bells, as often wont,
> Come swelling on the breeze, and to the sun
> Half-set, sing merrily their evening song
> Now dying all away, now faintly heard,
> And now with loud and musical relapse
> Its mellow changes huddling on the ear.

It is not in these languid and imitative lines that one feels the touch of inspiration, the creative and imaginative quality which Hurdis did, though intermittently and uncertainly, possess. It comes in the lines which immediately follow those I have quoted:

> So have I stood at eve on Isis' banks
> To hear the merry Christ Church bells rejoice.
> So have I sat too in thy honoured shades,
> Distinguished Magdalen, on Cherwell's brink,
> To hear thy silver Wolsey tones so sweet.
> And so too have I paused and held my oar
> And suffer'd the slow stream to bear me home
> While Wykeham's peal along the meadow ran.

They have not been quite forgotten; for they find a place in that delightful collection, the *Minstrelsy of Isis*: and so perhaps are an exception to the general statement that Hurdis has sunk wholly into oblivion.

It will be clear enough even from slight acquaintance with his manner and diction that he does not lend himself much to quotation. One short passage indeed, by some freak of taste, has had a really wide circulation, and is probably known to many who are quite ignorant of its authorship. It is his description of, or rather his reflection on, the artifice of a bird's nest.

> Mark it well, within, without,
> No tool had he that wrought, no knife to cut,
> No nail to fix, no bodkin to insert,
> No glue to join; his little beak was all.
> And yet how neatly finished!

But he has many felicities of phrase in his descriptions, and his close and sensitive eye for natural phenomena inevitably reminds one of the contemporary work of Wordsworth, who was but seven years his junior. I will quote a few lines from *The Favourite Village* describing an evening walk in early autumn in the Ouse Valley. They are of interest in connection with the poetical revolution which was then going on, if we set them beside Wordsworth's *Evening Walk*, written a few years earlier. In the Fenwick note, between fifty and sixty years afterwards, Wordsworth says of that poem that "the plan of it has not been confined to a particular walk or an individual place; a proof (of which I was conscious at the time) of my unwillingness to submit the poetic spirit to the chains of fact and real circumstance. The country is idealized rather than described in any one of its local aspects." This remark goes deep; it touches on the essential change, as regards the relation of art to nature, which was taking place in poetry as in the contemporary movement in the great school of the English water-colourists.

>   Be nothing heard
> Save the far-distant murmur of the deep—
> Or the near grasshopper's incessant note,
> That snug beneath the wall in comfort sits,
> And chirping imitates the silvery chink
> Of wages told into the ploughman's palm—
> Or gentle curlew bidding kind good-night
> To the spent villager, or e'er his hand
> The cottage taper quench—or grazing ox
> His dewy supper from the savoury herb
> Audibly gathering—or cheerful hind
> From the lov'd harvest feast returning home,
> Whistling at intervals some rustic air,

Or at due distance chanting in the vale
Exhilarated song. Such rural sounds
If haply notic'd by the musing mind,
Sweet interruption yield, and thrice improve
The solemn luxury of idle thought.
　　Oft at yon huddled town, that guards remote
The sounding ship-yard and contiguous port,
By sweet civility detain'd, the bridge,
At such late hour returning, let me pass;
What time aloft the moon, no more rotund,
Shines gibbous o'er the pure and still expanse
Of tide-uplifted Ouse, and lends to Night
An ample mirror, where her sober eye,
Her twinkling jewelry and face serene
Thrice placid and thrice beauteous, may behold.
　　If not abroad I sit, but sip at home
The cheering beverage of fading eve,
By some fair hand, or e'er it reach the lip,
With mingled flavour tinctur'd of the cane
And Asiatic leaf, let the mute flock,
As from the window studious looks mine eye,
Steal foldward nibbling o'er the shadowy down,
And take their farewell of the savoury turf.
Let the reluctant milch-kine of the farm
Wind slowly from the pasture to the pail.
Let the glad ox, unyok'd, make haste to field,
And the stout wain-horse, of encumbrance stript,
Shake his enormous limbs with blund'ring speed,
Eager to gratify his famish'd lip
With taste of herbage and the meadow brook.

In the earliest of Wordsworth's sonnets, the well-known one beginning "Calm is all nature as a resting wheel," the line about the horse which, when the cows are couched upon the grass "is up and cropping yet his later meal," was altered by him, at some time later than 1807, to "is cropping audibly his later meal." It is difficult to avoid the conclusion that meanwhile he had read *The Favourite Village*, or extracts from it in some review, and annexed Hurdis' "audibly gathering." If not, the coincidence is curious.

Cowper's Ouse, and the landscape surrounding Olney, were immortalized by him both in his descriptive or reflective poems and in a number of his exquisite lyrics. The Sussex Ouse, between Lewes and the sea, and the stretch of the South Downs through which it makes its leisurely way, one of the loveliest of southern English landscapes, are described in *The Favourite Village* with equal fidelity and with still greater detail. Within my own memory it was little changed from what it had been at the end of the eighteenth century, as then it was very much what it had been for hundreds of years earlier: the Downs, whether under tillage or in pasturage, were wholly unenclosed; ploughing was done by teams of black oxen, and corn threshed by flails in the flint-built and tile-roofed barns, some of these now derelict and ruinous, like the windmills in which the corn was ground, others, less fortunate, converted into week-end resorts for Londoners. In dedicating the poem to the Archdeacon of Lewes (whose curate he had been at Burwash) Hurdis speaks of it as "descriptive of those rural satisfactions and amusements to which, in the spirit of true taste, he has for many years given their due preference." It may be doubted whether taste, in this matter, has changed much for the better; the means of satisfying it are certainly disappearing with terrible rapidity.

His landscape, with all its intimacy, has largeness. Gilbert White, it will be remembered, speaks of "the vast range of mountains known as the Sussex Downs"; and so to Hurdis also they are a "nation of mountains." From his home "where yon enormous downs shoulder the eastern moon," they really have, in certain atmospheric conditions, just this effect: and he was familiar with them at all hours of day and night and all seasons of the year. In his descriptive scenes, especially perhaps those of night and early morning, he is unsurpassed for sensitive accuracy: even Wordsworth might be proud to own vivid touches that crowd one upon another; the full moon in autumn "as from a furnace rising red with heat,"

> And while it mounts the purple steep of heaven
> Glowing more ardent, and suspended high
> A globe intense of molten bullion hung
> Amid the gems of night:

the crescent moon "with reverted horn" in the eastern sky at dawn; or the wind on the cliff-top against which one can lean as if it were a solid wall; or the rainbow-coloured sparkles of hoar frost on the hedgerows as it melts under the winter sun; or the cloud of London smoke on the northern horizon with the whole width of the Weald between; or the perpetually varying lights and shades over the Channel.

Too many, it may be said, there are of these: it is true that Hurdis never learnt the lesson that the half is more than the whole. The trouble with him was that, as Pope said with incisive truth of Young, "he lacked common sense." Here and there his craze for cataloguing becomes almost ludicrous. The description of his own little library in *The Village Curate* opens charmingly. But having occasion to mention Johnson's *Lives of the Poets* as among its contents, he goes on—will it be believed?—to give a list of thirty-two of the fifty-two poets comprised in the "goodly band Johnsonian," with some account of the work of each. The comment sometimes runs into twenty or thirty lines, but generally is more restricted. At one point indeed his pen or his interest fails him; and one of the poets, a minor poet to be sure, is introduced and dismissed in what must be the shortest recorded notice of any author. It consists of two words: "Then Sprat."

As an artist in verse, Hurdis suffers from at least three defects; this accumulation of detail in his descriptions; the highly artificial diction which was then still prevalent and as it were consecrated by usage, and against which the main attack of Wordsworth in his famous prefaces as well as in his own practice was directed; and that *mollities* or sentimentality which was in part a note of the age, in part perhaps, as I have suggested innate in the Sussex temperament. In all these respects, while close parallels may be found between his work and that of his poetical master, the difference between Cowper and him is that between original and secondary inspiration.

It was a period in English poetry of transition, of uncertainty, of confusion. As in the middle of the seventeenth century, as again in our own time, it is difficult or impossible to trace a central current: the progress of poetry was forcing its way very slowly through many channels. How far this reflects an analogous confusion in the political and social evolution of national life is a theme which can only be suggested for consideration.

To resuscitate dead poetry is an idle effort. But so far as it was poetry in the full sense, so far as it was a creative interpretation of life and nature, no poetry can be dead. I do not know whether the poet—for he was a poet, though a minor one—who is the subject of this study can excite any revived interest now. But a little volume containing his two, perhaps his three, principal poems, and together with them the whole interchange of correspondence between him and Cowper as it has recently been made available, would be of interest and indeed of real value: the more so, if it were of any avail towards securing from devastation what is left of one of the loveliest and best-loved landscapes in England.

RUSKIN

[*Centenary Address*, 8 February, 1919]

WHETHER the practice of centenary celebrations is one to be commended or otherwise is a question on which there may be, and is, variety of opinion. It is raised in its most acute form when the celebration is of one who has been misunderstood or slighted in his own lifetime, for then it bears the aspect of a tardy and awkward reparation made to his ghost; and even those who celebrate it can hardly do so without some uneasy sense of being among those who build the tombs of the prophets and garnish the sepulchres of the righteous, and say, "If we had been in the days of our fathers, we would not have been partakers with them in the blood of the prophets."

But the occasion is one which suggests a fresh appreciation, an attempt at least at summing up a man's life and work, seen now more clearly as a whole in their effective value, and removed from the dust of contemporary prejudice. And the feeling I have mentioned is only to a limited degree applicable to our ceremony of to-day. In his lifetime, Ruskin compelled attention, even fame, and had not to meet with anything that can be called persecution. His name was universally known, his genius universally admitted. He had loyal friends and devoted followers; and it would be less than fair to these if one did not frankly admit that he often led them a dance and taxed their patience sorely. What he had to bear, and what he felt more keenly than insult or obloquy—though of these too he had his share—was a sort of good-natured and superior indulgence, which dismissed him as an eccentric and irresponsible man of genius, a writer with a wonderful gift of eloquence who generally talked nonsense, and a champion of absurd paradoxes. It was his bitterest and best-grounded complaint, that people read him for his style and paid no attention to his meaning; that he pleaded with them to choose between the way of life and the way of death, and they only said, What beautiful English he writes! "Lo, thou art to them," in the words of the Hebrew prophet, "as a very lovely song of one that hath a pleasant voice, and can play well on an instrument: for they hear thy words, but they do them not."

Now it is different. Those earlier and more ambitious works, whose dazzling eloquence captivated their readers and made him famous as a master of language, have had their day. It has faded, and they have in some measure ceased to live. A new generation has ceased to read *Modern Painters* with enthusiasm, or even with patience; it is no longer fascinated by the gorgeous elaboration of the *Stones of Venice*. His reputation as an exponent and interpreter of art was once unequalled. Time has not confirmed it; it is now even said, with some measure of truth, that he did not know what art meant.

It is as an interpreter, not of art but of life, that he now stands. Here his influence has been, and continues to be, immense. It is perhaps greater, so far at least as England is concerned, than that of any other single thinker or teacher. His social doctrine was germinal: it colours the whole movement of modern thought, and shapes the whole fabric of modern practice. The quotation from Ezekiel may be continued of him in the full weight of its meaning: "And when this cometh to pass (lo, it will come), then shall they know that a prophet hath been among them."

Like other prophets, Ruskin was a man of sorrows. He was the servant, not the master, of his message. The inspiration descended on him fitfully, with intervals of obscurity, confusion, or eclipse. Few men have ever been less fitted by nature, or enabled by temperament, to conquer circumstance, to pursue a steady course, to do large constructive work. The most dutiful and affectionate of children, he remained all his life a child: with the acute sensitiveness of childhood, with its passionate loves and loathings, with its terrible simplicity; and also with its touching helplessness and its distracting childishness. "No other man that I meet," Carlyle wrote of him to Emerson, "has in him the divine rage against iniquity, falsehood, and baseness that Ruskin has and that every man ought to have. Unhappily, he is not a strong man—one might say a weak man rather—and has not the least prudence of management." These words are like those of a wise and kind parent; and indeed the relationship between the two (Carlyle was twenty-four years older) was felt and spoken of by both as that of a spiritual father and son.

With their two names a third is instinctively joined when we regard the nineteenth century as a whole, that of Tolstoi. Tolstoi was perhaps the greatest of the three; at all events he has had the most potent influence over the world: and one that was for harm as well as for good. Turgenev, with his penetrating insight, noted of him that he was possessed by an immense spiritual arrogance. His whole life, through its manifold phases, was one of strangely sublimated selfishness: nothing was good enough for him. Carlyle, too, had in full measure the pride characteristic of his nation, and strongest among them in the class to which he belonged: though he knew it, and even ("Teufelsdröckh, beware of spiritual pride") could laugh at it. Ruskin's humility was as remarkable as his sincerity. He deferred to his juniors as much as to his elders; he was always willing to accept correction, and to believe himself mistaken.

All three were prophets, on whom the weight of their inspiration was an agony. All three lived to a great age, and with them all it ended in gloom. All three had for many years become the object of a cult among a younger generation. All three were consummate artists in language. Strangely enough, Carlyle was the only one of them who had any reverence for that art, to whom words were something divine and sacred. Tolstoi, the greatest artist perhaps of his age, despised and hated all art indiscriminately. Ruskin's attitude to art was more fluctuating: it at once attracted and repelled him. Even in his early writings, before he had put off the singing-robes of the poet to put on the sackcloth of the prophet, and was absorbed in the glory of art, he had raised in the most trenchant form that opposition between art and puritanism which is one of the great permanent antinomies in human life. But it was not till 1860 that the change (so we may call it) in his whole moral axis took full effect. It would be needless to recapitulate here

the well-known story of the appearance, from August to
November in that year, of the four papers headed "Unto
this Last" in the *Cornhill Magazine*; of the storm of outraged
protest from the whole reading public; of Thackeray's capitulation to it, and of their abrupt close. It is strange to
handle that old volume, and read in it, alongside of the instalments of *Framley Parsonage*, those four papers which may
almost be said to have changed the world; to realize how
deep into the roots of things, how far into the future, that
lonely mind saw. Our whole social legislation, and the whole
attitude of mind of which legislation is the result, have since
followed, haltingly and fragmentarily, the principles then
asserted for the first time. Nor have sixty years lessened their
vital and germinal force. Much of what was then taken for
monstrous paradox has become accepted truth, the mere
commonplace of social organization. Much more still awaits
fulfilment, and remains to us what it was for him, an obscure
and terrible inspiration, a sound of trumpets in the night.

Like others who have had a prophetic message (Carlyle and
Tolstoi are but two instances among many) Ruskin was
enormously voluminous. He could not help writing, and
could not help pouring out into what he wrote all that he
thought or felt. In the huge mass of his work there is much
that is of little value; there is much that detracts, by its wilful-
ness and whimsicality, from the effective value of the whole.
The childlike simplicity which is his great charm often takes
shape as freakishness and inconsequence. Flamboyant in his
youth, he becomes garrulous in his age. Even when he is at his
highest concentration he can never be trusted to withstand
the influence of some verbal or fanciful suggestion. No one,
I suppose, would sit down to read through the thirty-nine
volumes in which all his work has been collected by the pious
industry of Sir Edward Cook and Mr. Wedderburn. It is like
being faced with the lifelong accumulations of a painter's
studio; sketches and scribbles, tattered cartoons, vast canvases
thrown aside when they were half finished or barely begun,
false starts, repetitions, failures. Those who adventure into
this wilderness, "a maze trod indeed thro' forthrights and
meanders," may indeed hope—nay, may be assured—that they

will come every here and there on some unsuspected fragment of lovely outline or lustrous colour. But they will have a toilsome journey.

It is not necessary to make the attempt. For his best work and his most vital teaching lie in little compass. More and more, I should think, readers of Ruskin will concentrate on those writings of his—few, and, for him, brief—which are the masterpieces, and the permanently live forces. To know Carlyle, the vital and imperishable Carlyle, it is sufficient to know *Sartor Resartus, Past and Present,* and the *French Revolution.* To know Ruskin, the vital and imperishable Ruskin, even less is sufficient. I would not wish to say anything which might seem to slight or ignore the *Stones of Venice* or the *Seven Lamps.* The famous chapter "On the Nature of Gothic" in the second volume of the *Stones* presents the spirit of his beliefs with a force of truth and eloquence which makes it immortal. Nor is there any more delightful reading than his last work, the unfinished *Praeterita,* with its delicate fragrance, its pellucid atmosphere, its autumnal charm. And indeed one may say that there is hardly any writing of Ruskin's in which there is not something keenly felt, truly thought, memorably expressed. Of all his volumes, *Sesame and Lilies* was for long the most popular, and had the widest though not the deepest influence. Ruskin himself thought, as it is reported, that *Unto this Last* was the book of his which would stand the longest. His effective and permanent message is contained in the *Two Paths*—five lectures given in 1857-9—and in *Unto this Last,* the *Cornhill* articles of 1860. If we know these, we know Ruskin; and if we add to these the *Nature of Gothic* as a preface, and the *Crown of Wild Olive* as an epilogue, we know him, in all essentials, fully.

In the central period represented by these writings his powers were at their highest. He was not then, as he became later, shattered by the weight of his own prophetic burden. "Not a strong man," as Carlyle had in the early years gravely and tenderly noted, he succumbed to a weight of crowded thoughts, an agony of lacerated feelings: he became, in the full sense of words which may not be quoted lightly, a man of sorrows and acquainted with grief: stricken, smitten of God, and afflicted: cut off out of the land of the living. "I feel," he writes pathetically in 1884, "as if nobody could ever love me or believe me or listen to me or get any good of me ever any more." "The thoughts come into my head," he had written to the same correspondent several years earlier, "and if I don't set them down, they torment me—the angry ones chiefly."

The obsession of these angry thoughts, as he calls them, was indeed a constant torture to one so fragile and so highly strung. But their bitterness only struck inward. It never affected his boundless generosity in word and act, or impaired his noble courtesy. Newman's famous definition of a gentleman, one who never gives pain, applies to him. Towards no human being was he capable of bearing malice. From all, even from those who least understood him and were least in sympathy with him, he craved, and was touchingly grateful for, any fragment of affection, any scrap of appreciation. He never wilfully gave pain, though he was often distressed by the thought that he might have given it. Nor did he ever take amiss, or allow to rankle in him, any attack made on his work or on his teaching. No wonder that, just at the time when he was speaking of the torment of his angry thoughts, Burne-Jones wrote of him, "I am better in Ruskin's company than in that of any man."

Ruskin was above all things uniformly and transparently sincere. From first to last there was not a trace in him of self-seeking or envy, of conceit or pretence. No adverse criticism can be passed on his work, as regards either form or substance, which he has not anticipated himself and often put more pungently than any one else could put it. He takes for granted the same sincerity of spirit in others, and, by taking it for granted, he helps to create it. We are better in his company.

Thus his many-faceted genius gives expression, with equally trenchant force, to one side and another of the *insolubilia*, the fundamental antinomies of life and thought. He belongs to no school and confines himself to no system. His searchlight darts from point to point, throwing whatever it touches into startling illumination, and leaving it thenceforth something different for us. It is not necessary to agree with him, nor is he much concerned about being in agreement with himself, in any particular judgment. In these he was, one may say frankly, often fantastic and capricious. Many of his later annotations on his own writings are disavowals of what he had formerly asserted: for he was as far from any false pride as he was from any affected humility. It is part of his secret that he is (like life) so full of contradictions. An ardent and even fanatical Protestant, he is one of the great interpreters of medieval Catholicism. The champion and hierophant of the Pre-Raphaelite movement, he does not shrink from saying that the Pre-Raphaelites are all more or less affected by morbid conditions of intellect and temper. While he condemns and renounces the Renaissance and all its works, he steadily proclaims that in Titian and Velasquez art reached perfection. Going even further, in the same breath with which he glorifies art as the essence and flower of life, "that in which the hand, head, and heart of man go together," he also says in precise and unqualified words, that "the period in which any people reach their highest power in art is that in which they sign the warrant of their own ruin"; that "art followed as such is destructive of whatever is best and noblest in humanity"; that he has never—the courage of the famous words is as noble as their frankness is wonderful—has "never yet met with a Christian whose heart was, as far as human judgment could pronounce, perfect and right before God, who cared about art at all."

So, too, with regard to conduct, to the organization of human life. By religious and intellectual conviction no less than by temperament, Ruskin was a passionate lover of peace. But no one has written more burning or more memorable words than his on the duty of patriotism and the sacredness of soldiership. "You have put yourselves," he says to the cadets of the Royal Military Academy, "into the hand of your country as a weapon. You have vowed to strike when she bids you, and to stay scabbarded when she bids you: all that you need answer for is that you fail not in her grasp."

Or again, in *Unto this Last*:

The consent of mankind has always, in spite of the philosophers, given precedence to the soldier. And this is right.

For the soldier's trade is not slaying, but being slain. This, without well knowing its own meaning, the world honours it for. The reason it honours the soldier is because he holds his life at the service of the State. Our estimate of him is based upon this ultimate fact, of which we are well assured, that put him in a fortress breach, with all the pleasures of the world behind him and only death and his duty in front of him, he will keep his face to the front; and he knows that his choice may be put to him at any moment, and has beforehand taken his part, virtually takes such part continually, does, in reality, die daily.

And so, once more, a socialized commonwealth was what he presented, more and more fully as his thought plumbed deeper and ranged wider, not as a radiant and unapproachable ideal, but as a matter of obvious duty and of plain practical common sense. He is the prophet of the Socialist movement; he taught its leaders and inspired their followers. But the doctrines of Socialism, whether in its bureaucratic or its anarchic form, were to him false and even deadly. If this seems an overstatement, I can but quote his own very carefully chosen and very deliberate words:

All effectual advancement towards true felicity of the human race must be by individual, not public effort.

Division of property is its destruction; and with it, the destruction of all hope, all industry, and all justice.

The poor have no right to the property of the rich. Neither is the Socialist right in desiring to make everybody poor, powerless, and foolish, as he is himself.

The rich man does not keep back meat from the poor by retaining his riches; but by basely using them. Riches are a form of strength, and a strong man does not injure others by keeping his strength, but by using it injuriously.

Strangely reactionary doctrine from this source it may seem to some who have Ruskin's name often on their lips. But we must take, alongside of it, his presentation of the other side of the matter.

No agitators, no clubs, no epidemical errors, ever were or will be fatal to social order in any nation. Nothing but the guilt of the upper classes, wanton, accumulated, reckless and merciless, ever overthrows them. Of such guilt they have now much to answer for—let them look to it in time.

It is sixty years since these words were written, and they have lost nothing of their profound and terrible significance.

His own synthesis, his own statement of the truth for the individual and the community, he puts as incisively and even more briefly. First, as to the individual: "That your neighbour should or should not remain content with his position is not your business; but it is very much your business to remain content with your own." Secondly, as to the community: "My principles of political economy are all summed in a single sentence: Government and Co-operation are in all things the laws of life; Anarchy and Competition, the laws of death." From all classes alike, what Ruskin calls for is the controlling sense and the exact fulfilment of duty; and the reward he holds out for this is joy and peace.

Joy and peace he did not himself find; though there are those here among us whose affection and devotion did all that was humanly possible to give them to him. But he has helped, and may still help, many to find them. Their sources lie in each human soul, and no one can well indicate to another in what thought, or in what words, they are to be found. If I cite here two more passages from the core of Ruskin's writings, it is merely because they have to some certainly, and perhaps to many, been an actual refuge, a heightening impulse, in these last years, and for us upon whom the ends of the world have come.

In the awful week of 1914, two sentences in the *Crown of Wild Olive* rang, and rang true, for those on whom the call was suddenly made to face a momentous decision and accept their share in responsibility for it:

No man who is truly ready to take part in a noble quarrel will ever stand long in doubt by whom, or in what cause, his aid is needed. The principle of non-intervention as now preached among us is as selfish and cruel as the worst frenzy of conquest, and differs from it only by being not only malignant, but dastardly.

And in the days now present, equally momentous in their issues, we may well reflect on another passage from the same volume:

The wonder has always been great to me, that heroism has never been supposed to be in any wise consistent with the practice of supplying people with food or clothes. Spoiling of armour is an heroic deed in all ages; but the selling of clothes, old or new, has never taken any colour of magnanimity. Yet one does not see why feeding the hungry and clothing the naked should ever become base businesses, even when engaged in on a large scale. If one could contrive to attach the notion of conquest to them anyhow! so that supposing there were anywhere an obstinate race, who refused to be comforted, one might take some pride in giving them compulsory comfort! and, as it were, occupying a country with one's gifts, instead of one's armies.

And yet once more. The State is inaugurating a great constructional work in what Ruskin had so deeply at heart, National Education. I need make no apology for quoting another sentence of his, uttered when he was still the voice of a forerunner crying in the wilderness: "Do not hope to feel the effect of your schools at once. Raise men as high as you can, and then let them stoop as low as you need; no great man ever minds stooping." Had these words been more borne in mind for the last sixty years we should now be a more civilized commonwealth, a better and happier people, than we are. They apply now with equal force and with an added depth of meaning.

"No great man ever minds stooping": and the more he stoops the more he lifts others towards his own level. Those addresses of Ruskin, with their marvellous texture of impassioned rhetoric, lucid exposition, searching irony, and flashing wit, must have been—indeed they were—far over the heads of their immediate audiences. One may speculate as to the feelings with which a meeting of Bradford manufacturers listened to his description of the temple he suggests they should build to the Goddess of Getting On, and the long passage from Plato with which the address ends; or what working men really thought when he called their attention to passages in Aristophanes and Livy, or clinched his argument with lines cited (in the original Italian) from Dante. What he was in fact doing, there as elsewhere, was taking his hearers or readers into his unreserved confidence, stooping to them in order to lift them up beside him. He sowed, in the old saying, with the whole sack; and if the seed often fell among thorns or stony places, he did not care so long as some of it fell in good ground and struck root. By assuming intelligence and sympathy, as by assuming right feeling and high aspiration, he created them; and this is the secret not only of education, but of all human progress. There is an authentic record—well known, yet not so well known as it should be—of a conversation between Ruskin and the Duke of Argyll, in which, after listening with some impatience to Ruskin's eloquent pleading, the Duke crushingly, as he thought, observed, "You seem to want a very different world to that we experience, Mr. Ruskin." That, of course, was just Ruskin's case. Unless we want a world different from what it is, we are not likely to get it; and it is faith in its possibility which makes it possible.

Ruskin's vision was intermittent and often clouded. In the gloom which fell on his later years, his hope sank, his faith wavered; the burden of life became too heavy for him. Tenderness, he says, is the chief gift of all really great men; but his own tenderness, fragile and over-sensitive as he was, had from the first something excessive and even morbid. At last the tired brain succumbed; and the rest was silence. But he must be estimated, he takes his place among the living Powers —for it is the living and not the dead whom we celebrate—by those shining virtues which were mixed in him with human weaknesses. He claims remembrance, he calls forth our honour and our gratitude, not only as a brilliant writer, a subtle thinker, an inspired teacher, but as one who sought truth and loved goodness; who hated all cruelty, pride, and falsehood; who was unselfish, generous, dutiful; who shows us an example of utter transparency, of high courtesy, of courageous humility.

THE INTEGRATION OF SHAKESPEARE

[*An Address given to the Shakespeare Association,* 1933]

THE title of this paper, as well as the purport of what it attempts to set forth, was suggested by a notable lecture, "The Disintegration of Shakespeare," given at the British Academy some years ago by Sir Edward Chambers. That lecture registered a turning-point in Shakespearian studies. What it dealt with was the Canon, the body of dramatic work attributed to Shakespeare which was collected after his death. On the disintegration of that body of work, immense labour was bestowed for half a century or more by scores of researchers or students. Most of its conclusions are now discredited. To those who were content to be left in a facile orthodoxy, in the happy belief (to use Chambers' apt words) that "there was not much left to be done with Shakespeare, except perhaps to read him," it provided a mixture of amusement and annoyance. With others, however, it served a better purpose; it led them to examine apart the stability of their own doctrine, and of the grounds on which it was held.

The subject on which I now offer observations under this title is not chosen as a field of controversy, in which I am not a combatant, nor as the assertion of a dogma. It has a double function, in the first place as indicating a general trend in Shakespearian studies which as an observer I have watched in recent years with much interest; and further, as giving a name to an ideal towards which, not in that province of exploration alone, but more widely in all spheres of human activity, the efforts of the human mind to understand the world in which it is placed, and the motive forces of which it is the servant and the master, appear to be converging: slowly, it may be, and interruptedly, by methods of trial and error, and often going up blind alleys or working in the dark, but nevertheless finding fresh inspiration both from success and from defeat.

The disintegration of Shakespeare, a task on which so much energy was spent, and so much of that energy wasted, is often thought of as due to scientific and historical method, the two great inventions of the nineteenth century, being applied to the Shakespearian problem. This view will hardly bear scrutiny. The idolatry of a previous age, "inculcated from infancy," as Gibbon in a famous sentence remarked, "as the first duty of an Englishman," was largely the result of a change which had taken place in the movement of civilization. His plays became isolated from the life which they embodied. The Beauties of Shakespeare eclipsed Shakespeare.

The Romantic Revival increased a confusion which was already great. It did indeed disinter the Sonnets from their long oblivion. It reinforced interest in the plays. But the Canon, when studied at all, was studied superficially and carelessly. The successful candidate for the Chair of Poetry at Oxford in 1793 commended himself to the electorate by a pamphlet entitled *Cursory Remarks upon the Arrangement of the Plays of Shakespeare*. One sentence from it may suffice to indicate his ignorance of the whole subject and the fatuity of his own contributions towards it. "*The Winter's Tale*," he says, "was undoubtedly one of Shakespeare's earliest compositions. The faults of its metre and its language are so numerous that it must be ranked with *Antony and Cleopatra*, *Henry VIII*, *Coriolanus*, and *Cymbeline*, which four pieces I cannot help being strongly of opinion are the earliest efforts of our poet's verse."

It is almost incredible, but this represents the common condition into which Shakespearian study had sunk during the long night of the Ignorance. On that night, day had just broken. Malone's famous *Essay*, the foundation-stone of Shakespearian research and of the revitalization of Shakespeare, had already been published; and, what is difficult to credit but is nevertheless the case, the title-page of the pamphlet expressly states that the reading of Malone's *Essay* was the occasion of its composition. What Malone thought of it, if he ever saw it, may be left to the imagination.

The era of research and scholarly study had begun. But it was for long confined to a small circle of students or antiquarians. It did little towards the nationalization of Shakespeare. Towards that, more was effected by the concurrent era of aesthetic appreciation, in which Coleridge was the hierophant of what might almost be called a new religion. The two movements were, if not positively conflicting, disparate and divergent. Both lost touch with the dramatic value of the plays. The Elizabethan and Jacobean stage, with their surroundings, were gradually explored and partially reconstructed. But for long, little attempt was made to get behind the literary evidence or to ascertain how, under what conditions, for what audiences, with what effective results, the dramatic output of that whole period, and of Shakespeare himself as an actor-playwright, was produced. His plays, that is to say, the printed texts of his plays, were dissected, but not re-embodied. They were disintegrated, but not re-vitalized. Textual criticism flourished. The plays as documents became the subject of widespread and minute study. As literature also they gained wider appreciation. Shakespeare was established, for readers of all classes and all ages, as a great English classic. Edition after edition, of the whole Canon and of individual plays, poured out from the press. But Shakespeare as a dramatist, and the plays as live organisms, were largely ignored. The book of the words (and what a book of words it is!) got detached from the flesh and blood, from the voice and action, of which it is the record. Many of the plays were never re-incarnated on the stage at all; those that were, were generally presented in a mangled, hacked, distorted shape. They supplied a libretto for pageants in which dress, scenery, and the personality of a favourite actor or actress, were the chief interest. It was only the prestige attaching to the name of Shakespeare, and the ambition of actors and theatrical managers to associate themselves with it, that kept Shakespeare as a dramatist, and his work as drama, in existence at all.

It was not surprising, therefore, that the disintegrating process extended from the stage to the study. Once the Canon came to be thought of as a collection of works of literature, questions of authorship were inevitably raised. The full armament of scholarship, stimulated by its loudly proclaimed but short-lived success in disintegrating Homer, turned joyfully to the disintegration of Shakespeare.

Intoxicated by their discovery (for to them it seemed littl
less) that collaboration in the manufacture of plays existed i
certain known cases, and was indeed a customary feature i
that hive of industry where a new piece was being perpetuall
called for at short notice, investigators devoted themselves t
shredding up the plays of the Canon and assigning the frag
ments to different authors. In doing so, they were guide
partly by what seemed gaps or inconsistencies in constructior
partly, and more largely, by looking for, and finding accord
ingly, notes in language, versification, and paragraph-construc
tion characteristic of this or that contemporary playwrigh
But they strayed beyond their own field into that of literar
criticism. They refused to allow to Shakespeare anythin
which did not comply with measuring-standards of their ow
invention. What they considered that Shakespeare could no
or would not, or should not have written, they assigned t
someone else. In such procedure, as elsewhere, the adage hold
good that experiment is slippery and diagnosis difficult. Tha
Shakespeare's early work consisted largely in reshaping an
refurnishing existing plays, is certain. That in his later perio
he worked in concert with colleagues on the staff of the theatr
of which he was a shareholder and manager, is also certair
That he contributed one scene to *Sir Thomas More*, severa
scenes to the *Two Noble Kinsmen*, something, perhaps not ver
much, to *Henry VIII*, there is no reasonable doubt. Wher
Shakespeare is most himself, where he is writing, whethe
in prose or in verse, at the full stretch of his powers, his touc
is unmistakable. But his inspiration was not continuou
His work was not uniformly on a high level. It is paying hir
a very doubtful compliment to assume that he could no
or did not, ever write badly. It is contrary to reason to suppos
that he put the same intensity of imagination and expressio
into the whole body of a play as into the culminating point
The sense of dramatic values would in fact not only justify bu
demand great variation in this. In reading the plays as litera
ture, which is the way which has ever since the era of thei
production has been the ordinary approach to Shakespeare, :
requires active imagination and takes some pains to realiz
this element of dramatic value: and appreciation is inevitabl

impaired, is even deadened, by the presentation on the stage of mutilated or summarized or "improved" versions.

The recapture or rediscovery of the Shakespearian theatre, in the full meaning of that term, of the atmosphere, soil, and surroundings in which as a dramatist, an actor, and a producer, Shakespeare lived and the plays of the Canon came into being, is a task which in recent times has been pursued with immense industry and approached from many directions. It is not surprising that in its course it led at first to a further disintegration of Shakespearian study, that is to say, of Shakespeare. He that increaseth knowledge increaseth sorrow; or in a more limited way one might put it, analysis carries with it diminished appreciation. Values become distorted. Works of art treated as material for the laboratory lose their life when laid out on the dissecting-table. It would be needless to enlarge on the processes by which not only was the Canon reduced to a mass of crumbling fragments, but even the existence of Shakespeare as in any large sense or in any high degree its author was questioned and denied. Heresies multiplied, some of which even now retain a fitful life.

That joint-authorship was a common feature in the output of Tudor and early Stuart drama is undeniable. That Shakespeare took part in such collaboration—with Marlowe and Kyd and Peele and Greene in his earlier work, with Fletcher and Chapman and Massinger in his later—is not merely probable, but here and there approaches or even reaches certainty. But the process of disintegration was pursued to further consequences. If there was so much in the plays of the Canon which Shakespeare did not write, why need we suppose that he wrote any of them at all? From this daring conjecture, coupled with a natural reaction against the earlier idolization of Shakespeare as continuously inspired and infallible, a new heresy arose. The author of the plays was accepted as possessor of all human knowledge, as not merely a master of "the courtier's, scholar's, soldier's eye, tongue, sword," but as an accomplished lawyer, theologian, philosopher, politician. As such qualifications could not have existed in a mere plebeian and provincial who was only a member of the company of a London theatre, it was (and still is) contended that the authorship of the plays

produced and published under his name must be sough
among the higher circles of the Tudor aristocracy.

These fantasies are transitory and negligible. But they may
have been of incidental value in emphasizing what lies at the
root of the matter, and what had been greatly obscured, some
times quite lost sight of, in the intricacies of literary, linguistic
stylistic and aesthetic analysis: that is to say, that the content
of the Canon, while they are literature and as such, matter of
literary comment, analysis, and study, are primarily and
essentially records of the words which accompanied and
conveyed dramatic action; that they must be read and under
stood accordingly; that a play is a dramatic whole, a concrete
presentation of life, and as such, has like life itself its inconsis
tencies, its obscurities, its languors and excesses, its vulgaritie
and tediousnesses and absurdities; but, as in life itself also, that
all these are organic, and that without them, the play would not
represent reality, would not be alive with a life of its own.

In one of the most profound sentences of the *Poetics*
Aristotle with his usual nonchalance goes to the heart of the
matter. He is speaking of Homer, of the artist who created
the Iliad and Odyssey. The epic age, in the countries and
peoples which afterwards became Hellas and the Greeks, was
fertile in its production. Homer was one among many poets
as Shakespeare was one among a crowd of dramatists. It
would be a curious, indeed a too curious speculation to
conceive what our own attitude to Shakespeare, that is, to the
Shakespeare of the Canon, would be if all the contemporary
drama had entirely perished, and if we knew nothing except
by guesswork and inference, of the history, the political and
social life, the state of civilization, the material surroundings,
amid which the plays preserved in the Canon came into exis
tence. In such matters, Aristotle had as regards Homer and
the Homeric age much information accessible which has since
disappeared. But he was not greatly interested in them. He
lays his finger on the essential point when he says, briefly and
almost casually as is his wont, "Among the many excellencies
of Homer, one of the most eminent is that alone among poets
he clearly sees what a poet ought to do."

This point in the progress towards reintegration of Shakespeare we have now reached, or at least we are in sight of it. Alone among the crowd of his contemporary dramatists he clearly sees what a dramatist ought to do. The more that the Canon is read or studied with this in mind, the more that the articulation of the plays is apprehended, whether as made visible and audible by actors acting or even in the theatre of the mind, the more will the plays manifest themselves as organisms, as embodiments of organic life. That vitality is so powerful that it can bear, if one may not go further and say, demands for effectiveness, much dilution. Unrelieved high tension is not like life, which is as much as to say, is undramatic. Scenes in the plays which seem weak or commonplace or ineffective will often be found, when put to the test, to be not merely adjuncts but reinforcements to the total dramatic value of the play in which they are set. Whether this effect was in any particular instance calculated and deliberate, or was the outcome of a sort of unconscious dramatic instinct, or the playwright's sense of the stage, is another question. That it does not hold good everywhere, that Shakespeare now and then left in plays which he remodelled, perhaps even inserted in plays which he constructed, lumps of dead matter, may be frankly admitted. That in doing so he made concessions to fashion, indulged the worse as well as the better tastes of his audiences and patrons, interpolated his action with comments on current events or controversies, is perfectly true. One need not doubt that he good-naturedly wrote bombast for Burbage and bawdry for Kemp—up to a point. But that was because the bombast and the bawdry were expected, were even demanded, by the audience. And of some of the interstitial or relieving scenes one can quite fancy that he would merely say to himself as he inserted them, "gabble enough and good enough." Such a scene served its dramatic purpose for the immediate occasion; he may quite well have lifted it bodily from somewhere else. In any case, it was rubble in his masonry, incorporated by him with the hewn and dressed and marvellously carved stone to which it formed a backing, and even a reinforcement. By taking and using it thus, he made it his own. His pure poetry, his exquisite prose, he wrote for himself. To realize this—and perhaps it can only be realized adequately on the live stage—is to have made a solid advance in the reintegration of Shakespeare as a master-artificer, and of the Canon as the organic embodiment of his art.

In the integrated body of his work, all these things and others are part of the texture. Nor is it less important to realize that almost from the first he felt, and found, and took, the easiest way out of difficulties. He knew how far he might go safely in superfluities and inconsistencies and impossibilities. He constructs, as he writes, "with such a careless force and forceless care as if that luck in very spite of cunning bade him win all." He will get into what seems an inextricable entanglement, and then we find he has overleapt it or floated through it. His characters while on the stage are alive; when they are not, they do not exist. Infinite pains have been spent on filling in the interstices; in making something continuous, consistent, and as it were historical, out of his *Hamlet*, his *Iago*, his *Macbeth*. But Shakespeare was a dramatist, not a psychologist or a biographer.

He was a dramatist, and also a poet and a master of language. His poetical vocabulary he gathered from many sources; the use he made of it, the melody and intonation he put into it, were his own, and remained his own secret. Here a point deserves notice which in analysis of his verbal and metrical art has often been forgotten, and which bears directly on problems of disputed or mixed authorship in the Canon. It is this: just as he took all life, as it lay around him, for the texture of his dramatic creation, so he took all language as, whether spoken or written, it lay around him, for his dramatic use. That included, surely it should be useless to say, the language, the manipulation of words and phrases and rhythms used by his colleagues. We know that Virgil did not hesitate to lift whole phrases and lines, not only from earlier Latin poetry but from that of his contemporaries. Shakespeare clearly did the same. But both poets transmuted what they borrowed: it became in their hands Virgilianized or Shakespearianized. The disintegrators made the fatal mistake of treating the matter as though an organic work of art were merely the sum of its parts, and could be accounted for by analysis and dissection.

That process was carried so far with Shakespeare that it quickly collapsed under its own weight. Thus the chronicle series of *Henry VI* was parcelled out among no less than six hands other than his. The dissection of *Julius Caesar*, and the discovery in it of at least eight, was a process even more elaborate; it may be summarized as follows. A trilogy by Marlowe; conflation into a single play by Chapman and Drayton of parts two and three of the trilogy; complete recasting of part one by Chapman, and of part three by Dekker, Drayton, Middleton, Munday and Webster; revision of these by Shakespeare, and production, as two plays, on the transference of ownership of the copy to the Lord Chamberlain's company; finally, compression of the two plays into one, with insertions of his own, by Jonson. "Evidently," in Sir Edmund Chambers' acid comment, "the disintegration of Shakespeare is an open career for talent." It was left for Mr. Granville-Barker (and others whom he has guided or inspired), approaching the matter from the inside, to reinstate and vindicate the dramatic quality and the dramatic coherence of the whole play as we possess it.

But this was not all. Among those who accepted the authenticity of the Canon, curiosity about its author became more and more insatiable. A mythology about Shakespeare himself had already long existed. It swelled into prodigious and fantastic proportions. Clever guesses, precarious inferences, arbitrary interpretations were piled up into an illusory structure. Conjectures based on these interpretations of the plays were made into events in Shakespeare's own life; and the plays were then reinterpreted in terms of these imaginary events. As with the *Lives of the Saints*, each successive redactor added another story to the house of cards. There were as many Shakespeares as there were biographers of Shakespeare. Then the craze for disintegration found a fresh field. The plays, it being granted or at least not denied that they were his work, were allegorized. They were treated, in some cases as thinly veiled political pamphlets, and more largely, as a mass of topical allusions strung together on a thread of plot. If this were what Shakespeare gave us, he would not be worth our attention except as a quarry or source, nor would it matter much who was the author of the plays ascribed to him. Mr. Percy Allen, whose industry, learning and acuteness are unquestioned, claims to have proved "beyond all question" that Chapman's Bussy plays are a running commentary on *Twelfth Night, Macbeth*, and *Hamlet*; that Hamlet himself can be identified "conclusively" with the Earl of Oxford; that Olivia and Orsino are Queen Elizabeth and the Duke of Alençon, and Ophelia's death is, and is meant to be, a reproduction of what had happened some five and twenty years before in the house of Lord Burleigh. Others find that by manipulation of words and letters it can be shown that nothing that is so is so. All this comes of playing with a disintegrated Shakespeare, from which both literary and dramatic quality have disappeared, from which life has gone out.

This is a danger that attaches to all minute and over-specialized study. I shall not, I trust, be taken to mean that specialized study is to be condemned or even to be deprecated; if I did, I should not be addressing the Shakespeare Association, nor could I expect that the Association would listen to me. But it is, at least, it ought to be, a means, not an end. The body of Shakespearian work is art: Shakespeare was an artist. No research is idle which lays a more secure basis for the text of the plays, which throws light on the conditions under which they were composed and produced, which clears away accumulated rubbish or traditional misconception, which enables us to see and hear more intelligently the portraiture of human life and the cadences of human language of which the living art of Shakespeare is the supreme realization.

The re-integration of Shakespeare the author, the greatest single name in English literature, is being gradually but certainly effected. Scholarship has come to recognize its limits; and in particular, to fasten on the central truth that in letters, as in any work of art, what matters is not what the artist made it out of, but what he made it into; that the secret of life is life itself. But the full integration of Shakespeare the dramatist as a force, and of his art as something vital, can only be gained—if it can be gained; perhaps it might be better to say, can only be effectively approached—through the coalescence of the study and the theatre. The dramatic values in his work no doubt can be, and are, made the subject of closet-analysis. But they can only be tested and realized in action. Drama is, in fact as well as by etymology, action. Un-acted action comes near to being a contradiction in terms.

If I may here travel a little beyond the ground on which I can base any claim to be heard, I would add here some observations on a subject which is of interest both in itself and in its bearing on the process indicated in the title of this address. It is the establishment of a national theatre for Shakespeare. Such an institution may be regarded, from one side as a laboratory for experiment, from another as a training school for actors and dramatists, from another yet, and perhaps the most important, as an education for audiences. So far, what has been effected in all these directions is tentative and incomplete, especially in the last. It may be suggested that the efforts at a structure have been disappointing because the foundation on which it must be based has been inadequate. Action on the stage requires reaction in the auditorium. Otherwise, it might as well go on with the safety-curtain lowered throughout the performance. Action presented, that is to say, drama, does not carry except to those who respond to it, who are in some sense taking part in it, who are potential actors in it themselves. A national theatre, it may be urged, can only live and thrive as the culmination of a well rooted and widely diffused dramatic education, absorbed by, and taking effect through, the whole nation as audience. To a large extent this was the case with the religious drama of the Middle Ages. It was not so with the liberated and secularized drama of Tudor and Stuart England. The playhouses, and the companies who played in them, were in constant fluctuation. There were the Queen's men, the Lord Chamberlain's men, the Lord Admiral's men, and so on; there was also the Censorship. But there was no national theatre; and to a large section of the nation, the theatre was abhorrent. The whole situation was, and remained, chaotic. Indeed the closing of the theatres during the Civil War and the Protectorate came, one may be inclined to think, none too soon. The post-Restoration King's House, which later became the Theatre Royal Drury Lane, and later in Georgian times the Theatre Royal Covent Garden,

s

had special privileges which gave them a monopoly, but were not in any real sense national institutions. When the monopoly was abolished, the era of unrestricted competition among commercialized theatres began which has continued to the present day.

There are the makings of a national theatre in the full sense of the term now, slow and irregular in their growth, but with their roots struck in the life of the people. The superstructure will, short of imprevisible and incalculable revolutions in the whole framework of national life, rise on these foundations. For the drama, not as a technical art practised by professional performers, nor as an archaeological study pursued by professional scholars, but as a functional expression of actual life, is taking its place in the body, and in the soul, of the nation. The place to be taken by its greatest master in that process is secure. Not only is Shakespeare read, but scenes from his plays, and sometimes whole plays, are acted in practically all our schools: are acted, are brought back to life, are not elaborately tricked out, decorated, devitalized. In village institutes and similar institutions whether rural or urban, a like revivification is going on. The municipal theatre is becoming a feature of civic life. Its equipment is beginning to shake itself free of the old cramping tradition. Scenery and costumes, tricks of lighting and staging, are becoming recognized as adjuncts, not essentials.

The theatre, as distinct from the drama, is now the subject of large and varied experiment. To this movement, a great stimulus was given by Mr. Poel's courageous attempts to reproduce the Elizabethan stage and present Elizabethan plays on it as they were originally presented. But even if we could reconstitute that stage and setting with any certainty, the presentation would remain essentially artificial. Dramatic action in the drama of Shakespeare and his contemporaries was no doubt limited, and to a large extent determined, by the staging available. But it does not hinge on that. Even in Shakespeare's own life, staging in private and to a less degree in public theatres had large developments; of these he took advantage, and indeed without them, some portions of his later plays could hardly, if at all, have been put into action, and consequently, would not have been written. They give added range and freedom. It must not be forgotten that they also presented new temptations.

But the lure of archaeological reconstruction is perilous. If an Elizabethan stage, why not Elizabethan costume? Why not Elizabethan pronunciation? To get vital reality, one would have to go a step further yet, and reconstruct an Elizabethan audience: which is impossible. Free experiment is needed. It must be recognized as experimental, provisional, merely tentative. Sir Barry Jackson and Mr. Tyrone Guthrie among others, have shown how valuable, how stimulating, how suggestive such experiments may be. They have thrown real light on Shakespeare's art. They have aided the reintegration of Shakespeare not as a doctrine but as a practice. "The art of the theatre," Mr. Granville-Barker incisively says, "is the art of acting." A play's business is to interpret life. Shakespearian archaeology may be carried in practice to such an extent as to misinterpret life, to obscure or eclipse Shakespeare.

The power of the mere human voice to produce, with the utmost intensity and delicacy, the melodic and orchestrated effects of the verbal music in which action is interpreted and vivified, is limitless. Voice is action. The mere reading aloud of scenes from a play, or so far as time and other conditions permit, of a play in its entirety, with an imaginary background, no dresses, hardly any "properties," and just so much gesture and movement as is the instinctive response to the call of the words heard and altered, is an initiation into Shakespeare which cannot be over-valued. Its assiduous practice creates the intelligence on which dramatic representation in the fuller sense may be engrafted. This it creates both in the speaker and in the listeners. I may cite as an instance an unpretending association, the Sunday Shakespeare Society, founded nearly sixty years ago by Furnivall and still continuing in unabated vigour. Its main object, successfully carried out, is this reading aloud of the whole cycle of the Canon, and ancillary to that, occasional extension to plays of the same period by other dramatists. The cycle is completed once in every four years. The integration of Shakespeare is the result aimed at and to a large degree attained.

By multiplication of such communal activities, a powerful impulse may be given to the integration of Shakespeare in the fuller sense. A soil will be formed in which he will be rooted. The effective results of textual criticism, of historical investigation, of the whole enormous mass of comment, analysis, reconstruction, will merge in larger and more educated appreciation. Those who come after us, if not we ourselves, will be the inheritors not only of a dead world in which Shakespeare lived, but of the living and imperishable world which he created.

TRADITION AND DESIGN

[*A Lecture delivered to the Students of the Royal Academy,*
22 November, 1932]

ANY one who has felt the curiosity, or had the good sense, to look into the constitution of the Royal Academy will know that it has, from its first origins, recognized the alliance of the arts with one another, and also the continuity of art as the expression, through varied mediums and on different lines of approach, of the human spirit; its aim being to fix, to record, and to make intelligible in one or another language, something, at least, of the reality which underlies the transitory and evanescent pageant which presents itself to our senses; to interpret and stabilize experience through imagination, and to transform imagination into vision.

The Royal Academy of Arts, to give it its uncontracted title, was founded for the stated purpose of promoting the Arts of Design; these being defined, loosely, but quite conveniently, as painting, sculpture and architecture. It was to be a school, or a group of schools, of design. The courses of instruction to be given in it were prescribed under the names of a Summer Academy and a Winter Academy. The annual exhibition of works of art, which was also prescribed in the Instrument of Foundation (and which for the outer world, is all or pretty nearly all that the term Royal Academy means), was to some degree merely an incident. Its purpose was partly, no doubt, to stimulate public interest in works of contemporary art. But its primary object was to provide funds for support for the educational and charitable purposes of the institution. To emphasize this, any Academician who did not exhibit had to pay a substantial fine. Primarily, therefore, the Royal Academy was a State-aided school of design; collaterally, a society for the relief of indigent artists and their families; and incidentally, a body which organized annual exhibitions of works of art executed partly by its own members, and more largely, by all artists (so the regulations of the Instrument put it) "of distinguished merit." What constituted distinguished merit was prudently left undefined.

With this end in view, there was prescribed, in the constitution of the Academy, the formation of a library in which the records of earlier art, and of the civilizations, in many ages and countries, of which art has been the expression, should be available for study. With this end in view likewise, it was sought to widen the scope of the schools of design in which students of art received their training and equipment beyond mere technical instruction, so that design in the fullest sense might become a whole realm laid open before them. Professorships of Ancient History and of Ancient Literature in the Academy were created in the second year of its existence. This, even if it be regarded as little more than a gesture or a symbol, laid emphasis on the intimate connection between the arts of design and whole broad current of humanism. For mastery of design in the exercise of his own specific art, it is more than desirable, it is essential, that the artist's mind should be fertilized, his insight sharpened, his outlook widened by acquaintance with what has been done by his predecessors in the march of the human race. This means not merely the history of art, important as that is; not merely the literature of art, so far as such a thing exists. History and literature, which themselves are arts, are or should be linked up with art in its more restricted meaning. Their joint action extends over the whole sphere of the human spirit; it represents the pattern which is perpetually being woven anew, in which the design of the world receives fresh embodiments and interpretations, and which, reaching back over an immeasurable past, moves forward to an incalculable future.

Incalculable; for in art, as in history, and in life generally, we can make guesses at the future, but cannot anticipate it. According to what is, I understand, now the accepted doctrine of physical science, this incalculability is a fundamental law, or to put it otherwise, an ascertained fact, in the material universe. Movement or change is a matter not of inevitable sequence, but of probability. Until something has happened, there is no determined or determinable assurance that it will be one thing rather than another. Something similar obtains in the arts. In the mordant words of Ecclesiastes, "chance happeneth to them all." There is no inevitable sequence; movement is discontinuous and erratic. Even were it not the case that many movements go on, many schools or fashions arise, contemporaneously, and that these may be in sharp antagonism to one another, each movement or school or fashion is self-originated; and each, for what it is worth, settles down into its place in the complex fabric of tradition. This does not mean, however, either that the history of art is a futile study, or that works of art can be produced *in vacuo*; or that knowledge is no better than ignorance. The experience of each artist, the manner and degree in which he is influenced by existing art, past or present, primitive or decadent, classic or romantic, native or foreign, is a real thing.

The points on which stress was laid a hundred and fifty years ago, as it still has to be laid now, and which suggested the title for this address, are these two: first, that the arts with which the Royal Academy is concerned are expressly defined as the arts of design; design, alike in their theory and their practice, being not only essential but fundamental: secondly, that the promotion of these arts is only to be secured by, and must be based upon, the establishment of a continuous tradition founded on knowledge and appreciation of the past; a tradition which gathers up and hands on accumulated experience, not as a dead weight, but as a living and vitalizing force.

History has perpetually to be re-written. Works of literature mean something different to each successive age, and not only so, but to each individual reader. And in the arts of design likewise, design is not only being perpetually re-created, but being perpetually re-interpreted.

Two brief sentences may serve as texts for the subject under consideration. Both are taken from ancient literature; from the Greeks, of whom, both in literature and in art, we remain pupils, as our predecessors were and as our successors will be. They bear directly on the two words which were linked as the title of this lecture. One is from the greatest of Athenian poets: "Memory, the mother of the Muses." The other is from the prince of Greek philosophers: "Rightness consists in largeness and design." The first assigns its place and value to tradition. The second assigns its place and value to design. It will be worth while to pause and analyse both a little more closely.

"Memory," says Aeschylus, "is the mother of the Muses"; or in other words, is what gives birth to all the arts. The ordinary list of nine Muses includes for instance the Muses of History and of Astronomy. But there were other lists; in one of them there is a Muse with the suggestive name of Polymatheia, range of acquirement; the Muse who is

> opener of the mysterious doors
> Leading to universal knowledge.

And for the whole fellowship of the Muses there was an alternative name, the Mneiai, the Remembrances.

Memory is tradition; it is what remains vital and operative of inherited or transmitted and acquired experience. Partly tradition comes of itself; we cannot be rid of it; it is born in us and flows into us from all sides. Partly it has to be learned, studied, cultivated, consciously assimilated.

We may say in a celebrated phrase which has been much misconstrued, that "art happens." No doubt it does. But that does not carry one very far, unless one keeps it in contact with another and more important view; art means something, and does it; art creates.

What is art? Many answers have been attempted to this question and they mostly leave us pretty much where we were. But so much may be said; art is skilled production, *plus* something else. Skilled production by itself is at most only artifice: "artificium," the working of the machinery of art. What is the something else? It is the *élan vital*—an English phrase has perhaps yet to be invented to give the exact force of the French—which distinguishes art from mechanism, and transforms production into creation. The artist, as such, breathes into the material in which he works, the clay or the stone or the pigments laid on canvas, the breath of his own life. This is what is meant when we say that art creates.

The education of a painter, or a sculptor, or an architect,

is on its technical side the making acquaintance with, the obtaining mastery over, materials and processes. Tradition is obviously of the essence of this; it supplies to the craftsman the gathered experience wrested from the materials of their art by his predecessors. But as artist, or as creator, he is also dependent on a spiritual tradition. The rules or tricks of line and plane, of tone and colour, can be taught and learned by him as a workman (workman and craftsman mean the same thing). For the artist, as an artist, they are only the machinery which he can use, and the working of which he can master, as means towards embodying his own creative impulse. Here we come to the point. The creative impulse is there. The machinery is there. But they have to be brought into contact with one another. The establishment of this contact is the education of the artist. And it is an education which depends on, one may say, further which consists in, the inheritance of tradition, the entry into the stream of creative energy which vitalizes, from age to age, the work of the human race.

A startling saying was made some years ago by an artist of high distinction, one of our own Academicians. "The nineteenth century," he said, "will probably be memorable as the most barren of creation in the history of the civilized world." What he had in mind was the loss of tradition; for that implied the loss of the sense of design. Art that is not firmly rooted may flower, but does not fruit.

Loss of tradition brings with it this among other misfortunes, that some fragment or facet of it is rediscovered, is treated in isolation, and assumes an exaggerated importance, because there is no framework into which it fits, and it is not seen in relation to the larger truths of which it is a partial expression. As a corrective to the lure of novelties, the inquiry must be made whether they are in fact new.

This spiritual education may be guided, but it cannot be compelled. The wider that the apprehension of it is, the further back and deeper down that it goes, the better will be the chance of realizing its continuity and our own dependence upon it; the less will be the risk of being embedded in one particular tradition and becoming the victim of one particular fashion.

Fashion itself is a kind of tradition, a kind that is very easy to pick up, for it is the way in which the stream of tendency, or movement of energy, of which I have spoken makes its most immediate impact. "The predominancy of custom" (to use a phrase of Bacon's) is in one view a stabilizing, and in another a sterilizing or contracting influence. The fashion of being in the fashion is in fact, whether we like it or not, one of the things that are inherent in our very imperfect human nature: and the fashion of being out of the fashion is much the same thing, only turned the other way up. But tradition in its larger and nobler sense is the corrective of fashion. The fashions of the day or hour, of the group or school, are realized by acquaintance with the great tradition in its continuity as bubbles and swirls and eddies in the stream, appearing and disappearing and re-appearing. Deeper down, there is anchorage.

Every new age starts with an instinctive reaction against its predecessor. It claims to lead its own life, to make a fresh start into the unknown. Methods are discarded, schools are discredited; and others which had been forgotten or slighted resume their vitality. Since the consolidated tradition of the eighteenth century broke up, the world of art has expanded bewilderingly. Greek art was re-discovered and misunderstood. Close on the heels of that, medieval art was re-discovered and misunderstood as profoundly. Later still, the arts of Egypt, of India, of Japan and China, revealed themselves to add to the confusion. With every fresh view that has opened out, has come an increasing sense of disorientation. Where there were no boundaries there was no centre: for the centre was everywhere. A desperate effort was finally made in some quarters to reverse the engines, to blot out tradition, and get back to unsophisticated vision and uneducated execution. Events will show whether or not this is futile. Of some of these efforts it may be said, in the phrase of Ecclesiasticus: "there are also divers vanities." But so far as they are sincere, they have their purpose, their interest, and their value. What they ask, and ask justly, is that they should not be slighted. What may be required, and justly required of them, is that they should be tested.

I was much struck lately with a sentence in a letter written by an artist, in which he said that the art of painting seemed to be moving in the direction of the Sandwich Islands or some country where tattooing pure and simple is the National School of Art. This sounds, does it not, as if it were written very recently? It was in fact written nearly sixty years ago; and the writer was Rossetti. Research might discover that the same thing, or its equivalent, was said much earlier.

The fact is that tradition is what saves one from traditionalism just as in literature the classics keep one out of and above classicism.

The Parliamentary Secretary of the Board of Education recently laid stress on the object of education being to convey into thought, action, and production, the qualities of precision, order, balance, and lucidity. These are all included in the single word, design. But they do not exhaust its meaning. For design is creation, the work of a creator. It has innumerable embodiments, but one function. That function is to realize, to interpret, and to bring to the cognizance of the senses, some portion, some facet, of reality: of that pattern or structure which underlies phenomena, and by apprehending which the chaos of the phenomenal world is transformed or re-moulded into an ordered universe. The problem before the artist, only partially soluble at the utmost stretch of his power and will, is to fix evanescence; to condense, out of the flying vapours of the world, an image of perfection.

Thus we are led to the second of the two texts which I mentioned, the saying of Aristotle: "rightness (or goodness) consists in largeness and design." The largeness meant, of course, is not size, or measurement by scale, but the amplitude put into any work of art by the artist and reflecting, as it originates from, a similar quality of largeness in the artist himself. It applies alike to a cathedral or a coin, to a painting that fills a wall or one that covers a few square inches of paper. But it is the other constituent of the definition, design, with which we are now concerned.

The Greek word for which "rightness" or "goodness" is perhaps the nearest English equivalent, may also, and indeed usually is, rendered by the word "beauty." That of itself is a word of indefinable meaning. Of it, more than of most others, it may be said: "I know what it is, if you do not ask me." One of the nearest approaches that have been made towards defining it—and that is a description rather than a definition—is that it is "what satisfies." The saying is that of a poet; and none the worse for that. Another and a greater poet, Keats, as you will all remember, gave a still more succinct definition: "Beauty is Truth." That is a profound saying, but I will not try to follow out its implications. Why a particular sequence of notes in music is beautiful and another is not, is a mystery: but it is a fact. Music and painting are sister arts; and I have heard a great painter say that what was wanted in a picture was that it should sing. Melodiousness of design is a thing more easily felt than explained. Futile attempts used to be made to define a "line of beauty" drawn by pen or brush; the same is true of any attempt to account by mathematical formulae for the beauty, the satisfying quality, of a composition in two or three dimensions, of one or another complex of shapes, or colours, or tones.

It may be suggested indeed that in the education of the artist, and not merely while he is formally a student but throughout his whole life, the assiduous practice of linear design, or drawing in the more restricted sense of the word, is essential and irreplaceable, not merely as training of the hand, but as at the root of all design in its wider sense. The further assertion might even be hazarded, that without purity and suavity of line there can be no really great work of art.

It may be true, as is urged, that in nature there is no such thing as the line. Neither is there any such thing in nature, if by nature we mean what is cognizable by the senses, as a plane or a solid. That is just the difference between nature and art. The line as a vehicle of creative expression is fundamental in creative as well as in mechanical design. It is equally relevant, or equally irrelevant, to say as is also true, that there is no such thing in nature as colour. Colour and line are both ways of interpreting nature. The searching and creative draughtsmanship which gives mastery of line as a means of expression is fundamental in design. All forms of expression are conventions, that is to say, are based on a convention. Line is unique in the subtle and varied application which can be made of it to translate, as it were, into a single language the sense of planes and solids, of atmospheric effects and what are called tactile values. Crude inventions like cubism mean the use for art of raw material without subjecting it to distillation. But it would be beyond my present scope, and beyond my ability, to go further into this. I would only add, that just as largeness in any work of art is the projection into it of largeness in the mind of the artist, so perfection of design is the expression or embodiment of his whole organized intelligence.

Study makes designing possible, but does not create the faculty of design. It constructs and assembles the machinery; the motive force comes from within. In an Academy of Art, students learn the grammar of their subject, they go through their exercises and drill. That indeed goes on afterwards; and in fact many spend their whole lives on it, remaining art-students but never becoming artists. As training, it is admittedly indispensable. It launches the student on the stream of tradition; it equips him for using what creative powers he possesses by showing him, and helping him to understand, examples of creative power exercised by great artists. It depends on himself whether this experience, this entry into tradition, shall be deadening or vivifying.

There may be an exceptional or abnormal artist like Blake, who discards tradition and would do away with training. Art, Blake held firmly, is inspiration in its most literal sense. "I act by command," he said of his own work; and again, "I defy all competition, for no one can beat the Holy Ghost." In this attitude of mind it was natural to assert, as Blake elsewhere asserts, "There is no use in education. I hold it to be wrong. It is the great sin. It is the eating of the tree of the Knowledge of Good and Evil." Blake laid this down quite seriously, but it can hardly be called fruitful doctrine. The sterilizing effect of misdirected education, and the total absence of any effect at all from education which the recipient cannot take in (the word education, I may remind you, means feeding), is a different matter.

Of a former President of the Royal Academy, Benjamin West, Hazlitt relates, "I once heard him say in a public room that he thought he had quite as good an idea of Athens from reading the travelling catalogue of the place as if he had lived there for years." "I believe," Hazlitt pungently adds, "this was strictly true." If it was, or so far as it was, it shows how extremes meet. Blake and West were contemporaries.

This at least is certain. Design in its full sense must exist in the artist's mind before it takes visible and tactual embodiment. To put it more simply, the artist must have something to express before he can give it expression. He must know, or if one prefers to say so, must feel, what he means to do before he can do it. Creation in art is copying. But it is not copying things or their appearances; it is copying the impression made by the things or their appearances on the artist's mind, and materializing or translating that impression into sensible and communicable form. The artist's mind may be compared (of course incompletely) to a sensitive plate. But it is one which not only receives and stores impressions but discriminates and selects among them, elicits from them a design corresponding to the unembodied design which is in the mind itself, created there by the shaping spirit of imagination. The power of the executant is a separate thing. Its products are works of technical skill. All the technical skill in the world is, so far as art is concerned, only a means to an end.

This may be realized and notwithstanding misinterpreted. On one hand the immense and multitudinous volume of tradition, on the other hand the mathematics or super-mathematics of design, can exercise a pressure that provokes revolt. And so, attempts are made to sweep away tradition and to dispense with design; to dissolve the fabric built up by civilization and get back to an imagined state of nature. Desperate efforts are made to invent a new language, as if there were not too many languages already: in the hope to recover somehow through it the unclouded perception, the direct expression of the childhood of art, the age of innocence. Such artificial innocence, it may be feared, is only a further progress in sophistication. The vision of the child is a different thing from the childishness of the visionary. There is a famous couplet of Dryden's which may be applied here with the alteration of one word:

> The builders were with want of genius curst,
> The second temple was not like the first.

The second childhood is not like the first. Second childishness is one-half of a familiar line in Shakespeare. It is coupled by him in the other half of the line with mere oblivion.

The pyrotechnics of artistry flare up, dazzle, and fade; oblivion re-descends on them. Through their confusion the great lights burn steadily, and to the undazzled eye resume their lustre. By keeping them in sight, the artist may draw from them continuous inspiration, may light his lamp at theirs, nay become a part of the design which they create. Incidentally, he will be saved from the danger, to which so many of us succumb (not in the art of design alone), of becoming an imitator, not of this or that master, but of himself.

Art can only be explained or interpreted by art; and one art illuminates another. Ten lines of poetry seem to me to sum up, in the language of the sister-art, what was in my mind, and what I have endeavoured to put into words:

> And murmurs of a deeper voice
>   Going before to some far shrine
> Teach that sick heart the stronger choice,
>   Till all thy life one way incline
>   With one wide will that closes thine.
>
> And when the zoning eve has died
>   Where yon dark valleys wind forlorn,
> Come Hope and Memory, spouse and bride,
>   From out the borders of the morn,
>   With that fair child betwixt them born.

That fair child is Art.